Two Tudor Books of Arms; Harleian Mss. nos. 2169 & 6163

TWO TUDOR BOOKS OF ARMS.

HARLEIAN MSS. Nos. 2169 & 6163.

WITH NINE HUNDRED ILLUSTRATIONS.

Randle Halme

Thys wylam duke of normandye. as bothe old and lyth mencyon. By hys
tytylt and by hys chevalrye. made kynge by conqueft of theese albyon.
put scots to fleynge and take poffefyon. and bare thys reame full on
and .xx. yere kyng at home thus fayth the cronoclerye.

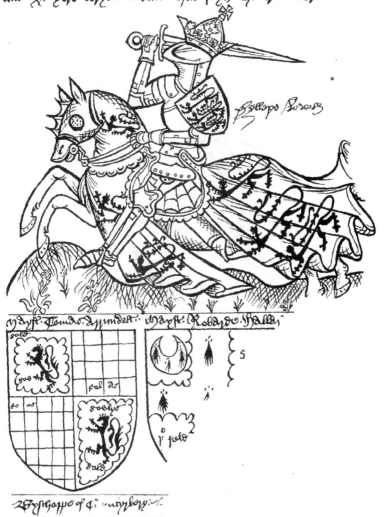

Sir Robert

Wyff: Fowle Aylmore. Wyff: Robert Halle;

Byshoppe of [...]

A TUDOR BOOK OF ARMS

TRICKED BY ROBERT COOKE BEING
HARLEIAN MANUSCRIPT No. 2169
BLASONED BY JOSEPH FOSTER,
HON. M.A. OXON.

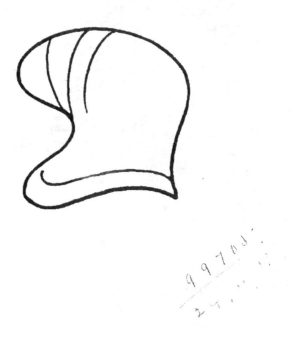

THE DE WALDEN LIBRARY

INTRODUCTION

~~~~~~~~~~~~~

IN projecting an "Heraldic Art Journal" a few years ago, I took occasion to print in various prospectuses, specimen illustrations from two notable "arms books," viz , Harleian MSS 2169 and 6163 My intention was to include examples from both of them in the journal, as they were very well calculated to afford an excellent series of studies, especially for those who had not the opportunity of readily consulting the manuscripts for themselves These illustrations attracted much attention among those interested in maintaining a high artistic standard for the armorist Several causes delayed their publication, among others the compilation of "Some Feudal Coats of Arms," a work which some consider might truly be styled "The Art of Heraldry" These "arms books" are here issued in their entirety as a companion to "Some Feudal Coats of Arms"

These manuscripts should appeal not only to the armorist, but to the self styled heraldic artist, whose art, as he practises it, is too often little better than the much abused coach-painting, without the paint His only authority is the spurious work in the pretentious books by which he is environed To consult an heraldic manuscript is beyond his wildest dreams, and, even if he does, he does not seem to possess that critical faculty which would enable him to discriminate between the excellent and the mediocre To him exaggeration is the Art of Heraldry, and hence to his own undoing he unconsciously drifts into heraldic caricature In a spirited drawing by the Tudor Arms painter he will see no art, no charm, but with an air of triumph will present his "comic cuts" as something vastly superior, and the public and his patrons, being equally uninformed are, alas ' equally pleased

As a case in point, I would recite an experience of my own More than a quarter of a century ago, the late Garter, King of Arms, allowed one of my draughtsmen to have access to some of the art MSS in the College of Arms, so that examples might be taken This resulted in "Foster's Peerage and Baronetage," containing a vast number of exquisite drawings, though many of them were only successful after the second or third attempt, yet caricatures, unfortunately, crept into its pages, as the hurried day of publication approached This, however, was only the beginning of the mischief, for imitators now swarm in England, Scotland and Ireland, each with his own peculiar notion of what heraldry should be, as if it never had been , but I defy any expert to detect the true heraldic spirit or touch in any of their fancy work, much less to identify, with any certainty, many of the charges which these imitators affect to represent, notably the beasts and birds Elsewhere we have seen the arms blocks of another utilized by the hundred without acknowledgment, and one is tempted to ask, is this the Art of Heraldry ? In the case of the deceased, surely a tribute is due to the work of his hands

In the British Museum catalogue of the Harleian MSS , No 2169 is erroneously described as an old heraldical book in small folio done in the time of King Henry VI, a description too often adopted by the unwary ("The Ancestor," III , 185) It is self-evident that Harl MS 2169, is *a copy* crudely tricked of a manuscript temp H VI , with which was incorporated, perhaps temp Ed VI , some rough gatherings by Robert Cooke, the father of Clarenceux Cooke (1567–92), and these "have from hence been entered into some other book " As to this "other book," its identity has long been a matter of common knowledge It was probably tricked for that "excellent improver and admirer of renowned antiquity," Sir Edward Brudenell, of Dyne (Dean), who died 24th February, 1584-5, and it now stands in the College of Arms, distinguished by the press mark L 8 Many of the tricks, charming and spirited to a degree, in the Harl MS 2169 are exquisite in L 8, marred though it is by the unconventional lyons, an early instance of the artist o'erleaping himself, for this vagary does not occur in Cooke's work-book   He was evidently prompted by the very natural desire to produce a better lyon than appears in his British Museum work-book, and so he could have easily done had he consulted earlier examples, rather than have relied solely on his own lively imagination   Lyons have always been the arms-painter's great difficulty, from those Tudor times down to this present

This Harleian MS 2169, acquired by the British Museum, was in the Randle Holme collection numbered, 6, "AUNCIANT COATES," B 4, 20   Wanley describes it as "a large collection of Armes of Foreign Kings, Saints, Nobles, &c., some of which are fabulous, as also of our English Nobility and Gentry, all mixed together ; which, notwithstanding that some be erroneous, and others want the names of the persons to which they did belong, are nevertheless of some use   The index begun by Jacob Chaloner and finished by the second Randle Holme " The autograph of Phellepe Bowthe occurs on the title page.

The tricks in this, as in most arms-painters' work-books, are very unequal, many of them spirited and admirable, others weak and crude   I have been allowed to annotate these pages from Cooke's finished copy, and have thus been enabled to rescue many missing names (see pages 4, 18, and 19) and a few coats which are quite additional (see page 121)   On the other hand Cooke excludes not only the three equestrian figures at the commencement of the MS but also the curious "passion plates" of pages 107 and 109   In L 8 an attempt has been made to rearrange and classify the arms of this work-book, and most of the unnamed arms are also placed by themselves, though in an inferior manner ; one effect of this is to obscure the identity of the manuscripts ; they do not commence with the same names, but whole pages are in the same order, and the last coat is the same in both   It is noteworthy that the name of Smith is conspicuous by its absence from these MSS   It has been inserted in L 8, hence its appearance in the Index

Should this volume be of real utility to the art student, I shall have much cause to be thankful   The best examples were selected for illustration, then difficult subjects were singled out for representation, and a few were ultimately inserted to meet the exigencies of particular pages   I have retained the blazons of the original artist (temp H VI ?), which occur on the face of the illustrations, as they are of considerable interest   The current blason is adopted in the text because, being intelligible, it serves as a protest against the unpicturesque mimicry of those blazons to which we are introduced under "What is believed" in "The Ancestor," Vol vii, pp 184 187, and with which we are unintelligibly threatened, even in the "Victoria History of the Counties of England"

The classified lists which follow are intended to introduce the armorist at once, strange though we think them, to the names of the Kings, Saints, Worthies, Knights of the Round Table and others, whose fabulous ensigns, contained in the manuscripts here printed, were the creation and delight of the (Tudor) arms-painters, those "painter-fellows," who were at all times a thorn in the side of the heralds

For the publication of this volume heraldic students are indebted to the munificence of Lord Howard de Walden

JOSEPH FOSTER,

Hon M A , Oxon

21, BOUNDARY ROAD LONDON, N W.

SOME FABULOUS COATS OF ARMS

Saints, the Nine Worthies, Knights of the Round Table, Kings and Emperors

* An asterisk denotes an illustration

Prelates, Abbots, Masters of St. John of Jerusalem, Lord Mayors, and some Impersonal Arms—London Companies, Cities, Towns, etc

" Strangers "

Smyth

B

Original folios 4. 5. 6. of the Manuscript are missing. As the "pe de grewe" referred to below does not appear in L. 8, it may be safely inferred that it was not in the original MS. from which Cooke made his original arms-book, Harl. MS. 2169. The names of prelates Stafford 4, Neville 4 and Wainflete 4 occur in the Index ; their arms, tricked in MS. L. 8. College of Arms, are as follows:—

(1) John Stafford, Archbishop of Canterbury. Or, a chevron gules, a bordure engrailed sable.
(2) Robert Nevill, Bishop of Durham. Gules, on a saltire argent two annulets interlaced the uppermost gules the other argent.
(3) William Wainflete, Bishop of Winchester. Lozengy ermine and sable, on a chief of the second three lilies slipped argent.

Harl. MS. 2169, folio 4.

The pe de grewe be reyght lyne
Found and prevvyd by anerytaunce
How Kynge Herry the Sexyth nowghtcoleyne [1]
Ys trewe kynge of ffraunce.

The following twelve, rather rudely tricked, have been added by a similar hand (others by the same occur on f.64 st seq.). These may refer to the city and its citizens.

1. Azure, two lucies saltireways argent ducally gorged or. The STOCK-FISHMONGERS of LONDON; merged in the later FISHMONGERS, shield (see page 98 for the earlier shield). The field, sable in *Papworth*.

2. Per fess gules and argent (in L.8), a pale counter-coloured, three pineapples 2 and 1 or. Blasoned by some, quarterly (6) gules and argent, three, &c.

3. Per chevron crenellée or and azure, three eaglets displayed counter-coloured. JOHN DARBY, Sheriff of London 1446, Harl. MS. 1349 f.42.

4. Per chevron crenellée or and sable, three eaglets displayed counter-coloured.

5. Per pale argent and azure, two lyons couchant (? passant) tails cowed counter-coloured.

6. ROTE, *in later hand*. "Enbelyfe," *i.e.*, per bend sinister argent and sable, a lyon rampant counter-coloured.

7. Argent, on a pile botonnée sable a gilly-flower argent, stalked and leaved.

8. Per fess or and azure a pale counter-coloured, three fleurs de lys 1 and 2 argent. Blasoned by some, quarterly (6) or and azure, three, &c.

9. "Enbelif," *i.e.*, per bend azure and argent, an eagle displayed counter-coloured, armed or.

10. Paly crenellée (6) argent and gules.

11. TALLOW CHANDLERS, *in later hand*. Per fess azure and argent a pale counter-coloured, three doves 2 and 1 (of the second), each with an olive branch in its beak (or). Blasoned by some, quarterly (6) azure and argent, three, &c.; granted by John Smart, Garter, 24th Sepr., 1456.

12. Gyronny (6) azure and argent, three popinjays (? proper *vel* azure) 2 and 1 in the argent. SIR WILLIAM STOCKER, Lord Mayor of London 1484—*Papworth*.

[1] Perhaps "now living" in the original.

Folio 4b.

1. ROY DE SYPYR (Cyprus). Argent four bars azure, over all a lyon rampant queue tourchée gules, crowned——"The arms of Jerusalem quartly wt. all," are tricked in the margin.

2.* THE KYNGE OF SAVASTOFOLO (*alias* Constantinople, in the Index). Azure, "an ymage of Seynt Gorge" argent. See preceding page.

3. ROY DE ERMONYE. A lyon rampant crowned.

4. ROY DE NORREWAYE. Azure, three hulks or, at the prow and stern a dragon's head gules. See also page 7b.

5. ROY DE DACYE. Quarterly ; (1.) Or, three lyons passant in pale azure. (2.) Azure, three crowns 2 and 1 or. (3.) Argent, a gryphon segreant gules. (4.) Gules, a lyon rampant or, holding a battle-axe erect ; over all on a cross argent, an escocheon or charged with two lyons passant gardant azure.

6. BRUTE. Or, a lyon passant gules, erroneously tricked rampant. "The (fabulous) armys of Brewte the ffirst yt ever conqwerd Yngelond."

7. S. LAWNCELOT DE LAKE. Per pale gules and argent two bendlets of the second—— fabulous.

8. S. GAWAYNE, THE GOOD KNIGHT. Vert, three gryphon passant or ; "part wt. GAWAYNE" sable fretty argent, a label (3) gules——fabulous. See also No. 9. f.5, and No. 8, f.32.

9.* UTER PENDRAGON. Argent, a wyvern vert armed gules——fabulous.

Folio 5.

1. THE GENTYLL SOWDAN. Or, a pellet charged with a lyon passant argent crowned (? gules)—fabulous.

2.* THE SOWDEN OF BABYLOYNE. Sable, out of a chalice or, "a tortose" argent. "Part wt. the chaleys," the mutilated indication of a coat, possibly intended for an impalement, *viz.*, a hand and arm issuant in bend sinister gules, grasping a dragon's head at the neck, the arm charged with 2 bars or, all fabulous.

3.* ROY DE TACE. Azure, a hare embelif or.

4. ROY JASPER DE COLOYNE. Azure, a waxing moon and between the horns, a mullet all or.

5. ROY MELCHER DE COLOYNE. Azure, seven mullets 3, 3, 1, or.

Original folios 4. 5. 6. of the Manuscript are missing.   As the " pe de grewe " referred to below does not appear in L. 8, it may be safely inferred that it was not in the original MS. from which Cooke made his original arms-book. Harl. MS. 2169.   The names of prelates Stafford 4, Neville 4 and Wainflete 4 occur in the Index ; their arms, tricked in MS. L. 8. College of Arms, are as follows :—

(1) John Stafford, Archbishop of Canterbury.   Or, a chevron gules, a bordure engrailed sable.
(2) Robert Nevill, Bishop of Durham.   Gules, on a saltire argent two annulets interlaced the uppermost gules the other argent.
(3) William Wainflete, Bishop of Winchester.   Lozengy ermine and sable, on a chief of the second three lilies slipped argent.

Harl. MS. 2169, folio 4.

The pe de grewe be reyght lyne
Found and prevvyd by anerytaunce
How Kynge Herry the Sexyth nowghtcoleyne [1]
Ys trewe kynge of ffraunce.

The following twelve, rather rudely tricked, have been added by a similar hand (others by the same occur on f.64 et seq.).   These may refer to the city and its citizens.

1. Azure, two lucies saltireways argent ducally gorged or. The STOCK-FISHMONGERS OF LONDON; merged in the later FISHMONGERS, shield (see page 98 for the earlier shield).   The field, sable in *Papworth.*

2. Per fess gules and argent (in L.8), a pale counter-coloured, three pineapples 2 and 1 or.   Blasoned by some, quarterly (6) gules and argent, three, &c.

3. Per chevron crenellée or and azure, three eaglets displayed counter-coloured. JOHN DARBY, Sheriff of London 1446, Harl. MS. 1349 f.42.

4. Per chevron crenellée or and sable, three eaglets displayed counter-coloured.

5. Per pale argent and azure, two lyons couchant (? passant) tails cowed counter-coloured.

6. ROTE, *in later hand.* " Enbelyfe," *i.e.,* per bend sinister argent and sable, a lyon rampant counter-coloured.

7. Argent, on a pile botonnée sable a gillyflower argent, stalked and leaved.

8. Per fess or and azure a pale counter-coloured, three fleurs de lys 1 and 2 argent. Blasoned by some, quarterly (6) or and azure, three, &c.

9. " Enbelif," *i.e.,* per bend azure and argent, an eagle displayed counter-coloured, armed or.

10. Paly crenellée (6) argent and gules.

11. TALLOW CHANDLERS, *in later hand.* Per fess azure and argent a pale countercoloured, three doves 2 and 1 (of the second), each with an olive branch in its beak (or). Blasoned by some, quarterly (6) azure and argent, three, &c. ; granted by John Smart, Garter, 24th Sept., 1456.

12. Gyronny (6) azure and argent, three popinjays (? proper vel azure) 2 and 1 in the argent. SIR WILLIAM STOCKER, Lord Mayor of London 1484—*Papworth.*

[1] Perhaps "now living" in the original.

Folio 4b.

1. ROY DE SYFYR (Cyprus). Argent four bars azure, over all a lyon rampant queue fourchée gules, crowned—" The arms of Jerusalem quartly wt. all," are tricked in the margin.

2.* THE KYNGE OF SAVASTOFOLO (*alias* Constantinople, in the Index). Azure, " an vmage of Seynt Gorge" argent. See preceding page.

3. ROY DE ERMONYE. A lyon rampant crowned.

4. ROY DE NORREWAYE. Azure, three hulks or, at the prow and stern a dragon's head gules. See also page 76.

5. ROY DE DACYE. Quarterly; (1.) Or three lyons passant in pale azure. (2.) Azure, three crowns 2 and 1 or. (3.) Argent, a gryphon segreant gules. (4.) Gules, a lyon rampant or, holding a battle-axe erect; over all on a cross argent, an escocheon or charged with two lyons passant gardant azure.

6. BRUTE. Or, a lyon passant gules, erroneously tricked rampant, " The (fabulous) armys of Brewte the ffurst yt ever conqwerd Yngelond."

7. S. LAWNCELOT DE LAKE. Per pale gules and argent two bendlets of the second—fabulous.

8. S. GAWAYNE, THE GOOD KNIGHT. Vert, three gryphon passant or; " part wt. GAWAYNE " sable fretty argent, a label (3) gules——fabulous. See also No. 9, f.5, and No. 8, f.32.

9.* UTER PENDRAGON. Argent, a wyvern vert armed gules—fabulous.

Folio 5.

1. THE GENTYLL SOWDAN. Or, a pellet charged with a lyon passant argent crowned (? gules)—fabulous.

2.* THE SOWDEN OF BABYLOYNE. Sable, out of a chalice or, " a tortose " argent. " Part wt. the chaleys," the mutilated indication of a coat, possibly intended for an impalement, viz., a hand and arm issuant in bend sinister gules, grasping a dragon's head or the neck, the arm charged with 2 bars or, all fabulous.

3.* ROY DE TACE. Azure, a hare embelif or.

4. ROY JASPER DE COLOYNE. Azure, a waxing moon and between the horns, a mullet all or.

5. ROY MELCHER DE COLOYNE. Azure, seven mullets 3, 3, 1, or.

Original folios 4. 5. 6. of the Manuscript are missing.   As the "pe de grewe" referred to below does not appear in L. 8, it may be safely inferred that it was not in the original MS. from which Cooke made his original arms-book, Harl. MS. 2169.   The names of prelates Stafford 4, Neville 4 and Wainflete 4 occur in the Index ; their arms, tricked in MS. L. 8. College of Arms, are as follows :—

(1) John Stafford, Archbishop of Canterbury. Or, a chevron gules, a bordure engrailed sable.
(2) Robert Nevill, Bishop of Durham. Gules, on a saltire argent two annulets interlaced the uppermost gules the other argent.
(3) William Wainflete, Bishop of Winchester. Lozengy ermine and sable, on a chief of the second three lilies slipped argent.

Harl. MS. 2169, folio 4.

The pe de grewe be reyght lyne
Found and prevvyd by anerytaunce
How Kynge Herry the Sexyth nowghtcoleyne [1]
Ys trewe kynge of ffraunce.

The following twelve, rather rudely tricked, have been added by a similar hand (others by the same occur on f.64 et seq.).   These may refer to the city and its citizens.

1. Azure, two lucies saltireways argent ducally gorged or. The STOCK-FISHMONGERS OF LONDON; merged in the later FISHMONGERS, shield (see page 98 for the earlier shield). The field, sable in *Papworth.*

2. Per fess gules and argent (in L.8), a pale counter-coloured, three pineapples 2 and 1 or. Blasoned by some, quarterly (6) gules and argent, three, &c.

3. Per chevron crenellée or and azure, three eaglets displayed counter-coloured. JOHN DARBY, Sheriff of London 1446, Harl. MS. 1349 f.42.

4. Per chevron crenellée or and sable, three eaglets displayed counter-coloured.

5. Per pale argent and azure, two lyous conchant (? passant) tails cowed counter-coloured.

6. ROTE, *in later hand.* "Enbelyfe," *i.e.,* per bend sinister argent and sable, a lyon rampant counter-coloured.

7. Argent, on a pile botonnée sable a gillyflower argent, stalked and leaved.

8. Per fess or and azure a pale counter-coloured, three fleurs de lys 1 and 2 argent. Blasoned by some, quarterly (6) or and azure, three, &c.

9. "Enbelif," *i.e.,* per bend azure and argent, an eagle displayed counter-coloured, armed or.

10. Paly crenellée (6) argent and gules.

11. TALLOW CHANDLERS, *in later hand.* Per fess azure and argent a pale counter-coloured, three doves 2 and 1 (of the second), each with an olive branch in its beak (or). Blasoned by some, quarterly (6) azure and argent, three, &c. ; granted by John Smart, Garter, 24th Sepr., 1456.

12. Gyronny (6) azure and argent, three popinjays (? proper *vel* azure) 2 and 1 in the argent. SIR WILLIAM STOCKER, Lord Mayor of London 1484—*Papworth.*

[1] Perhaps "now living" in the original.

Folio 4b.

1. ROY DE SYTYR (Cyprus). Argent four bars azure, over all a lyon rampant queue fourchée gules, crowned——" The arms of Jerusalem quartly wt. all," are tricked in the margin.

2.* THE KYNGE OF SAVASTOPOLO (*alias* Constantinople, in the Index). Azure, "an vmage of Seynt Gorge" argent. See preceding page.

3. ROY DE ERMONYE. A lyon rampant crowned.

4. ROY DE NORREWAYE. Azure, three hulks or, at the prow and stern a dragon's head gules. See also page 76.

5. ROY DE DACYE. Quarterly ; (1.) Or, three lyons passant in pale azure. (2.) Azure, three crowns 2 and 1 or. (3.) Argent, a gryphon segreant gules. (4.) Gules, a lyon rampant or, holding a battle-axe erect ; over all on a cross argent, an escocheon or charged with two lyons passant gardant azure.

6. BRUTE. Or, a lyon passant gules, erroneously tricked rampant. "The (fabulous) armys of Brewte the ffirst yt ever conqwerd Yngelond."

7. S. LAWNCELOT DE LAKE. Per pale gules and argent two bendlets of the second—fabulous.

8. S. GAWAYNE, THE GOOD KNIGHT. Vert, three gryphon passant or ; "part wt. GAWAYNE" sable fretty argent, a label (3) gules——fabulous. See also No. 9, f.5. and No. 8, f.32.

9.* UTER PENDRAGON. Argent, a wyvern vert armed gules—fabulous.

Folio 5.

1. THE GENTYLL SOWDAN. Or, a pellet charged with a lyon passant argent crowned (? gules)—fabulous.

2.* THE SOWDEN OF BABYLOYNE. Sable, out of a chalice or, "a tortose" argent, "Part wt. the chaleys," the mutilated indication of a coat, possibly intended for an impalement, *viz.*, a hand and arm issuant in bend sinister gules, grasping a dragon's head at the neck, the arm charged with 2 bars or, all fabulous.

3.* ROY DE TACE. Azure, a hare embelif or.

4. ROY JASPER DE COLOYNE. Azure, a waxing moon and between the horns, a mullet all or.

5. ROY MELCHER DE COLOYNE. Azure, seven mullets 3, 3, 1, or.

Original folios 4, 5, 6, of the Manuscript are missing. As the "pe de grewe" referred to below does not appear in L. 8, it may be safely inferred that it was not in the original MS. from which Cooke made his original arms-book. Harl. MS. 2169. The names of prelates Stafford 4, Neville 4 and Wainflete 4 occur in the Index; their arms, tricked in MS. L. 8. College of Arms, are as follows:—

(1) John Stafford, Archbishop of Canterbury. Or, a chevron gules, a bordure engrailed sable.
(2) Robert Nevill, Bishop of Durham. Gules, on a saltire argent two annulets interlaced the uppermost gules the other argent.
(3) William Wainflete, Bishop of Winchester. Lozengy ermine and sable, on a chief of the second three lilies slipped argent.

Harl. MS. 2169, folio 4.

The pe de grewe be reyght lyne
Found and prevvyd by anerytaunce
How Kynge Herrv the Sexyth nowghtcoleyne [1]
Ys trewe kynge of ffraunce.

The following twelve, rather rudely tricked, have been added by a similar hand (others by the same occur on f.64 et seq.). These may refer to the city and its citizens.

1. Azure, two lucies saltireways argent ducally gorged or. The STOCK-FISHMONGERS OF LONDON; merged in the later FISHMONGERS, shield (see page 98 for the earlier shield). The field, sable in *Papworth.*

2. Per fess gules and argent (in L.8), a pale counter-coloured, three pineapples 2 and 1 or. Blasoned by some, quarterly (6) gules and argent, three, &c.

3. Per chevron crenellée or and azure, three eaglets displayed counter-coloured. JOHN DARBY, Sheriff of London 1446, Harl. MS. 1349 f.42.

4. Per chevron crenellée or and sable, three eaglets displayed counter-coloured.

5. Per pale argent and azure, two lyons couchant (? passant) tails cowed counter-coloured.

6. ROTE, *in later hand.* "Eubelyfe," *i.e.,* per bend sinister argent and sable, a lyon rampant counter-coloured.

7. Argent, on a pile botonnée sable a gilly-flower argent, stalked and leaved.

8. Per fess or and azure a pale counter-coloured, three fleurs de lys 1 and 2 argent. Blasoned by some, quarterly (6) or and azure, three, &c.

9. "Eubelif," *i.e.,* per bend azure and argent, an eagle displayed counter-coloured, armed or.

10. Paly crenellée (6) argent and gules.

11. TALLOW CHANDLERS, *in later hand.* Per fess azure and argent a pale counter-coloured, three doves 2 and 1 (of the second), each with an olive branch in its beak (or). Blasoned by some, quarterly (6) azure and argent, three, &c.; granted by John Smart, Garter, 24th Sepr., 1456.

12. Gyronny (6) azure and argent, three popinjays (? proper *vel* azure) 2 and 1 in the argent. SIR WILLIAM STOCKER, Lord Mayor of London 1484—*Papworth.*

[1] Perhaps "now living" in the original.

Folio 4b.

1. ROY DE SYPYR (Cyprus). Argent four bars azure, over all a lyon rampant queue fourchée gules, crowned——." The arms of Jerusalem quartly wt, all," are tricked in the margin.

2.* THE KYNGE OF SAVASTOPOLO (*alias* Constantinople, in the Index). Azure, " an ymage of Seynt Gorge " argent. See preceding page.

3. ROY DE ERMONYE. A lyon rampant crowned.

4. ROY DE NORREWAYE. Azure, three hulks or, at the prow and stern a dragon's head gules. See also page 76.

5. ROY DE DACYE. Quarterly ; (1.) Or, three lyons passant in pale azure. (2.) Azure, three crowns 2 and 1 or. (3.) Argent, a gryphon segreant gules. (4.) Gules, a lyon rampant or, holding a battle-axe erect ; over all on a cross argent, an escocheon or charged with two lyons passant gardant azure.

6. BRUTE. Or, a lyon passant gules, erroneously tricked rampant. "The (fabulous) armys of Brewte the ffirst yt ever conqwerd Yngelond."

7. S. LAWNCELOT DE LAKE. Per pale gules and argent two bendlets of the second—— fabulous.

8. S. GAWAYNE, THE GOOD KNIGHT. Vert, three gryphon passant or ; "part wt. GAWAYNE" sable fretty argent, a label (3) gules —— fabulous. See also No. 9, f.5, and No. 8, L.42.

9.* UTER PENDRAGON. Argent, a wyvern vert armed gules—fabulous.

Folio 5.

1. THE GENTYLL SOWDAN. Or, a pellet charged with a lyon passant argent crowned (? gules)—fabulous.

2.* THE SOWDEN OF BABYLOYNE. Sable, out of a chalice or, " a tortose " argent, " Part wt. the chaleys," the mutilated indication of a coat, possibly intended for an impaleuient, riz., a hand and arm issuant in bend sinister gules, grasping a dragon's head at the neck, the arm charged with 2 bars or, all fabulous.

3.* ROY DE TACE. Azure, a hare embehfor.

4. ROY JASPER DE COLOYNE. Azure, a waxing moon and between the horns, a mullet all or.

5. ROY MELCHER DE COLOYNE. Azure, seven mullets 3, 3, 1, or.

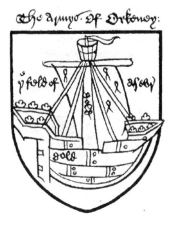

6.* ROY BALTEZER DE COLOYNE.   See illustration.

7.* The Armys of ORKENEY. Azure, a lymphad or, sail argent.

8. ROY DE GRYFFON. Azure, a gryphon segreant or ; erroneously tricked passant.

9. S. GAWAYNE THE GENTYLL; above this name is written "Roy de Marroke." Azure, three lyons heads erased or. See also No. 8, f.32.

Folio 5b.

THE IX WORTHY CONQWEROURYS.

1. ECTOR DE TROYE. Sable, two lyons combatant or—fabulous.

2. ALYXAUNDYR MAGNUS. Gules, a lyon (erroneously tricked rampant) sejant in a chair of state argent, holding a battle-axe azure—fabulous. This impossible trick has even victimised the herald, acting for THE VICTORIA HISTORY OF THE COUNTIES OF ENGLAND. See ANCESTOR, No. 3, page 194.

3. JULYUS SESARE. Or, a double-headed eagle displayed sable, armed gules—fabulous.

4.* ROY DAVYTH. Azure, a harp or—fabulous.

5. DEWER JOSEWE. Lozengy argent and gules, a wyvern sable. (*A note in later hand.*) Party per bend sinister or and gules, a batte displayed *sable*. Per GERARD LEIGH—fabulous.

6.* JUDAS MACHABEUS. Or, three Cornish choughs proper—two in pale only tricked—fabulous.

7. ROY ARTHUR. Gules, three crowns in pale or—fabulous.

8. ROY CHARLEMAYNE. Azure, florettée or, for OLD FRANCE, *dimidiated with*, or, a double-headed eagle sable—fabulous.

9. GODEFRAY DE BOILOYNE; (the Recoverer of Jerusalem). The fabulous arms of Jerusalem (No. 5 prox.), *dimidiated confusedly with*, gules an escarboncle or—fabulous.

Folio 6.

All the Kyestyn Kyngys yn ondyr offer theyr degre.

1. THE POPE OF ROOME. MARTYNE DE COLUMNIS (1417). Gules, a column argent environed with ribbon, crowned or. See No. 3, f.68.

2. PRESTER JOHN. Azure, the Crucifixion the cross or. Styled Emperour et Roy de Inde in Harl MS. 619, f 82. "One of the magi."

3. EMPEROWRE OF ROME ET DE ALMAYNE. Or, an eagle displayed sable.

4. THE EMPEROWRE OF COSTANTYNE LE NOBLLE AND OF GRACE. Or, a cross between four fire steels gules. See page 5 and Harl. 6163, f.i.

5. ROY DE JEREUSALEM. Argent, a cross potent between four like crosses or.

6.* ROY DE FRAUNCE. Azure, three fleurs de lys or.

7. ROY DE ENGLETARE ET DE FRAUNCE. FRANCE and ENGLAND quarterly. See also page 14.

8.* ROY DE SPAYNE ET DE CASTYLE. Gules, a castle or; *quarterly with* [LEON], argent, a lyon rampant purpure. See page 8.

9. ROY DE ARRAGON ET DE CECGYLE. Paly (10) or and gules—a note adds, but 4 paly, *i.e.,* 4 palets.

Folio 6b.

1. ROY DE PORTYNGALE. Sable, five false escocheons in cross azure, each charged with as many plates saltireways, on a bordure gules six castles or. Indications of a cross pattée vert, have been attempted.

2 ROY DE NAVARRENE. Gules, the Navarrese net, chains or; *quarterly with* azure, florettée or, a bend gobony argent and gules.

3. ROY DE BEAUME. Argent, a lyon rampant queue fourchée gules, crowned or.

4. Roy de Hongerye. Argent, three bars gules; *impaled with* France, azure, florettée or.

5.* Roy de Poyle. Gules, a king armed cap-a-pie on a prancing charger argent.

6. Roy de Naplys. France (as No. 6, f.6) with a label (3) gules; *impaled with* Jerusalem, as No. 5, f.6.

7. Roy de Cescyle the Olde, Per saltire or and argent four palets gules, on each flank an eagle displayed sable crowned or.

8. Roy de Cescyle, Dewke de Angove. (Duke of Gwyer added in L. 8, f.54). Quarterly of six; (1.) Argent, three bars gules. (2.) France as No. 6, f.6, for Naples. (3.) Jerusalem as No. 5, f.6. (4.) France as No. 6, f.6, within a bordure gules, for Anjou. (5.) Azure, crusily and two barbel addorsed or. Bar. (6.) Or, on a bend gules three eaglets displayed argent. Lorraine. A note in L. 8 states—"he beareth Anegos for his 4th coat and Loraine on an inescocheon.

9. Roy de Scottys. Or, a lyon rampant (tail inturned) within a double tressure flory counterflory all gules.

Folio 7.

The lordys that bene past, here aforetyme.

1. Roy Edward Sc. Azure, a cross pattée between five (four in L. 8. f.16b) martlets or; and also a rough trick of these arms, *impaling* France and England — Edward and Yngelond.

2. Seynt Gorge. Argent, a cross gules.

3. Kyng of Ingland. Gules, three lyons passant (not gardant) or; Seynt Ed———d Kynge, struck through.

4. Dewke of Lancastyr. England, with a label (3) of France.

5.* Dewke of Excestre. Bewfort—France and England, within a bordure gobony ermine and azure. See No. 7, 1,8, Name altered to Bishop of Winchester in L. 8, f.7b.

6. Erle of Hertforde (Earl of Northampton 1337). Azure, on a bend cotised (argent) between six lyoncelles rampant or, three mullets pierced. See No. 4, f.11b.

7. Roy de Denmarke. Or, three lyons passant gardant azure.

8.* Erle of Hontyngeton. England, within a bordure argent florettée or (*sic*). Coat and name defaced —attainted.

9. Erle of Warrenne. Chequy or and azure.

Folio 7b.

1. Erle of Warrewyke, Sir Gye (*over it Sir Harry Percy!*). Chequy or and azure, a chevron ermine; being the arms of Neubourg borne in the first quarter by Richard, Earl of Warwick, 1401-39. See No. 6, f.32.

2. Erle of Hampton, Sir Bevvys (*over it Sir Symond Mounforthe Earl of Leceter!*). Argent, a chief gules three roses 2 and 1 counter-coloured. ("The famous and Renowned History of Sir Bevis of Hampton.") See also No. 7, f.32.

3. Erle of Marche. Azure, three bars or, a false escocheon argent; on a chief of the second two palets between as many esquires of the first. See also No. 9, f.32.

4. Erle of Ulstyr. Or, a cross gules.

5. Erle of Genevvyle. Azure, three barnacles open or, on a chief ermine a demilyon rampant issuant gules. See also No. 1, f.32b.

6. Erle of Arrondell. Gules, a lyon rampant or; *quarterly with,* chequy or and azure.

7. Erle of Cornewayle. Argent, a lyon rampant gules, crowned—a bordure sable besantée.

8. Erle of Lyncolne. Or, a lyon rampant purpure. Henry Lacy, *in later hand.*

9. Erle of Penbroke. "Berle," *i.e.* barry (though tricked as 4 bars) argent and azure "vii. or ix." martlets bordurewise—8 in trick—gules. Wyllmus Valence *in later hand.* See also No. 7, f.32b.

Folio 8.

1. Erle Marchall——Mowbray. Gules, a lyon rampant argent, armed azure.

2. Erle of Woscestre.——Bechampe. Gules, on a fess between six crosses crosslet, 3. 2. 1. or, a crescent sable.

3. Erle of Mortayne and Bologne. Paly (6) vair and gules, on a chief or an eagle displayed sable. *Substituted in a later hand,* for Erle of Penbroke; paly (6) argent and vert, on a chief or an eagle displayed sable. See also No. 7, f.32b. Count of Blois.

4. Bygot, Duke (*sic*) of Northefolk. Per pale or and vert, a lyon rampant gules; in the margin an indication of a "gurge" is tricked untinctured. See also No. 2, f.32b.

C

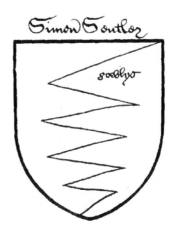

5. COUNT DE A[LBE]MARLE. Gules, a cross patonce vair. Will. Le Grose, Earl of Amarle and Howderness in L. 8.

6. THE LORD BURNELL. Argent a lyon rampant, and a bordure sable.

7. COUNT DE PERCH, BEWFORDE (THOMAS DE BEAUFORT, DUKE OF EXETER). FRANCE and ENGLAND *quarterly*, a bordure gobony argent and azure florettée or. See No. 5, f.7.

8.* COUNT DE CAMBRYGGE. FRANCE and ENGLAND *quarterly*, a bordure (argent) entoyre of lyoncelles rampant (purpure).

9. COUNT DE SALYSBERY, MOUNTTEGEW. Argent, three fusils conjoined in fess gules; *quarterly with*, or, an eagle displayed vert.

Folio 8b.

1. COWND DE RYCHEMONDE. Chequy or azure, a quarter ermine, a bordure gules—ALLAN FERGAUNT, *in later hand*.

2. LO. HARCOURT, *in later hand*. Or, three bars gules.

3. LORD WAKE. Barry (6) or and gules, in chief three torteaux.

4. SIMON MONTFORT, COUNT DE LEYCESTYR. Gules, a lyon rampant queue fourchée argent.

5. LORD MERMYON. Vair, a fess gules.

6. COUNT DE CHESTYR. Azure, three wheat sheaves (or) banded (gules) in L. 8.

7. LORD FORNYVVALE. Argent, a bend between six martlets 3 and 3 gules.

8.* SIMON SENTLEZ, COUNT DE HUNTINGTON 1174-84 per pale indented argent and gules; *in later hand*. Originally written COUNT DE LEYCESTYR. Per pale indented ermine and gules.

9. COWNT DE CLARE, SIR GYLBERT—or, three chevronels gules, a label (3) azure—E. GLOSTER, *in a later hand*.

Folio 9.

"*Thes beth the vij Kyngys armys that dwellyd yn Yngelond all attonys.*"

1. SEYNT OSWALDE, ROY DE NORTHWMBERLONDE — a cross between four lyons rampant—fabulous. See No. 2, f.9b.

2.* ROY DE KENT. Gules, three se axes *vel*, cutlasses argent, handles or—fabulous.

3. ROY DE ESSEX. Gules, three crowns or. L.8. ZEBBE (a 665) is added.

4.* ROY DE SOWTHSEX. Azure, three trefoyles raguled 2 and 1 argent—fabulous.

5. ROY DE NORTHFOLKE. Argent, three crowns 2 and 1 gules—fabulous.

6. ROY DE MARCHELOND (MERCIA) LYNCOLLCHYRE. Azure, three crowns 2 and 1 argent—fabulous.

"*Here be vj of the Kyngys that dwellyd all att oo tyme yn Yngelonde And Seynt Edwardys armys was the seiynth.*" See No. 1, f.10.

7. COUNT DE STAFFORDE. Or, a chevron gules.

8. LORD SENTAMOUNT. Or, fretty sable, on a chief of the second three besants.

9. LORD BASSETT. Or, three piles meeting in base gules, a quarter ermine.

Folio 9b.

1. SC. CUTHBERTUS, EPISCOPUS. Azure, a cross patonce between four lyons rampant —. See No. 5, prox. and next page.

2. SC. OSWALDUS. Purpure, a cross or between four lyons rampant. See No. 1, i.o.

3.* SENT MYHELL, arrays. Azure, the device of the Trinity argent, inscribed sable. See page 12.

4. SC. THOMAS OF CAUNTERBERY. Argent, three (beckits) Cornish choughs proper; *impaling* on the sinister the arms of the See of Canterbury, as No. 1, f.3.

5. *SC. COTHBERD OF DEPHAM. Azure, a cross patonce or, between four "lyonsens" rampant argent. See No. 1 above.

6. SC. W(ILFRID) OF YORKE. Or, seven mascles conjoined 3. 3. 1. gules.

7. SC. THOMAS (Bishop) OF HERFORDE, DE CANTHILUPO. Gules, three leopards faces reversed jessant de lys or.

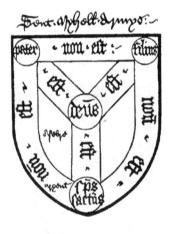

8. MAYSTER SCROPE, Buyschoppe of Yorke. Azure, a bend or, a label (3) argent.

9. BYSCHOPPE SPENSER OF NORWYCHE. Argent, a bend sable, a crescent for difference ; *quarterly with*, gules, a fret or.

Folio 10.

1. SC. EDMONDE KYNGE OF YNGELONDE. of olde tyme. Azure, three crowns 2 and 1 or—fabulous.

2.* MAYSTER BOWET, Byschopp of Yorke. Argent, three " rayndere " heads cabossed 2 and 1 sable.

3.* MAYSTER W. ASKEWE, Byschoppe of Salysbery. Sable, a fess gules between three asses passant argent.

4.* BYSCHOPPE HARREWELL. Argent, a fess undée sable between three hares' heads gold (? gules). Bishop of Bath and Wells—1369.

5. SEYNT TOMAS OF AKERYS. Azure a cross formée per pale gules and argent.

6. THE ABBEY OF HYDE YN WYNCHESTYR. Argent, a lyon rampant sable, on a chief of the second four keys addorsed 2 and 2 of the first.

7. ABBOT OF THORNTON CURTAYS. Azure, three escutcheons 2 and 1 of the arms of MARCH, see No. 3, f.7b, with the false escocheon gules, in chief a crosier erect or.

8.* ABBOT OF SELBY. Sable, three swans 2 and 1 argent, armed gules.

9. BYSCHOPPE OF LONDON. Argent, seven mascles 3. 3. 1. gules ; borne within a bordure by ROBERT BRAYBROOKE, bishop—1382.

Folio 10b.

1. LORD OF OFFORD. Or, a cross lozengy sable.

2. FYTZGEROD. Per pale indented argent and azure.

3. COUNT DE MORTAYNE. Ermine, a chief indented gules.

4.* LORD OF GYNES. (Gwyes.) Vaire or and azure.

5. COUNT DE SENT POULE. Paly (10) vair and gules, on a chief or, a label (5) azure.

6. COUNT DE PROVENSE. Paly (10) or and gules—tricked as five pallets.

7. Gules, three pallets vair, a chief or. A later hand has named the trick, COMES BLOYS, adding an eagle on the chief.

8. COUNT DE HONTYNGTON. Argent, crusily fitchée (3, 2, 1,) sable on a chief azure, two mullets pierced or.

Folio 11b.

1. LORD MENELL.   Azure, three bars gemelles and a chief or.

2. Or, billettée sable, a label (5) gules.

3. NORTON, *added.* Paly (6) argent and azure, on a chief or, three martlets gules.

4. WYLLM. BOHOUN, ERLE OF NORHAMTON (*substituted in a later hand* for Count de Worcest.). Azure, on a bend argent cotised or, between six lyoncelles rampant of the third, three mullets pierced gules. See also No. 5, f.7.

5. COUNT DE KENT. ENGLAND within a bordure argent.

6. LE MOUNT HERMER. Or, three false escocheons 2 and 1 vair each charged with three barrulets gules.

7. Lozengy sable and or, on a quarter gules a lyon passant argent ; for lozengy, a " fret of saybll " is blasoned.

8. COUCY, EARLE OF BEDFORD (*in a later hand*). Vair, four barrulets gules. In his seal, barry (6) vair and gules.

9. COUNT DE KYME. Gules, crusily and a chevron or.

9. RATHERFELD PYPPARD. Argent, two bars azure, on a quarter of the second a cinquefoyle pierced or.

Folio 11.

1. LORD DENCOURTE. Azure, billettée and a fess dancettée or.

2. LORD SAYMER. Argent, two chevronels gules ; *quarterly with* NEVILL—on a saltire a crescent.

3. LORD BOWRCHER, ROBSARDE. Vert, a lyon rampant or ; *quarterly with* BOURCHIER, see No. 4. f.14b.

4. LORD MATREVVERES. Sable, a fret or.

5. LORD MAULEY, *substituted for* WASTNEYS. Or, a bend sable.

6. LORD BARDOLFFE, S. WYLYAM PHELYPE Per cross gules and argent, in the quarter an eagle displayed or—*quarterly with* BARDOLF, azure, three cinquefoyles pierced or.

7. FERRERS. Vaire or and gules, a bordure azure entoyre of fers-de-cheval (6) argent.

8. GYRONNY (12) or and azure, a quarter ermine.

9. LORD GRAUNSOUN. Paly (6) argent and azure, over all on a bend gules three escallops or. LORD GRANDISON.

[FOLIO 10b.—MS. L. 8, COLLEGE OF ARMS.]

Folio 12.

1. LE CARDYNALL DE ENGELETABE, FRANCE and ENGLAND quarterly, within a bordure gobony argent and azure ; surmounted of a Cardinal's hat. For HENRY BEAUFORT, son of JOHN OF GAUNT.

2. ROY HERREY THE VJ. FRANCE and ENGLAND quarterly, surmounted of a regal coronet. See also page 7.

3.* LE CARDYNALL DE YORKE. Gules, three wheat sheaves 2 and 1 or, a bordure engrailed of the last ; surmounted of a Cardinal's hat. KEMPE, *in later hand.*

4. DEWKE DE CLARAUNCE. FRANCE and ENGLAND quarterly, a label (3) ermine.

5. DEWKE DE BEDFFORDE. FRANCE and ENGLAND quarterly, a label (5) per pale ermine and floretée (FRANCE).

6. DEWKE DE GLOWSESTRE. FRANCE and ENGLAND quarterly, within a bordure argent.

7. DEWKE DE EXCESTYR. ENGLAND within a bordure of FRANCE.

8. DEWKE DE YORKE. FRANCE and ENGLAND quarterly, a label (3) argent, on each file as many torteaux.

9. DEWKE DE NORTHFOLKE. ENGLAND, with a label (3) argent.

Folio 12b.

1. DEWKE DE BOKYNGHAM. FRANCE and ENGLAND, within a bordure (a marginal note, the armys of Dewke of Glowsestyr, see No. 6, last past), *quartering* or, a chevron gules, STAFFORD, all *quarterly with* the ERLE OF HERFFORDE (in marginal note), three mullets pierced in bend between two cotises, six lyon celles rampant three in chief and as many in base. See also No. 5, f.7, and No. 4, f.11b.

2. DUKE OF SOMERSETT, *in later hand.* FRANCK and ENGLAND quarterly, within a bordure gobony argent and azure, BEAUFORT *impaled with* BEAUCHAMP *quartering* NEW-BURGH untinctured. See next.

3. DUKE OF WARWYKE, *in later hand.* Gules, a fess between six crosses crosslet; *quarterly with,* NEWBURGH, chequy or and azure, a chevron ermine, *impaled with* CLARE and DESPENSER quarterly —no tinctures.

4.* PRYNCE OF WALYS (S. Tomas Howe *struck out* and HOWELL DDA *added*). Argent, three lyons passant regardant tails cowed and erect gules. Note, "Set hym bynethe ye olde armys." See also No. 4, f.32.

5. The Armys of GYAN. Gules, a lyon passant gardant or, armed azure. GUIENNE.

6. DUKE OF SOFOKE, *in later hand.* (Azure), a fess between three leopards faces or; *quarterly with,* WINGFIELD, argent, on a bend gules three pairs of wings conjoined argent. BRYENAC an GYAN deleted, the trick pasted over with POLE and WINGFIELD. See also No. 8 prox., and No. 5, f.32.

7.* LE BAGES DEU ROYE. Sable, three ostrich feathers argent with golden pens, each enfiled by a scroll or, bearing the motto "hic hoff."

8.* BRIAK en GYAN armes (in footnote) substituted for DEWKE DE SOMERSETT. Or, two gryphons legs fessways, erased sable. See also No. 5, f.32, and next page.

9.* THE BASTARD OF CLARAUNCE (the *name apparently deleted*). "Enté asewre a chief of gowlys," *i.e.,* per chevron gules and azure, in chief two lyons counter combatant gardant or, in base a fleur de lys of the third. See also No. 3, f.33; and page 17.

Folio 13.

1. COUNT DE ARBONDELL. Gules, a lyon rampant or; *quarterly with,* sable, a fret or.

2. COUNT DE WARREWYKE. Gules, a fess or between six crosses crosslet—BEAUCHAMP, *quarterly with* NEWBURGH, chequy or and azure a chevron ermine. See also No. 3, f.12b.

3. LE VVYSCOUNT DE BEAUMOND. Azure, florettée and a lyon rampant or ; *quarterly with*, azure three wheat sheaves (*vel* "garbys ') 2 and 1 or.

4. LORDE HASTINGS (substituted for, The olde Kynge of Man). Gules, a maunch or. In MS. L. 8, f.13, the coat of Chetwynd appears in this place.

5. LORD SPENSER. Argent, a bendlet sable ; *quarterly with*, gules a fret or.

6. LORD ROOS. Gules, three "bowgys" (water bougets) 2 and 1 argent.

7. LORD TALBOTT. Or, a lyon rampant within a bordure engrailed gules ; *quarterly with*, STRANGE, gules two lyons passant in pale argent.

8. LORD OF AWDELEY. Ermine, a chevron gules ; *quarterly with*, gules, a fret or ; " Thys quarter before chef," *i.e.* in the first quarter.

9. LORD GRAY, CODNORE. Barry (6) argent and azure, in chief three roundles, GREY ; *quarterly with* HASTINGS *quartering* VALENCE.

Folio 14.

1. LORD LOVVELL. Barry undée (6) or and gules, *quarterly with* HOLLAND, azure florettée and a lyon rampant argent.

3. COUNT DE NORTHUMBERLOND. Or, a lyon rampant azure ; *quarterly with*, gules, three lucies hauriant argent.

4. COUNT DE WESTEMERLOND. Gules, a saltire argent.

5. COUNT DE DOVVENECHYRE (Devon). Or, three torteaux ; *quarterly with*, or a lyon rampant azure.

6. COUNT DE OXYNFFORD. Per cross gules and or, in the quarter a mullet pierced argent.

7. COUNT DE SCHROWYSBERY. I. and IV., a lyon rampant within a bordure engrailed ; *quarterly with*, two lyons passant in pale— II. and III. a bend between six martlets ; *quarterly with*, a fret ; over all an escocheon of BEAUCHAMP.

8. COUNT DE SALYSBERY. Three fusils conjoined in fess ; *quarterly with*, or an eagle displayed—*all quarterly with* NEVILL, gules, a saltire argent, a label (3) gobony ; " Salysbery by fore chef," *i.e.*, in the first quarter.

9. COUNT DE URMOUNDE. Or, a chief indented azure—BUTLER, ERLE OF ORMONDE.

Folio 13b.

1. COUNT DE WYLCHYRE, S. JAMES BOTTELER. Or, a chief indented azure, a label (3) argent.

2. COUNT DE WORCESTYR — TYPTOFTE. Argent, a saltire engrailed gules—" Quartly wt the armys of Salesbery." See No. 5, f.41b.

2. LORD DE LA WARRE. Gules, crusily fitchée and a lyon rampant argent ; *quarterly with* CANTELUPE, azure, three leopards faces reversed jessant de lys or.

3. LORD FEWATYR. Or, a fess between two chevrons gules, FITZWALTER.

4. LORD WYLBY. Sable, a cross engrailed or, WYLLOUGHBY ; *quarterly with* BEK, gules, a cross moline argent.

5. LORD CLYFFORDE. Chequy or and azure, a fess gules.

6. LORD FERRERES OF GROBY. Gules, seven mascles conjoined 3. 3. 1. or.

7. LORD OF WELLYS. Or, a lyon rampant queue fourchée sable, armed gules.

8. LORD CALYS (SCALES). Gules, six escallops 3. 2. 1. argent.

9. LORD SOUCH. Gules, besantée a quarter ermine.

Folio 14b.

1. LORD BOTREWSE. Argent, a gryphon segreant gules armed azure, BOTREAUX ; *quarterly with* DE MOELS, barry (6) argent and gules in chief three torteaux.

2. LORD BERKELEY. Gules, crusily formée (6 and 4) and a chevron argent.

3. LORD FANHOPE. Ermine, a lyon rampant gules, crowned or, a bordure engrailed sable, besantée. CORNEWALL.

4. LORD BOWCER. Argent, a cross engrailed gules between four "bosches"
(water bougets) sable. BOURCHIER. A marginal note "wt lord bemond le vvyscount a
fore baronys." See No. 3, f.13b.
5. LORD TYPTTOFTE. Argent, a saltire
engrailed gules. See No. 2, f.13b.
6. LORD HUNGERFORDE. Barry (6) argent
and sable, in chief three pellets.
7. LORD STRAUNGE. Gules, two lyons
passant argent, armed azure.
8. LORD CROMEWELLE. Argent, a chief
azure, a bend (vel baston) gules ; quarterly
with TATESHALL, chequy or and gules, a chief
ermine.
9. LORD PONYNGYS. Barry (6) or and
vert, a baston gules ; quarterly with FITZ
PAYNE, gules, three lyons passant argent, a
baston azure. A marginal note "to be
mendyd," i.e., corrected. In L.8. Quarterly
1 and 4 or, three piles azure, BRYAN ; 2.
POYNINGS ; 3, FITZ-PAYNE.

Folio 15.

1. LORD MORLAY. Argent, a lyon rampant
sable, crowned or.
2. LORD DODDLEY. Or, two lyons passant
azure, POMERI ; quarterly with SUTTON,
argent, a cross pattée azure. LORD DUDLEY.
3. LORD KLYNTON. Argent, on a chief
azure two mullets pierced or, CLINTON ;
quarterly with SAY, per cross or and gules.

4. LORD POWES. Or, a lyon rampant
queue fourchée gules, armed azure.
5. LORD MOLAYNYS. Paly wavy (6) or
and gules ; quarterly with, sable, two bars
argent, in chief three plates.
6. LORD SWDELEY. Or, two bendlets
gules ; quarterly with, gules, a fess compony
argent and sable, between six crosses crosslet
fitchée at the foot or.
7. LORD GRAYE OF WYLTON. Barry (6)
argent and azure, a label (5) gules.
8. LORD FEHEWE. Chevrony fretty (a
mistake for three chevrons interlaced), and
a chief—FITZHUGH ; impaling MARMION,
vair a fess gules.
9. LORD GRAY, Rethen. Barry (6) argent
and azure, in chief three torteaux.

Folio 15b.

1. LORD DARCHY. Azure, crusilly and
three syse-foyles pierced argent. DARCY.
2. LORD CROPE OF BOLTON. Azure, a
bend or, SCROPE ; quarterly with TYPTOFTE,
argent, a saltire engrailed gules.
3. LORD OF DAKYR. Gules, three escallops 2 and 1 argent, DACRE ; quarterly
with VAUX of Gillesland, chequy or and gules.
4. LORD SCROPE OF UPSALE. Azure, a
bend or, a label (3) argent.

5. THE BARON OF GRAYSTOKE. Barry (8)
argent and azure, three chaplets of roses gules,
buds or.
6. LORD CAMEWSE. Or, on a chief gules,
three plates. CAMOYS.
7. LORD OF BARGEVVENNE. Gules, a fess
between six crosses crosslet or, a crescent
sable, BEAUCHAMP ; quarterly with WEST-
MORLAND, gules, a saltire argent. NEVILL.
LORD OF ABERGAVENNY.
8. LORD HERYNGETON. Sable, fretty
argent ; blasoned "sylvyr the frette."
HARINGTON.
9. LORD LATEMER. Gules, a saltire argent,
NEVILL ; quarterly with LATIMER, gules, a
cross patonce or ; impaling BEAUCHAMP
quarterly with NEWBURGH as No. 3, f.12b.

Folio 16.

1. LORD LYLE. Gules, a lyon passant
argent crowned or, LISLE ; quarterly with
TYES, argent, a chevron gules.
2. LORD FAWCONBERGE. Argent, a lyon
rampant azure, armed gules ; quarterly with
NEVILL, gules, a saltire argent.
3. LORD FERRERES OF CHARTLEY. Vaire,
or and gules.
4. LORD BEAUCHAMPE. Gules, a fess
between six martlets or. S. JOHN BEACHAMPE
OF POWYK.

D

5. LORD COBBHAM. Gules, on a chevron or, three lyoncelles rampant sable.

6. LORD STORTON. Sable, a bend or between six fountains.

7. LORDE VVESSEY. Or, a cross sable, VESCI ; *quarterly with* BROMFLETE, sable, a bend flory counterflory or.

8. LORD SEYNT AMONDE. Or, lozengy (blasoned " a fret ") sable, on a chief of the second three besants ; *quarterly with* BEAU-CHAMPE, gules, a fess between six martlets or. S. WYLYAM BEAUCHAMPE.

9. LORD FEWARREYNE. Quarterly per fess indented ermine and gules, FITZWARREN ; *quarterly with* BOURCHIER, argent, a cross engrailed gules between four water bougets sable. SR WYLYAM BOURCER. ROCHE pryore, imperfectly deleted.

10. LORD OF SEYNT GONYS. Blanc.

Folio 16b.

1. LORD EGREMOYNE. A lyon rampant, on his shoulder a fleur de lys. PERCY *quarterly with* LUCY, three lucies hauriant. " Northumbyrland armys wt difference."

2. LORD REVVERS. Barry (6) gules and argent, on a quarter of the first an eagle displayed or. LORD RIVERS.

3. LORD BONVVVLE. Sable, seven mullets 3. 3. 1. pierced argent.

4. LORD SAYE. Per cross or and gules (in the margin, a bordure argent). SAVE ; *quarterly with* FIENNES, azure, three lyons rampant or.

5.* THE BARON OF CARREW. Or, three lyons passant sable.

6. THE BARON OF HYLTON. Argent, two bars azure.

7. S. GYLBERD UMFERVVYLE OF NORTHUM-BERLOND. Gules, crusily bottonée and a cinquefoyle pierced or.

8. S. ROBARDE OF OGLE OF NORTHUMBER-LAND. Argent, a fess between three crescents gules, OGLE ; *quarterly with* BERTRAM, or, an orle azure.

9.* S. THOMAS LAVMLEY. Argent, a fess gules between three popinjays proper.

Original leaf 20 of this Manuscript has been torn out, the following eleven names occur in the Index, and the blasons have been derived from MS. L. 8 College of Arms

ARDEN, WILLIAM. Chequy or and azure a fess ermine.

ASTWYCKE, WILLIAM, BEDFORDSHIRE. Argent, three crosses botonnée sable.

BEKKE, possibly the same coat as on page 38,

CORNEWALL, BRYAN OF HARFFORDSHYRE.
Ermine, a lyon rampant gules, a bordure
sable, bezantée.
DAINHAM. In L. 8, f. 35b, Wyllm. Domham.
Sable, on a chevron argent three ravens
proper.
FYLOLL OF DORSETSHIRE. Vair, a quarter
gules.
GRAUNFORT, RICHARD OF SOWSEX. Gules,
a lyon rampant argent, a bordure en-
grailed sable.
LANGLEY, possibly Bishop of Durham, as on
page 51.
LOCKTON THOMAS OF Co. CAMBRIDGE. Argent
a chevron azure.
PEVVERELL. Gules, three lyons rampant or,
a bordure engrailed or. L. 8, f 35b.
Erroneously indexed as Powtrell.
SLEYCLOWE. ? Strelley.

Folio 17.

1. S. WYLYAM EWERYS OF YE BYSCHE-
PRYKE OF DERHAM. Per cross or and gules,
on a bend sable three escallops argent.
EVERS or EURE.
2. S. WYLYAM BOWYS OF YE BYSCHE-
PERYKE OF DERHAM. Ermine, three bent
bowes erect gules.
3. NEVELL (in *later hand*). Gules, on a
saltire argent a rose. LORD BERGAVENNY.

4. S. ROBARDE KNOLLYYS OF NORTHHUM-
BERLAND. Gules, a lyon rampant argent, a
bordure engrayled of the second.
5. S. JOHN SORTEYS OF NORTHUMBER-
LOND. Argent, crusily fitchée and three
covered cups 2 and 1 sable.
6. S. JOHN COYNYERYS OF YORKECHYRE.
Azure, a maunch or.
7. S. WYLYAM ELMEDENE OF THE BISHO-
PERYKE OF DERHAM. Argent, on a bend
sable three crescents of the field.
8.* S. ROBARD CLAXTON OF THE BYSCHI-
PERYKE OF DERHAM. Gules, a fess between
three hedgehogs (orchonys · urchin) passant
argent.
9.* S. EMONDE HERON OF NORTH-HUMBER-
LOND. Gules, three heron 2 and 1 argent,
beaks and feet or.

Folio 17b.

1. S. JOHN CONSTABYLL, YORKECHYRE.
Barry (6) or and azure. vij peeys, in the
margin.
2. S. JAMYS STRANGWAYS, YORKECHYRE.
Sable, two lyons passant gobony (6) argent
and gules.
3. S. ROBARDE OWTHREYGHT. YORKE-
CHYRE. Gules, on a cross pattée or, five
mullets pierced of the first, OUGHTRED ;
quarterly with BURDON, azure, crusily and
three burdons erect all or.

4. S. TOMAS METHAM, YORKECHYRE. Per cross azure and argent, a fleur de lys in the quarter or.

5.* S. ROBARDE KNOLLYS, YORKECHYRE. Gules, on a chevron argent three roses of the first.

6. S. JAMYS PYKERYNGE, YORKECHYRE. Ermine, a lyon rampant azure crowned or.

7. S. JOHN SALVVAYNE, YORKECHYRE. Argent, on a chief sable, two mullets pierced or.

8. S. ROBARDE WATERTON, YORKECHYRE. Ermine, three bars gules, as many crescents 2 and 1 sable.

9.* S. JOHN OF MELTON, YORKECHYRE. Azure, a cross patonce voided argent.

Folio 18.

1. S. JOHN BARTRAM, NORTHUMBERLAND. Or, an orle azure, tricked rather as azure, a false escocheon or, all within a bordure of the second.

2. S. JOHN SAYVVYLE, YORKECHYRE. Argent, on a bend engrailed sable three owls argent; *quarterly with* THORNHILL, gules, two gemelles and a chief argent.

3. S. WYLYAM NORMANVVYLE, YORKE-CHYRE. Argent, on a fess cotised gules three fleurs de lys of the field.

4. S. JOHN PERCEHAYE, YORKECHYRE. Gules, a chevron ermine between three lyons rampant or, those in chief respectant, the arms defaced. LANGTON, see No. 1, f.20, inserted in error for PERCEHAYE; argent, a cross moline gules. See "Some Feudal Coats of Arms."

5. S. ALYSAUNDYR FOLGHAM, DERBY-CHYRE. Sable, a bend between six escallops 3 and 3 or.

6. S. HARRY PERCY, YORKECHYRE; "the olde armys." Azure, five lozenges conjoined in fess or.

7. S. RAWFE RADCLYFF OF LANCASTER-CHYRE. Argent, two bendlets engrailed sable.

8. S. WYLYAM LUMLEY OF YE BYSCHOP-PERYKE OF DERHAM. Gules, a fess between three popinjays argent.

9. S. ROBARD ROOS OF MYDHERST, SOWSEX. Gules, three water bougets ermine.

Folio 18b.

1. GOY OF ROCLYFF, YORKECHYRE. Argent, a chevron between three lyons heads erased gules.

2. TOMAS WESCHYNGTON OF YE BYSCHOP-PERYKE OF DERHAM. Gules, three bars and in chief as many mullets pierced all argent.

3. WYLYAM ROMONBY, YORKECHYRE. Ermine, a fess gules.

4. S. TOMAS OF STANLEY, LANCASTER-CHYRE *struck through* (see No. 8, i.19b). Per pale or and sable, a lyons gamb issuant from the sinister counter-coloured.

5.* TOMAS GRA, YORKE CHYRE. Argent, on a bend cotised azure, three gryphons passant or. The blason on the trick is confused.

6. MAYST, JOHN MAWRSCHALL, YORK CHYRE. Azure, three whet chevys (wheat sheaves) argent.

7. JOHN OF NEWSAM, YORKE CHYRE. Sable, on a fess argent three crosses crosslet botounée of the first.

8. S. WYLYAM OF RYTHER OF YORKE-CHYRE. Azure, three crescents 2 and 1 or; *quarterly with*—a lyon rampant.

9. S. TOMAS BOSSEVELL OF YORKE CHYRE. Argent, five fusils conjoined in fess gules.

Folio 19.

1. JOHN CATTON (LAUTON, *in later hand*) OF DERHAM CHYRE. Argent, a fess between six crosses crosslet fitchée 3 and 3 sable.

2.* S. GYLBERD HALSALE (LANCASTER *added*). Or, three dragons heads erased azure, langued gules.

3. S. JOHN BERRON OF LANCASTERCHYRE. Argent, three bendlets enhanced gules. BYRON.

4. ROBARDE ELYS, YORK CHYRE. Or, on a cross sable five crescents argent; *quarterly with* EVERBINGHAM, gules, a lyon rampant vair.

5. S. JOHN DAVVELL OF YORK CHYRE. Argent, a fess flory counterflory sable.

6. WYLYAM STRYKELONDE. Sable, three escallops 2 and 1 argent.

7. RYCHARD OF BARTON OF LANCASTER CHYRE. Ermine, on a fess gules, three annulets or; *quarterly with*, paly (6) argent and vert.

8. S. TOMAS OF STANLEY, LANCASTER CHYRE. Or, on a chief indented azure three plates, LATHOM; *quarterly with*, argent on a bend azure three harts heads cabossed or.

9.* WYLYAM PELLESON, YORKE CHYRE. Sable, a fess between three pelicans argent vulning themselves proper. See page 22.

Folio 19b.

1. WYLYAM PRESTON OF LANCASTER CHYRE. Argent, two bars gules, on a quarter of the second a cinquefoyle pierced or.

2. WYLYAM LATON. Sable, a fess gules (*sic*) between three escallops argent.

3. S. JOHN PYGOT. Gules, three picks erect 2 and 1 or.

4. S. JOHN LANGFORD. Paly (6) argent and gules, on a chief azure a lyon passant gardant or.

5.* Tomas Gower. Azure, a chevron between three talbots saliant ("embelit") argent. Gower may be a misreading of the herald painter for Talbot. See also No. 7, f.20b.

6. Tomas Crathorne. Argent, on a saltire gules five crosses pattée sable.

7.* S. Tomas Lambton. Gules, a fess between three lambs passant argent.

8.* Tomas Berrewyk. Argent, three bears heads erased sable, muzzled gules.

9. S. Hewe of Anysley. Paly (6) argent and azure, a bend gules. Annesley.

Folio 20.

1. S. John of Langton, York chyre. Gules, a chevron ermine between three lyons rampant or, those in chief respectant. See No. 4, f.18.

2. S. Wylyam Plomton, York chyre. Azure, five fusils conjoined or, on each an escallop gules.

3. S. John Claryvays of Kroft, Yorke chyre. Sable, a saltire or. Clervaux.

4. S. Rawf Barthorpe, Yorke chyre. Sable, a chevron or between three crescents ermine.

5. S. Emonde Darrell, Yorke chyre. Azure, a lyon rampant or.

6. S. Rycharde Buttler, Lancaster chyre. Azure, a bend between six covered cups 3. 3. or.

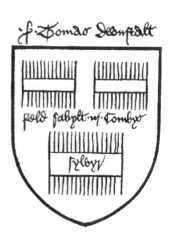

7. S. JOHN BUTTLER, LANCASTER CHYRE. Azure, a chevron between three covered cups or.

8. S. JOHN RADCLYFFE, LANCASTER CHYRE. Argent, a bend engrailed sable.

9. S. ALYSAUNDYR LOWNDE, YORKE CHYRE. Azure, fretty argent, a bordure or, entoyre of torteaux.

Folio 20b.

1. S. JOHN KYRELEY (KIGHLEY), YORKE CHYRE. Argent, a fess sable.

2. S. JOHN OF ETTON, YORKE CHYRE. Argent, five bars gules, on a quarter sable, a cross patonce or.

3. S. RYCHARDE HAWGHTON OF LANCASTER CHYRE. Sable, three bars argent.

4. THE BARON OF NEWTON, LANCASTER CHYRE. Argent, three chevronels gules. LANGTON.

5.* S. TOMAS AYSTON, LANCASTER CHYRE. Argent, a mullet sable. ASSHETON.

6.* S. TOMAS DWNSTALL OF LANCASTER CHYRE. Sable, three combs 2 and 1 argent. TUNSTALL.

7.* S. EMONDE TALBOTT, LANCASTER CHYRE. Argent, three squirrels sejant 2 and 1 purpure. This is not a usual Talbot coat. See also No. 5, f.19b; and next page.

8. S. Jafferey Massey of Lancaster chyre. Per cross argent and gules.

9. S. John Sorteys, Yorke chyre. Argent, on a chevron between three escallops sable as many crescents of the first. Surtees.

Folio 21.

1.* S. Tomas of Bowthe of Lancaster chyre. Argent, three boars heads erased and erect 2 and 1 sable.

2. Harry Wwaveser, York chyre. Or, a fess dancettée sable. Vavasour.

3. Stevvyn Haytfelde, Yorke chyre. Ermine, on a chevron sable three cinquefoyles pierced or. Stephen Hatfeild.

4. John of Portyngeton, Yorke chyre. Gules, on a fess argent three "chovvys" (choughs) proper.

5.* Hopkyne Mawleverere, Yorke chyre. Sable, three levriers courant argent collared.

6.* Tomas Constabyll of Cattysfosse, Yorke chyre. Gules, ten fusils conjoined 5. 5. sable; blasoned as "ij fecys fesele of sabyll."

7. Tomas Dalarevver, Yorke chyre. Vair, a bordure sable, besantée.

8. Robarde Manerys, North umberlond. Or, two bars azure and a chief gules. Sir Richard also in L. 8.

9. WYLLYSTHROPPE, YORK CHYRE. Azure, a chevron between three lyons passant gardent argent.

Folin 21b.

1. JOHN FYTZ HENRY, YORKE CHYRE. Argent, a cross engrailed sable.

2.* SCHORTHOSE, YORKE CHYRE. Gules, three tilting spears erect argent, with pennons flotant.

3. POLLARD (RAWF ACCLUM), byschopperyke of Derham. Ermine, a cross engrailed sable. POLLARD, *in later hand.* Acclum misplaced, see No. 5.

4. WYLYAM CHAUNCELER (SKELTON added on the shield), byschopperyke of Derham. Azure, a fess between three fleurs de lys or.

5. RAWFE ACCLUM, YORK CHYRE. Gules, a maunch and six cinquefoyles bordurewise 3 2 1 pierced argent.

6. JAFFEREY MYDDYLTON, LANCASTER CHYRE. Argent, a saltire engrailed sable.

7. JOHN PASLEUE, YORKE CHYRE. Argent, a fess sable between three mullets pierced of the field.

8.* TOMAS LYYS OF THE BYSCHOPPERYKE OF DERHAM. Ermine, five fusils conjoined in fess gules. L.8. f.52b, *impaling* — a bend ermine.

9.* JOHN MONKTON, NORTHWMBERLAND. Sable, on a chevron between three martlets or, as many mullets pierced of the first.

Folio 22.

1.* TOMAS HAWKYSWORTH, YORKE CHYRE, Sable, three " spare " (sparrow) hawks 2 and 1 argent.

2. HEWE OF LYGHT, LANCASTER CHYRE. Azure, two bars argent.   HUGH LEIGH.

3. S. JOHN NEVYLL, BYSCHOPERYKE OF DERHAM — on a saltire argent, a fleur de lys azure.

4. JOHN OF BOROWE, YORKE CHYRE. Azure, three fleurs de lys 2 and 1 ermine.

5. ROGER LASSELYS, YORKE CHYRE. Argent, three chaplets of roses gules.

6. WYLYAM VVYPOUNT OF THE BYSCHO-PERYKE OF DERHAM. Gules, six annulets 3. 2. 1. or.

7. JOHN TWAYTYS, YORKE CHYRE. Argent, on a fess sable between three fleurs de lys gules, as many besants (blasoned torteaux).

8. JOHN MOWBRAVE, NORTHUMBERLOND. Gules, a lyon rampant argent, a bordure gobony or and of the second.

9. NYCOLL ENTYWESYLL OF THE BYSCHO-PERYKE OF DERHAM. Argent, on a bend engrailed sable, three mullets pierced of the first.

" downe all shyres." . A reference to L. 8,

Folio 22b.

1. DAVLVAFF (BALIOL) LORD OF BARNARD CASTLE. Gules, an orle ermine.

2. S. ROBARDE ROOS OF YNGMANDTHORPE. Azure, three water bougets or.

3. JOHN NEVELL, YORKE CHYRE. A saltire charged with a mullet; *quarterly with*, per cross or and argent, in each quarter five fusils conjoined in fess gules.

4. WATVR CALVVERLEY OF LANCASTER CHYRE. Sable, a false escocheon between six owls 3. 2. 1. bordurewise argent.

5.* NEWMARCHE, the olde armys of. Argent, a wind mill sail in bend throughout sable.

6. JOHN HORSSLEVE, NORTH VMBERLONDE. Gules, three horses heads couped, 2. 1. argent.

7. JOHN MVSGROVVE, WESTMERLAND CHYRE. Azure, six annulets 3. 2. 1. or. MVSGRAVE.

8. COTHBERT COLVYLE, NORTH VMBERLONDE. Argent, three chevronels sable, besantée.

9. HEWE AVSTLAYE OF THE BYSCHOPRYK OF DERHAM. Gules, on a chevron argent, a popinjay vert.

Folio 23.

1. WVLYAM SCARGYLL, YORKE CHYRE. Ermine, a saltire gules.

2. WVLYAM ELTOFTE. Argent, three chess-rooks 2 and 1 sable.

3. S. GYGGARD COUNT DE HON. Or, billettée and a lyon rampant azure. Sir Giuchard d'Angle K.G. cr. Earl of Huntingdon for life 16 July 1377.

4. ROBARDE PRENDERGEST, NORTHUMBERLONDE. Gules, a bend argent.

5. ROBARDE HOLME, YORKE CHYRE. Barry (6) or and azure, on a quarter argent a chaplet gules; *quarterly wt.* WASTNEY armys.

6. ROBARDE BOWTH, NORTHUMBERLOND. Argent, crusily fitchée and three horse shoes 2 and 1 sable.

7.* RYCHARDE FYSCHEBORNE OF THE BYSCHOPPERYKE OF DERHAM. Argent, a fleur de lys sable.

8. S. GERVVAYS OF CLYFFTON, NOTYNGHAM CHYRE. Sable, a lyon rampant argent eight sisefoyles bordurewise of the second, blasoned as cinquefoyles.

9.* HARRY PRESTON OF CRAVYN. Argent, a chevron engrailed sable, between three wolf heads erased of the second.

"downe all that hathe names."

Folio 23b.

1. RAWLYN VAUX, CUMBERLONDCHYRE. Argent, a bend chequy or and gules.

2.* EDWARD CLAYTON, LANCASTER CHYRE. Gules, on a bend sable three roses or.

3.* JOHN OF SWYNOWE, NORTHUMBER-LOND CHYRE. Argent, three swine passant 2 and 1 sable armed or.

4.* NYCOLAS BLAUNTON (BLAKISTON) OF THE BYSCHOPPERYKE OF DERHAM. Gules, three cocks 2 and 1 argent.

5. S. WYLYAM RYTHER OF YORK CHYRE. Azure, three creacents 2 and 1 or.

6.* JOHN SAYER OF THE BYSCHOPPERYKE OF DEXAM CHYRE. Gules, two barrulets lozengy conjoined, between three sea mews 2 and 1 all argent.

7. COSTANTYNE MAHAWTE. Argent, a lyon rampant gules over all a fess sable.

8. RYCHARDE ARNOLDE OF HOLDYRNESSE. Sable, three escallops 2 and 1 argent.

9. NYCOLAS BELYNGHAM, LANCASTER CHYRE. A hunting horn.

Folio 24.

1. TOMAS HASKETT, LANCASTER CHYRE. Argent, on a bend sable three wheat sheaves (garbs) of the first. HESKETH.

2.* RYCHARDE REDMAYNE, YORKE CHYRE (*over it* "Lanc," *added*). Gules, three cushions tasselled 2 and 1 argent.

3. RAWFE STANDYSCHE, LANC. Sable,
three standing dishes 2 and 1 argent ; *quarterly with*, argent, a saltire sable within a
bordure of the second.

4. TOMAS MOSTON OF HOWDEN CHYRE. A
chevron between three crosses flory sable.

5. S. ANTON SEYNT QWYNTYNE OF
HOLDYRNESSE. Or, a chevron gules and a
chief vair.

6. S. RAWFE BYGOT. Or, on a cross gules
five escallops argent.

7.* WYLYAM FAYREFAX, YORK CHYRE.
Argent, a chevron between three " hyndys
hedys " erased gules.

8. JOHN FETZ WYLYAM OF YORK CHYRE.
Lozengy argent and gules.

9. WYLYAM TAYLBOYS, LYNECOLL CHYRE.
Argent, a saltire gules, on a chief of the second
three escallops of the first.

Folio 24b.

1. S. ALYSAUNDYR NEVYLL, YORKE CHYRE.
Gules, on a saltire argent, a mullet sable.

2.* S. TOMAS FOLTHORPE, YORKE CHYRE.
Argent, on a cross moline sable, a crescent for
difference. FULTHORPE. See next page.

3. S. PYERSSE TYLYALL OF COUMBYR-
LANDE. Gules, a lyon rampant argent, over
all a bendlet azure

4. S. CYRSTOFFYR CORWENE OF COMBER-
LAND. Argent, fretty gules, a chief azure ;
lozengy, in the trick.

5. WYLYAM THORYNBOROWE. Ermine, a
fret and a chief gules ; lozengy, in the trick.

6. CHARLYS MORTON. Quarterly per fess
indented gules and ermine, in the quarter a
goat's head erased of the second.

7. MORYSBY, WESTMERLANDE. Sable, a
cross argent, in the quarter a cinquefoyle
pierced (of the second).

8. TOMAS SALKELL OF COMBERLAND. Vert,
a fret argent.

9. TOMAS MYDDYLTON OF YORKCHYRE.
Argent, a fret and a quarter sable ; lozengy,
in the trick.

Folio 25.

1. RYCHARD SALKELL OF WESTMERLAND.
Argent, a fret and a chief gules ; lozengy, in
the trick.

2. JOHN HOWTON (HOTHAM). Or, on a
bend sable three mullets pierced argent.

3. S. WYLYAM MOUNTFORT. Argent, a
lyon rampant azure within eight crosses
crosslet bordurewise gules.

4.* WYLYAM WYSTOWE. Sable, a chevron
between three pitchers *vel* possenets argent.

5. RYCHARD WYLBYRFOOSE OF YORK
CHYRE. Argent, an eagle displayed sable,
armed gules.

6. HARRY CLYFFORD, GLOUCESTER CHYRE.
Chequy or and azure, on a bend gules three
lyoncelles rampant gardant or.

7. S. JOHN ABBNALL, GLOWCESTER CHYRE.
Azure, a chevron ermine. Ascribed also to
Sir John Lodbrooke of Warwicks. in E. ij. roll.

8. S. ROBARD NEVYLL, YORKECHYRE OF
FERNLEY. Argent, a saltire gules.

9. THOMAS CYSCYLE, YORKE CHYRE YN
HOWDENCHYRE. Azure, three roses 2 and
1 or.

Folio 25b.

SOWTH CONTRE.

1. S. UMFFREY STAFFORDE, DORSSET
CHYRE. Or, a chevron gules, a bordure engrailed sable.

2. S. PHELYPE CORTENEV, DEVVNCHYRE.
Or, three torteaux and a label (3) azure.

3. S. JOHN BREWSE OF SOWSEX. Azure,
crusily botonnée and a lyon rampant or.
BRAOSE.

4. S. JOHN DENHAM, DEVENCHYRE. Gules,
five fusils conjoined in fess ermine.

5. S. WILLIAM STORMVE OF WORCESTER
CHYRE. Argent, three demi-lyons rampant
2 and 1 gules.

6.* S. Percyvvall Sowdane " of Walys, Voryner." Gules, a soldan's head in profile couped argent, wreathed : quarterly with, sable, three pales wavy fitchée at the ends argent.

7. S. John Lyle, Hampchyre. Ermine, on a chief azure three " lyonseuse " rampant argent.

8. S. Harry House of Sowcex. Ermine, three bars gules.

9. S. John Sengone (St. John) of Walys. Argent, on a chief gules two mullets pierced of the first.

Folio 26.

1. S. John Greynder of Glowcester chyre. Or a fess between six crosses botonnée gules.

2. S. Hewe Halsam of Sowsex. Argent, a chevron engrailed gules between three leopards faces of the second ; quarterly with, paly (6) or and sable.

3. S. Tomas Chaworthe, Notyngham chyre. Azure, two chevronels or.

4. S. John Popham, Hampchyre. Argent, on a chief gules two harts heads cabossed or.

5. S. Wylyam Mountfort, Warrewyk chyre. Bendy (8) or and azure, a bordure gules.

6. S. Morres of Berkeleye, Cambryge chyre. Gules, crusily and a chevron argent. Also for Sir Maurice of Hants, l. 8. f. 31.

7. Carmynowe, Devenechyre. Azure, a bend or, a crescent for difference.

8. S. Rawfe Chottysbroke, Oxynford chyre. Ermine, on a chief per pale dancettée or and gules, a rose of the third. Shottisbroke.

9. S. Rycharde VVernun of the Peke, Derbychyre. Argent, a fret sable and a quarter gules——fretty, in trick.

Folio 26b.

1.* S. Wylyam Porter of Lyncolich. Sable, three bells 2 and 1 argent. See page 32.

2. S. Harry Frowyke of Myddylisex chyre (Lord Mayor 1435 and 1444). Azure, a chevron between three leopards faces or.

3. S. John Mwngomery of Walys. Gules, a chevron ermine between three fleurs de lys or.

4. S. Edwarde Stradling of Walys. Paly (6) argent and azure, on a bend gules three cinquefoyles pierced or.

5. Alyxaundyr Sparrowe of Myddyllsex chyre. Argent, three roses 2 and 1 purpure.

6.* S. Raynolde Cobham of Sowtherey chyre. Gules, on a chevron or, three estoyles pierced sable.

7. JOHN NANFAN OF CORNEWAYLE. Sable, a chevron ermine between three wings argent; *quarterly with*, argent, two wolves passant azure.

8.* JOHN CATVRMAYNYS, OXYNFORD CHYRE. Azure, a fess between quatre mayne (mains) 2 2 or; *quarterly with*, argent, two "mongrelys" passant gules: the "mongrelys" resemble talbots; all for QUATRE-MAYNE.

9.* TOMAS OF YEDDYNGE, MYDDYLSEX CHYRE. Sable, a falcon close argent, belled or.

Folio 27.

1. JAFFEREY CHAWSERYS, OXYNFORD CHYRE. Per pale argent and gules, a bend counter-coloured; THE POET CHAUCER. See also No. 4, f.30.

2. WYLYAM WARBYLTON, HAMPCHYRE. Lozengy or and azure.

3.* TOMAS GOLLOFFYR, OXYNFORD CHYRE. Argent, two bars undée gules, on a bend sable three crescents or.

4. TOMAS VEDALE, HAMPCHYRE. Gules, a cross moline argent, UVEDALE; *quarterly with* (SCURES), azure a fret or.

5. JOHN NEWBOROWE, DORSSET CHYRE. Bendy (6) or and azure, a bordure engrailed gules.

6. WYLYAM BEOCASE OF HAMPICHYRE, bore, sable, a lyon "enbelife" gardant or ; *quarterly with*, sable, two lyons passant gardant argent.

7. TOMAS DELAREVVER, BARKECHYRE. Azure, two bars dancettée or.

8. TOMAS BAYNARDE, WYLCHYRE. Or, three eagles displayed gules.

9. ROBARDE LONGE, WYLCHYRE. Sable, a lyon rampant between eight crosses crosslet bordurewise argent.

Folio 27b.

1. TOMAS BULLOK, BARKECHYRE. Gules, a chevron argent between three bull heads cabossed of the second, horned or.

2. RAWFE LEUNEHAM, BARKECHYRE. Sable, six fleurs de lys 3. 2. 1. or.

3.* JOHN NORDVS, BARKECHYRE. Argent, on a chevron sable between three raven heads erased proper, as many crescents —— .

4. TOMAS FACCHELL, BARKECHYRE. Ermine, four bendlets azure. VACHELL.

5.* JOHN BEEREWE, HAMPCHYRE. Gules, on a bend argent three leopards faces erased sable, langued or. BURGH.

6. JOHN BASKET, HAMPCHYRE. Azure, a chevron ermine between three leopards faces or.

F

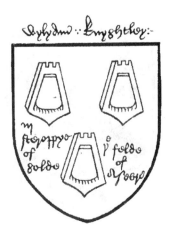

7. RYCHARDE COOKE, SOUSEXCHYRE. Gules, three crescents 2 and 1 argent and a quarter ermine; *quarterly with*, or, a cross azure. The quarter is rather—argent, a chess-rook between four ermine spots.

8.* JOHN COLYNGTON, SOUSEXCHYRE. Sable, six lyoncelles rampant 3, 2, 1, or.

9. JOHN SHYPLEY, SOTHEREYCHYRE. Gules, a chevron compony counter-compony argent and sable ("checche") between three fleurs de lys or.

Folio 28.

1.* WYLYAM KNYGHTLEY, NORTH HAMP-TONCHYRE. Azure, three stirrups 2 and 1 or.

2. GYFFORDE, HAMPCHYRE. Argent, nine torteaux 3, 2, 3, 1.

3. EDWARD POWMBRAY OF DEVENESCHYRE. Or, a lyon rampant gules, a bordure engrailed sable, POMEROY ; *impaling* BEVILE, argent, three pellets 2 and 1 each charged with a bend of the field.

4. NYCOLAS UPTON, WYLCHYRE. Argent, on a saltire couped sable five annulets or.

5. TOMAS ARDARNE, DERBY CHYRE. Gules, three crosses crosslet fitchée or and a chief of the second.

6. JOHN COPPYLSTONE OF DVENECHYRE. Argent, a chevron engrailed gules, between three leopards faces azure langued gules.

7. TOMAS HAWLEY OF DEVVENCHYRE. Gules, fretty and a quarter argent.

8.* WYLYAM WYLYNGHAM, WARREWYKE-CHYRE. Or, on a chevron sable between three antelopes heads couped of the second, spotted gules, a crescent argent for difference.

9. TOMAS PORTER OF SWLHYLL (SOLIHULL). WARREWYKCHYRE. Gules, on a quarter azure, a fesse counter embattled argent ; *quarterly with*, barry undée (6) argent and gules, a bordure sable besantée.

Folio 28b.

1. THE PRYORY OF KYLMAYNE OF YRLANDE. Argent, on a saltire gules a cross moline anchored of the first.

2. S. WYLYAM OLDEHALE, LYNCOLLE-CHYRE. Gules, a lyon rampant queue fourchée ermine.

3. BROKYSBY, NOTYNGHAMCHYRE. Sable, three bars undée argent and a quarter gules. "Conisence ij. hartes," L. 8, f.27b.

4. S. JOHN BACCOD, NOTYNGHAM CHYRE. Gules, crusily or, three lucies hauriant argent.

5. S. JOHN BACCOD, NOTYNGHAM CHYRE. Argent, two chevronels azure.

5. WYLAM HYLL, SOMERSET CHYRE. Gules, a lyon rampant or, over all a bend gobony argent and azure.

7. MAYST. ROBARD BEAUMONT, NORTH-HUMBERLAND. Azure, a fess argent between three leopards faces or.

8. JOHN COURSUN, WARREWYECHYRE. Argent, on a bend sable three popinjays or, a crescent for difference : "with a bordure engrailed sable," is written below the shield. See No. 2, f.30.

9. TOMAS BANDERV, HAMPCHYRE. Azure, a chevron between in chief two cocks argent and in base a lyon's head erased or.

Folio 29.

1. S. WYLYAM WYNDESORE, LANCASTER-CHYRE. Argent, a saltire sable.

2. S. FOWKE FYTZWARRYNGE OF DORSSETT CHYRE. Quarterly per fess indented argent and gules.

3. S. ROBARD BRUS. Or, a saltire and a chief gules.

4. S. TOMAS KYRVELL, KENT CHYRE. Or, two chevrons and a quarter gules.

5. S. ROBARD HARCOURT, OXYNFORD-CHYRE. Gules, two bars or.

6. S. RYCHARD LEUGENORE, SOWLEX-CHYRE. Azure, three chevronels or. LEWKS-NOR.

7. S. JOHN WETYNGTON, WORCESTER CHYRE. Gules, a fess counter-compony or and azure, an annulet of the second.

8. JOHN HYDE, NORTHAMPTON CHYRE. Azure, a chevron between three bezantes or.

9. SABERTON OF KENTT CHYRE. Argent, a chevron gules between three boars heads couped sable.

Folio 30b.

1.* S. JOHN CORKYNE OF DERBYCHYRE. Argent, three cocks 2 and 1 gules.

2. TOMAS DELAHAYE OF HEREFORDCHYRE. Azure, an estoyle of eight points radiated or.

3. S. TOMAS BEAUMONT OF DEVENECHYRE. Gules, two bars vair.

4. CHAUMBRUN. Or, on a bend sable three horse shoes argent.

5. S. JOHN HOLLAND OF THROPWATER, NORHAMPTONCHYRE. Azure, floretée and a lyon rampant gardant argent, a crescent for difference. THOMAS in L. s. f.286.

6. WYLYAM WAKE, NORHAMPTONCHYRE. Argent, two bars gules, in chief three tor-teaux.

7. ROEGER OF THORYNTON OF NORTHUM-BERLAND. Sable, a chevron argent and a chief indented of the second.

8. RYCHARDE SWINAM OF LANCASTER CHYRE. Argent, a fess between three chess-rooks sable.

9. CONESTABYLL OF FLAYNBOROWE. Quarterly gules and vair, over all a bend or.

Folio 30.

1. S. WATYR DEWERSE OF HERFFORD CHYRE. Argent, a fess gules and in chief three torteaux. DEVEREUX.

2. JOHN CORSUN OF DERBYCHYRE. Argent, on a bend sable three popinjays or. CURZON. No. 8, f.28*b.*

3. S. NYCOLL PERPOYNT OF DERBY CHYRE. Argent, a lyon rampant sable, six cinque-foyles bordurewise pierced gules.

4. JAFFEREY CHAWCERYS OF OXYNFORD CHYRE. Argent, a chief gules; over all a lyon rampant or, for BURGHERSH; "quartelye the wylle," *i.e.* wheel, intended for. ROET; *rightly,* gules three wheels or, *in a later hand.* See No. 1, f.27, for Chaucer coat.

5.* TOMAS CORNEW OF DEVENECHYRE. Argent, a chevron between three hunting horns sable.

6. RICHARD OF ASKE, YORKCHYRE. Or, three bars azure.

7. WYLYAM HARDY, YORKCHYRE. Argent, on a bend per bend azure and sable, a bendlet or; *quarterly with,* argent, a chevron gules between three spear heads sable.

8. TOMAS BRAKYNBERY OF THE BYSCHOP-FERYRE OF DERHAM. Azure, fretty or.

9. GORGE POPELEY, YORKE CHYRE YN CRAVVYN. Argent, on a fess sable three eagles of the first.

Folio 30b.

1. DEWKE DE BOURGOYNE. Quarterly I. and IV. FRANCE, within a bordure gobony; *quarterly with,* bendy (6) and a plain bordure. II. and III. per pale, *incomplete,* on an escocheon a lyon rampant. FLANDERS. See No. 5, f.31.

2.* LE DOLFFYNE DE FRAUNCE, FRANCE; *quarterly with,* or, a dolphin hauriant embowed azure.

3. LE DEUK DE ORLYAUNCE. FRANCE, and a label of three points argent, but blasoned as of five points.

4. DEUKE DE LAUNCON (ALENCON). Azure, florettée—and a bordure gules, platey.

5. DEUKE DE BERRYE, *altered to,* TROPE. Or, an eagle displayed per pale gules and sable.

6. DEUKE DE ANGERYS (BARE, *written above it*). Azure, crusily—and two barbel addorsed or.

7. DEWKE DE BAYRE (HEYNYSBERY, *in later hand*). Or, four bars gules (blasoned as 6 pieces); *impaling,* gules crusily and two barbel addorsed or; *all quarterly with,* gules, a lyon rampant queue fourchée renowée argent, crowned or; over all on an escocheon a lyon rampant. See No. 8, prox.

8.* DEWKE DE MELAN. The crowned biscia ("bis") of Milan swallowing a man; "torayd yn vij vowts," tricked as of six volutes.

9.* DEWKE DE BRYTAYNYE. Ermine.

Folio 31.

1.* COUNT DE SEYNTPOULE. Argent, a lyon rampant crowned, queue fourchée renowée gules.

2. DEWKE DE LOREYNE. Or, on a bend gules three "merlettys" displayed argent, the "alerions" of LORRAINE are probably intended, though the birds are tricked and blasoned, eagles, in a later hand.

3. SEYNT DENYSE DE FRAUNCE. Gules, a cross argent.

4. THE ERLE OF DOWGGLES YN SCOTLAND. Argent, a human heart gules, on a chief azure three mullets pierced or. DOUGLAS.

5. COUNT DE FLAUNDRYS. Or, a lyon rampant sable. See No. 1, f 30b.

6. THE ERLE OF BOWHAN. Azure, three garbs "of comyn" or. BUCHAN.

7. DEWKE DE BOKRONE. Azure, florettée or aud a bend gules.

8. DEWKE DE BERRY. Azure, florettée or aud a burdure engrailed gules.

9. DEWKE DE CLEVE. Gules, a false escocheon argent, over all an escarboucle or.

Folio 31b.

1.* JOHN MARTYNE OF KENT CHYRE. Argent, three talbots passant sable.

2. JOHN BORDEVVYLE OF SOWSEX. *altered to* KENT. Gules, a chevron vair, between three cinquefoyles pierced or. THOMAS in L. 8. f.33.

3. JOHN GORYNGE OF SOWSEX. *altered to* KENT. Argent, a chevron between three annulets gules.

4.* J. MAWDELY. Sable, a chevron ermine between three shoveller heads erased argent.

5. WYLYAM WATTON, KENT CHYRE. Argent, a lyon rampant gules, on a bend sable three crosses crosslet fitchée of the first.

6. S. GYLYS DAWBANEY. Gules, a bend fusily argent.

7. NYCOLAS BROKHULL, KENTCHYRE. Gules, a cross argent between twelve crosses crosslet fitchée or.

8. JOHN KENTWOOD. Gules, three cinque-foyles pierced ermine.

9. JOHN BEKER OF SOWSEX. *altered to* KENT. Barry (6) argent and sable, on a quarter of the second a leopards face or.

Folio 32.

SOWTH CONTRE.

1. THE BANER OF OWRE LADY. The Virgin and Child. FABULOUS.

2. SEYNT BARTHELMEW SPYTTYLL (HOSPITAL). Per pale argent and sable, the Crucifixion, *sine* cross.

3. OURE LADY ARMYS. Intended for a cross crosslet grieced between a pair of wings, on a chief the legend, *aue gracia plena.* FABULOUS.

4. PRYNCE OF WALES (HO'LL DUA *in later hand*). Argent, three lyons passant regardant tails cowed gules. See also No. 4. f.12b. One lyon struck out in L. 8, f.61.

5. BRYGRAC EN GEVAN. Or, two gryphons legs barways talons to the dexter erased sable. See also No. 8, f.12b.

6. S. GYE OF WARREWYK. Chequy or and azure, a chevron ermine. (Natl. Dict. Biog. xxiii. 386). See also No. 1, f.7b.

7. S. BEVVYS OF HAMPTON. Argent, a chief gules three roses 2. 1, counter-coloured. Rather tricked as per fess gules and argent, &c. See also No. 2, f.7b.

8. S. GAWAYNE the good knight. Azure, three lyons heads erased or. See also No. 9, f.5.

9. ERLE OF MARCHE. The arms of Mortimer as No. 3. f.7b.

Folio 32*b.*

1. COUNT DE GENEVVYLE. Azure, three horse barnacles open or, on a chief ermine a demi-lyon rampant issuant gules. See page 9.

2. COUNT DE NORFOLK (BOKYNGHAM, *deleted*) ERLE BIGOT, *in margin*. Per pale or and vert, a lyon rampant gules. See page 9.

3.* COUNT DE WALYNGKFORD. Burelly (10) gules and argent, on a chief of the second three lyons rampant sable, over all, tracery suggestive of the Navarrese net, and terminating in a bordure, all or.

4.* Gyronny (12) or and gules, and a chief azure, in the dexter a demy lyon passant gardant of the first.

5. S. FRAUNCYS DE COURT (COUCY *in later hand*) COUNT DE PENBROKE *probably in error*. Paly (6) argent and vert, on a chief or, an eagle displayed sable. See also No. 3, £8.

6. ———— YORKCHIRE. Azure, besantée and a lyon rampant or.

7. COUNT DE PENBROKE; VALENCE, *in later hand*. Burelly (10) argent and azure, eight martlets bordurewise gules. See page 9.

8. COUNT DE GLOWCESTYR. Or, three chevronels gules.

9. WYLYAM OF OXYNFORDE, YORKECHYRE. Azure, three leopards faces or, a chief per pale dancettée of the second and first.

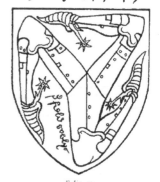

Folio 33.

1.* THE ARMYS OF THE ILE OF MAN. Gules, three legs "iune sayle" argent, spurs ("eprone") or. Marginal note "sporrys and the Kneys golde."

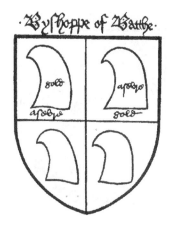

2. Or, a fess gules and six fleurs de lys 2. 2. 2. counter-coloured. DANBY of Yorks, in later hand.

3. THE BASTARD OF CLARRAUNCE. Per chevron gules and azure, in chief two lyons rampant combatant, and in base a fleur de lys, all or. See also No. 9, f.32b.

4. PYROT. Or, a gurges gules.

5. GRAVE VAN GUIZ DE ALMAYNE (BURGO, E. OF KENT, in later hand). Lozengy gules and vair ; imperfectly tricked.

6. GORGES, in later hand. Azure, a gurges (whirlpool or whirl-pitte) argent.

7. S. THOMAS BLOUNT, STAFFORDCHYRE. Barry undée (6) sable and or.

8. TOMAS SKYLFORDE. Or, three bars dancettée sable.

9. S. WYLYAM STORMYE, HAMPE CHYRE. Argent, three demi-lyons rampant gules.

Folio 33b.

1. S. WYLYAM GASQWOYGE (GASCOIGNE), YORK CHYRE. Argent, on a pale sable, a fish head couped or.

2. S. TOMAS GRESLEY, LEYCESTER CHYRE. Vaire argent and gules.

3. S. XPYSTOFFYR CORWENE. Argent, a fret gules (lozengy in trick) and a quarter azure. Fretty in L. 8, f.37.

4.* S. BRYAN STAPYLTON, YORKE CHYRE, Gules, three swords conjoined at the pomel, points to the dexter and sinister chief and to the base, proper.

5.* TOMAS BAXTERD, NORTHUMBERLAND, Vert, three squirrels sejant vorant 2 and 1 argent.

6. ROBARD STRANGWAYS, YORKECHYRE, Sable, two lyons passant gobony (6) argent and gules, crowned.

7. S. ROWFE BOWLMAR, YORKE CHYRE. Gules, billettée and a lyon rampant or.

8.* (JOHN DE DROKENESFORD, 1309-29), "a byschoppe of Bathe." Quarterly azure and or, four caps counter-coloured.

9. ROUFE STANDYSCH, LANCASTER CHYRE, Sable, three standing dishes 2 and 1 argent.

Folio 34.

1.* S. FRAUNCYS OF ALDENHAM, HAMP-CHYRE, "beryth azeure a stremer of gold." Azure (3) sternys (stars) or.

2.* S. ADAME FRAUNCYS OF THE YLF OF WYCHT. (LORD MAYOR 1352-3). Per bend or and sable, a lyon rampant counter-coloured.

3.* S. JOHN GODDARDE, "beryth a poynt of sabyll, a chefe of gouly entté grele, iij eglys hedy of sylvyr, ye bekys gold," *i.e.*, per chevron engrailed gules and sable three eagle heads erased argent, beaked or. See page 42.

4.* DANIERS (substituted for S. JOHN SAVVAGE), LANCASTER CHYRE. Argent, a pale indented sable.

5. S. BRYAN SANDFORDE, NOTYNGHAM CHYRE. Ermine and sable entté, &c., *i.e.*, per chevron sable and ermine, in chief two boars heads regarding each other and couped or.

6.* S. JOHN STEWARDE OF WALYS. Azure and gules entté (*i.e.*, per chevron) three lyons heads, etc. 2, 1 erased all or.

7.* THORPE, YORKECHYRE. Or, on a chief "entté pycche," &c., *i.e.*, per chevron azure and or a gryphon passant argent.

8. RAWFE RESTWOLDE, BARKCHYRE. Per saltire gules and ermine.

9.* JOHN GREYBY, HOXYNFORD CHYRE. Ermyne, two flaunches azure on each three wheat herys (ears) paleways or.

John Gjorby

Rorlox

Folio 34b.

ROCLEY beryth ix peseys gold.

ROCLEY beryth iiij pecys.

1.* ROCLEY. Or, on a cross quarter pierced azure four roe heads couped of the first.

2. HOLWELL OF WALYS (substituted for SOUTHWELL). Per chevron gules and ermine, in chief three chess-rooks of the second.

3.* PYERSE OF CAWODP, YORKE CHYRE, Per chevron crenellée grady sable and argent, three buck heads 2 and 1, counter-coloured.

4. RICHARD WHITGREVVE, STAFFORD-CHYRE; "beryth Staffor and sylvyr ix pecys lune et laut," *i.e.* azure, on a cross quarter pierced or, four chevrons gules of STAFFORD.

5. TOMAS STOKYS. Per chevron vert and ermine, a chevron engrailed counter-coloured.

6.* S. WYLYAM LYNDE, BARKECHYRE, otherwyse callyd S. ADAME BUXHULL, *in later hand.* HYNDE in L. 8, f.34b. Or, a lyon rampant azure "maskelyd yn sylvyr." See next page and also Storgon, No. 3, prox.

Pyerse of Cawodp

7.* RYCHARDE MYDDYLMORE, WARREWYK-CHYRE. Per chevron argent and sable, in chief two moorcocks of the second.

8. ROGER BREUSE, MYDDYLSEX, *otherwise called* RYCHARD WERYMAN, *in later hand.* Per saltire azure and gules, a cross potent (?) or.

9.* FRAUNCYS HERSTON, SOUTHEREY CHYRE. Per chevron sable and argent, three harts salient 2 and 1 counter-coloured those in chief respectant, attires or.

Folio 35.

1.* ROBARD NORTON, RYCHEMOND CHYRE. Sable, three piles fleurettée at the points issuant from the sinister base bendways argent.

2. TOMAS NEWTON, SOTHEREY CHYRE. Vert, on a cross quarter pierced gules, four leopards' faces or.

3.* STORGON, SOTHEREYCHYRE. Azure, three sturgeons naiant or, "maskylyd yn au nette" gules. See also WALYNGEFORD and LYNDE, No. 6, i.34b.

4. ————————, of SOWTHEREY. Per bend sinister sable and argent, a lyon rampant counter-coloured.

5.* PYERSE DEWRANT, DE GWASCOWYNG. Azure, four bends "potance" argent.

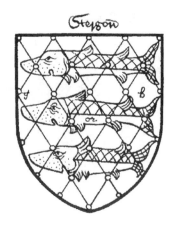

John Olney

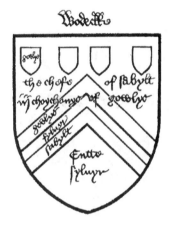

Wodecke

John Castton

6. JOHN POLE. Per pale or and sable, a saltire engrailed "of the same."

7.* JOHN GARTHER, SOWTHEREY CHYRE. Ermyn (ermines) a cross quarter pierced ermine. See page 45.

8. JOHN MOLSOO, SOUTHEREY CHYRE. Argent, a chevron per chevron or and sable between three fleurs de lys erminois (*sic*) blasoned as "ij cheveronys of gold and sabyll."

9.* JOHN OLNEY, SOTHEREYCHYRE. (LORD MAYOR 1446). Gules, besantée two flaunches sable, each charged with a lyon rampant gardant argent, crowned gules armed azure.

Folio 35b.

1. (EVTTON, CHECHIRE *in later hand*). Quarterly argent and sable, a cross patonce counter-coloured.

2.* WODECOKKE, BARKECHYRE. Per chevron sable and argent, two chevronels gules and of the first, in chief three (four tricked) false escocheons of the third.

3. (READE *in later hand*), OXYNFORD CHYRE. Per chevron three unicorn heads 2 and 1 couped.

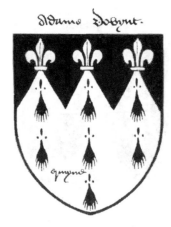

4. NYCOLAS BLACBORNE, YORK CHYRE. Gules, a lyon rampant chequy ermine and erminois, crowned and armed or.

5. ALAM, YORK CHYRE. Argent, three saltorelles ("sawtreys") engrailed 2 and 1 sable. The reverse borne by LEXINTON, lord of Laxton, L. 8, f. 21.

6. TOMAS PYKE, ECEX CHYRE. "Restaurator Eccl. Bartholomei juxta Byrsam" (MS. L. 8), c. 1438; an alderman of London. Gules, three piles wavy meeting in base argent, a bordure engrailed of the second.

7.* JOHN CARLTON. Argent, a fess gules between three harts trippant 2 and 1 sable.

8. Six staves saltireways 2 and 1, each couple between four leopards faces.

9. GORGE RYGMAYDYN. Argent, three harts heads cabossed 2 and 1 sable.

Folio 36.

1.* MAYDYSTON, MYDDYLSEX. Ermine, two battle axes saltireways sable.

2. JAFFEREY GOODLUK, LYNCOLL CHYRE. Azure, on a chevron engrailed ermine be tween three escallops argent as many torteaux.

3.* ADANE DOVYNT, SOWTHEREYCH. Ermine, a chief dancettée sable, fleurtée at the points.

4.* WYLYAM STOKYS, ECEXCHYRE. Sable, three eagles displayed argent, beak and feet gules, a chief dancettée of two points argent,

5. JOHN MACWORTH, STAFFORDCHYRE, Per pale indented sable and ermine, a chevron gules, fretty or.

6. JOHN GRENE, YORKE CHYRE. Or, fretty gules (tricked lozengy) a fess per fess dancettée point in point azure and ermine.

7. JOHN GARGRAVVE, LANCASTER CHVR. Argent, on a chief indented gules, three crosses botonnée fitchée.

8.* JOHN WOODE, KENT CHYRE. Argent, an alaunde (or wolfe added) salient sable collared or.

9. JOHN DENYSS, SOMERSSET CHYR. Vert, on a saltire engrailed argent, between four crosses botonnée fitchée of the second, a fleur de lys or.

Folio 36b.

1. BILLERS (smudged out), LEYCESTER CHYRE. Per pale gules and sable, a lyon rampant argent. See also No. 8, f.46b.

2. TOMAS QUYXLEY, RYCHEMOND CH. Gules, an orle argent, over all a bend ermines.

3. ROBARDE NORTHFFOLKE, YORKECHYRE. Per pale gules and argent, two bars counter-coloured.

4. WYLYAM FOSTER, BYCHOPBRYKE OF DERHAM. Gules, a chief crenellée argent.

5. GORGE STYDOLFE, SOWSEXCHYR. Argent, on a chief sable two lyons heads erased or.

6.* GORGE PALMYS, YORKCHYRE. Gules, three fleurs de lys 2 and 1 argent, a chief vair.

7.* TOMAS BARNEWELL, SOTHEREY CH. Per pale argent and gules, two beavers courant in pale counter-coloured.

8. ———— DE ALMAYNE. Per chevron enttè (the point or base) gules, the chief per pale or and azure.

9.* ———— DE GALEYS. Sable, two leopards counter salient argent " in their kynde."

Folio 37.

1. S. JOHN HARPLEY, NORTHFOLKECH.; ("gold and silver berle, &c."). Or, five bars argent, three chevronels engrailed sable.

2.* S ROBARDE CHARLTON, WYLCHYRE. Argent, a chevron engrailed sable, between three gryphons heads erased of the second.

3. TOMAS NEWMAN NORHAMPTONCH. Azure, three demy lyons rampant couped ermine.

4.* TOMAS BARE DE CALAYS. Per pale argent and sable, a boar passant in fess counter-coloured.

H

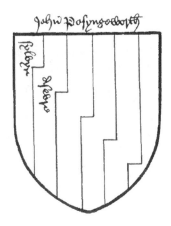

5.* JOHN POSYNGEWORTH. Paly (6) angled argent and azure.

6. WYLYAM DE AYNO, OXYNFORD CHYRE. Sable, a saltire fleurtée at the ends argent between four lyons passant gardant or.

7. JOHN THORNEBERY OF SOWTHEREYCH— (gules) on a bend engrailed (argent), three roundles ermines. WILLIAM in L. 8, f.32.

8. WYLYAM PERKYNYS OF BARKE CHYRE. Or, billettée (? erminois), a fess dancettée sable. PARKYNGE in L. 8.

9. FAYRFAX (added) OF YORKECHYRE— three bars gemelles, over all a lyon rampant; "ondowne." A reference to L. 8, in which this coat does not appear.

Folio 37b.

1.* S. JOHN SANDRYS. Argent, a cross raguly and truncated sable. SANDYS.

2. S. EDWARDE TROMPYNGTON. Azure, crusily and two trumpets pileways or.

3. S. JOHN HARPEDENE. Gules, on a mullet argent, a besant thereon a martlet sable, in the trick; blasoned, porte gowlys une molet de argent a v poyntys perce de dore.

4. W. WELLYS. Lozengy ermine and vert, a lyon rampant gules.

5. RYCHARDE CURSUN. Paly (6) argent and sable, on a chevron gules a cross crosslet or.

6. PYERSE OF HALL. Ermine, two bars gules, three false escocheons 2 and 1 or.

7. BORTON (TANNATT, *in later hand*, see also No. 8, f.39). Per fess sable and argent, a lyon rampant counter-coloured.

8. JOHN MAYNSTON. Sable, a bend embattled counter embattled argent.

9. TOMAS CODERYNGTON. Argent, a fess embattled counter embattled sable, fretty gules, between three lyons passant of the last; the fess is tricked lozengy rather than fretty.

Folio 38.

1. S. JOHN CHYDYOCC. Quarterly per fess indented ermine and gules.

2. S. WYLYAM PEYTO. Barry (6) per pale indented argent and gules counter-coloured.

3. S. ——— WETYNGHAM. Per fess vert and or, a fess argent, over all a lyon rampant gules. The tinctures vert and argent are inadvertently transposed.

4. TOMAS GLOWCESTY(R). Gules, a cross chequy———.

5. JOHN BOROWEHOPPE. Argent, a chevron of "FRANCE," *i.e.,* azure, thereon three fleurs de lys or. BROWNHOPE in L. 8, f.38b, note.

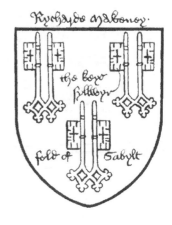

6.* WATYR SKYRLOWE. Argent, a cross sable, "pale, fece, seve" (severed). Blasoned by some, argent, three barrulets and as many pallets in cross disjointed sable. One of these names Bishop of Durham, 1388-1406.

7. TOMAS HERTTYLL. Barry (6) vert and argent.

8. JOHN THROGMERTON. Gules, on a chevron argent three bars gemelles sable.

9. TOMAS LANGLEY. Paly (6) argent and vert. Another coat, with a mullet for difference, or, for the *Bishop* of Durham, in L. 8, f.6b.

Folio 38b.

1.* S. TOMAS TREVVET. Argent, a "trevet" sable.

2. NYCOLAS POYNYS. Quarterly per fess indented azure and argent.

3. JOHN KERKEBY. Per pale argent and gules, on a chief sable a lyon passant or.

4. Argent, three roses 2 and 1 gules, on a chief of the second two cygnets (synettys) of the first.

5. JOHN WALDYVE. Or, three leopards faces 2 and 1 sable.

6.* RYCHARDE MAKENEY. Sable, three pairs of keys addlorsed 2 and 1 argent.

7.* WYLYAM TAWKE, BASYNGESTOKE. Per
pale azure and gules, four chevronels counter-
coloured, a cross botonnée fitchée argent.

8. JOHN BLENKYNSOPPE. Argent, a fess
between three garbs sable ; and in the trick,
a fleur de lys for difference.

9.* ARBLASTER. Ermine, an arquebus
gules.

Folio 39.

1. S. RYCHARD MOLYNEKYS. Azure, a fer
de moline or.

2. S. TOMAS, LORD DE STRATFELD ("argent
and asewre beurle," &c.) ; argent, six bars
azure, over all a lyon rampant gules.

3.* S. RYCHARD GETHEN. Argent, a
chevron azure between three "revenys of
sable."

4.* MATHEWE GOGH. Azure, three boars
passant 2 and 1 argent.

5. HUMFFREY SMERT. Ermine, three chess-
rooks 2 and 1 gules.

6.* NYCOLAS FYTZ JOHN. Sable, a chevron
gules between three lucies heads erect and
erased argent.

7. JOHN WALWAYNE. Gules, a bend
ermine.

8. TOMAS BORTON (BURTON in L. 8, f 39b).
Per fess sable and argent, a lyon rampant
counter-coloured. TANNATT, in later hand.
See also No. 7, L.37b, and for BALLARD,
No. 9, f.40.

9. ROBARD ROLSTON. Bendy (6) gules
and vert, a chevron ermine.

Folio 39b.

1.* Barry paly billety argent and sable,
on a chief of the second three mallets of the
first.

2.* THE ARMS OF EWERST (GRENFEILDE,
added). Gules, three organ rests or; see
page 54.

3. FETZ HERBARDE. Gyronny (12) argent
and gules, a bordure sable besantée. These
arms were borne by Thomas Peverell. See
Some Feudal Coats of Arms.

4. TOMAS TRORLEY. Vert, ten escallops
4. 3. 2. 1. argent.

5.* Gules, masoned or, on a chief azure, a
demy lyon rampant issuant of the second.

6. RYCHARDE BALDYRSTON. Argent, a
lyon rampant queue fourchée purpure.

7. HARRY WYLTON OF WYLCHYRE. Gules,
a bend vair between six escallops or.

8. NEWTON (DERBY., *added*). Two cross-
bones saltireways. See page 54.

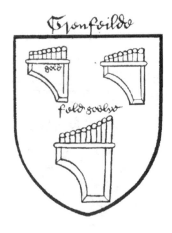

Tronfoilde

f 39ᵇ no 5

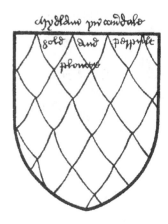

Rychayd Depnoy

0. MAYSTER STEVVYN OF THE SEE, YORKE-CHYRE. Azure, two bars undée ermine " and no more " ; in correction of the blason on the shield " aseur iij fecys oundy." DE LA SEE or AT SEE.

Folio 40.

1.* MYDLAM YN COVERDALE. Or and pur-pure " plomte," *i.e.*, plumeté.

2. NYCOLL ALDYRW(I)KE. Sable, a pale engrailed or, between six crosses formée 2, 3, 2, argent.

3. LAWRANCE FETTON. Argent, a quarter gules, over all on a bend azure three garbs or. *The quarter and the tinctures in later hand.* FITTON.

4.* RYCHARD VERNEY (CO. WAR., *added*). Gules, three crosses pattée pomettée voided or, a chief vaire ermine and ermines. See No. 8, f.39, and No. 9, f.11.

5.* TOMAS METSOUNT (MOTFOUNT or MOT-SOUNT). Argent, a cross undée sable, *i.e.*, a pale and a fesa per cross undée.

6. JOHN NORTON. Per pale ermine and gules, a saltire engrailed counter-coloured.

7.* SHARINGBURY (*in later hand*) ; *blanc*, a lyon triple-bodied gules.

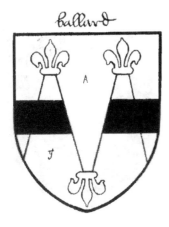

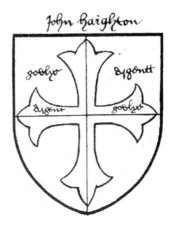

8.* NOTTINGHAM (*in later hand*). Azure, a lyon gardant double bodied sejant crowned, tails cowed erect or; see page 55. John of Northampton, Lord Mayor of London 1381-3.

9.* BALLARD (CHESCHER, *in later hand*); *blanc*, a pile, between two piles reversed fleurtée at the points gules, a fess surmounted by the centre pile, sable (*sic*).

Folio 40b.

1. S. ROGER LECHE. Ermine, on a chief dancettée gules three crowns or.

2. JOHN MORLAY, LANCASTER CHYRE. Sable, a leopards face reversed or, jessant de lys argent.

3.* "JOHN HAIGHTON, CHESHER," added. Quarterly gules and argent, a cross patance counter-coloured.

4. LANGLEYE, STAFFORD CHYRE. Or, a chief gules, over all a lyon rampant vair.

5.* TOMAS BURDON, DERHAM CHYRE. Argent, two burdons (palmers staves) saltire-ways sable, forks (prongs) or.

6. JOHN SOWMERS, NORHAMPTON; under it SOWTHEREYCH. Quarterly gules and azure a cross patonce argent.

7. DAVY MATHEWE OF WALYS. Per fess gules and argent, three roses in fess counter-coloured. COOKE adds L. 8, f.35b. " is the last that hath any name of their shyres."

8.* JAMYS BEDEFORD, DERHAMCHYRE. "ermyne," three bars "ermyne," i.e., ermines.

9. WYLYAM OF STROUDE, SOWTHERKY CHYRE. Azure, semée of arrows paleways flighted to the base or.

Folio 41.

1. S. TOMAS EPPYNGHAM. Vert, a false escocheon between six martlets 3, 2, 1, bordurewise argent.

2.* MAYST GYLBERD KYMER, DORSSET CHYRE. Argent, a wolf salient azure, a bordure sable, besantée.

3. JOHN OF CAVYLE, HOWDENCHYRE. Gules, a fess flory counter-flory argent.

4. JOHN PECCAM. Ermine, a chief quarterly or and gules.

5. ALYXAUNDYR TWYER, HOLDYRNESSE. Gules, a cross vair.

6. JAMES FLOWRE, NORHAMTONCH. Ermine, a cinquefoyle pierced sable.

7.* WYLYAM MOUNSEWYS, HOLDYRNESSE. Gules, a cross moline or.

8. ———————, YORKECHYRE. "sylvyr entté," i.e., per chevron sable and argent, in chief two covered cups of the last.

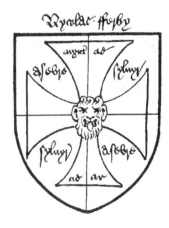

9. MACKWILLIAMS, added; DE ALMAYNE.
Per bend gules and argent, three roses in bend
counter-coloured.

Folio 41b.

1. WEST, SOWSEXCHYRE. Argent, a fess
dancettée sable; "une chevverond daunce"
in blason.

2.* NYCOLAS FERBY, YORKECHYRE. Quarterly azure and argent, on a cross formée
counter-coloured a leopards face.

3. JOHN MAULEVERER OF ALLYRTON.
Sable, three levrières courant argent, collared.

4.* TOMAS GRENWOD, YORKE CHYRE.
Argent, a cock sable.

5.* ROBARDE OTTYR, YORKECHYRE. Azure
three otters passant or.

6. WYLYAM VVYNSENT, (D)ERHAMCHYRE.
Argent, two bars gules, on a quarter (canton)
of the second a trefoyle or.

7. MAYST. TOMAS MORTON, YORK CHYRE.
"Berley," *i.e.* borulée (12) argent and gules,
niue martlets 4. 2. 3. bor-lnrewise sable.
The martlets blasoned as *heth cockys.*

8.* TOMAS WASTENEYS, NOTYNGHAM CH.
Sable, a lyon rampant queue fourchée argent,
armed gules.

0.* MAYST. ELWELL, YORKE CHYRE. Argent, two "cheyns" saltireways linked in the centre by an annulet all sable, a crescent for difference.

Folia 4b.

1. MAYST. HARRY BOLTON, YORKECHYRE. Argent, on a bend engrailed gules, three leopards faces ("rasyd") of the first.

2.* TOMAS HOLTOGATE, YORKECHYRE. Gules, a chevron engrailed argent, between three hounds (talbots) sejant of the last.

3.* HARRY BAKTON, SOWTHEREYCH. (LORD MAYOR 1416 and 1428). Ermine, on a saltire sable, an annulet masoned or, enclosing an ermine spot. See page 66.

4.* S. TOMAS GRENE, NORTH HAMPTON-CHYRE. Azure, three bucks trippant or. See page 60.

5. ————, SOWTHEREYCH. "Sylver a chefe entty of sabyll," etc., *i.e.*, per chevron sable and argent, in chief a lyon passant gardant or.

6. WYLYAM OF NALTON, YORK CHYRE. Or, three boars passant sable, armed argent. NEWTON in L. s. f.22b.

7. S. JOHN DEPDENE, YORKCHYRE. Ermine, on a chief azure three lyoncels rampant argent.

8.* RYCHARD BURTON OF MYLFORD. Sable, three dexter gauntlets argent, in chief as many rings interlaced 2 and 1 of the last.

9. THE ARMYS OF MANCHESTYR, LANCAST CHYRE. Gules, three bendlets enhanced or. BYRON bears them argent and gules.

Folio 42b.

1. PYERSSE DE LA HAYE, YORKECHYRE. Argent, three escallops in bend gules, between two cotises sable. The escallops are erroneously tricked on a bend argent.

2.* JOHN CASSOUSE, SOUTHEREY. Or, a boar passant sable in front of an oak-tree fructed vert.

3.* TOMAS SMETON, YORK CHYRE. Azure, three plough shares argent.

4. HUMFREY CHERLETON, YORKCHYRE. Or, a lyon rampant gules.

5. ————, YORKCHYRE. Argent, a buck salient sable.

6.* MAYST. ROGER KEYS, YORKCHYRE. Per chevron gules and azure, three keys 2 and 1 erect, wards to the sinister or.

7. ——— DE ALMAYNE (*in later hand*). Gules, a cross quarter pierced ermine. *Sometimes blasoned* quarterly of nine pieces gules and ermine.

John Chysoke

Tomas Smoton

Mayst Roger Boys

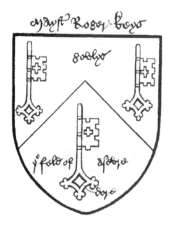

lord van Cappott

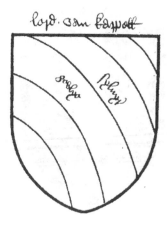

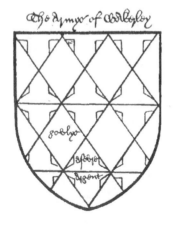

8, ————————, YORK CHYRE. Gyronny (8) sable and ermine.

9.* LORD VAN KAPPELL OF ALMAYNE. Bendy arched (6) argent and gules. See page 61.

Folio 43.

1.* THE BYSCHOPPE OF BRYGWATER. Sable, three mitres or, between two piles arched in point, out of dexter and sinister base, argent.

2. ————————, OF ALMAYNE, trick defaced. See No. 9 prox.

3. HUBERK (in later hand), LEYSCESTER CHYRE. Argent, on a bend sable nine annulets interlinked in triplets or.

4.* JOHN MYCHYLGROVVE, SOUSENCHYRE. Quarterly or and azure, a falcon belled argent.

5. COLVVYLE, SOTHEREYCHYRE. Argent, on a cross gules five lyoncelles rampant of the first.

6. LORD CANTELAWE. Azure, three leopards faces reversed jessant de lys or. CANTELUPE.

7. HERE VAN APENZBERG, DE ALMAYNE. Per bend sable and or.

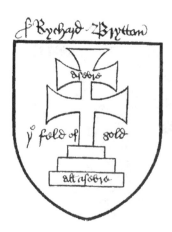

8. WYLYAM ROSSELEYN, YORK CHYRE. Argent, on a bend gules three round buckles, tongues to the sinister base, of the first.

9.* THE ARMYS OF WAKERLEY. Lozengy vair and gules.

Folio 43b.

1. S. WYLYAM TRACY. Barry (6) or and gules.

2.* S. RAYNOLD DE BERSON. Argent, three bears heads couped sable, muzzled —.

3.* S. RYCHARD (*substituted for* WYLYAM) BRYTTON. Or, a cross patriarchal pattée on three grieces azure.

4. Blanc.

5.* REX ALYXAUNDIRE DE ALMAYNE. Azure, three crowns, each surmounted of a boar passant all or.

6. RYCHARD GRENE OF SOWSEXCH. Gules, crusily and three cinquefoyles pierced or.

7. S. JOHN BARRE OF HEREFORDCHYRE. Gules, three bars gobony (4) argent and sable.

8. S. RYCHARD PENERYON OF HEREFORD-CHYRE. Or, three bars azure, a bend gules.

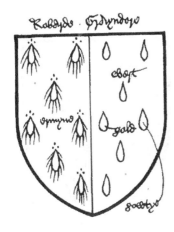

9.* ROBARDE GRAYNDORE OF GLOUCES-
TERCHYRE. Per pale erminois (vel pean), and
vert, guttée d'or.

Folio 44.

1. THE BYSCHOPE OF LYNCOLLNE. Per
pale argent and azure, on a chevron gules
three lyoncelles passant gardant or.

2.* THE ARMYS OF CHEYPTON MALETT,
SOMERSETCH. Argent, three mallets 2 and 1
gules.

3.* MARCHES STIRIE DE ALMAYNE. Vert,
a gryphon segreant, sans wings, argent,
armed or.

4. S. JOHN HAKELETT, SOMERSET CH.
Argent, on a bend cotised gules three mullets
pierced or.

5. LORD OF DEROLSEN DE ALMAYNE. Per
pale azure and or, an eagle displayed counter-
coloured.

6.* LORD OF HUMME DE ALMAYNE. Per
fess argent and gules, the chief dancettée of
4 and the base of 2 all throughout counter-
coloured.

7.* ————————— DE ALMAYNE. Or, a
talbot erect per fess sable and argent.

8. Per saltire azure and argent.

9.* REX WEIMARIE, D'ALMAVE. Gules,
two bars (? or), potent throughout sable,
"gold the mase."

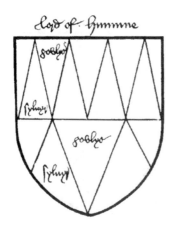

Folio 44b

1. AN OLDE LORD ; " or ij fecys endentyd gold and ascure " (*sic*). Tricked lozengy or and azure two bars counter-coloured.

2. TOMAS CLARELL, YORKCHYRE. Gules, six martlets 3. 2. 1. argent.

3. RYCHARD OF BANK OF KRAVVYN (CRAVEN). Sable, a cross or, between four fleurs de lys argent.

4. WYLYAM DRYRY OF NORTHFOLK. Argent, a quarter gules, over all a bend azure between two cinquefoyles pierced of the second.

5. JOHN ERYTH OF KENT CHYRE. Quarterly gules and or, over all a cross engrailed counter-coloured.

6. REX DE TRENACLIE OF ALMAYNE. Gules, three swords points meeting in a mount at the base azure, hilts or. ? TRINACRIA = SICILY.

7. " KYNGE STEVENE that lyth at FFEVYRSAM ; beryth, aseure a sagettary of golde " - fabulous.

8. COMES DE HOYA, HY ALMAYNE. Or, two bears legs and feet to the chief, conjoined in base sable.

9. LANT GRAVIUS DE HASSIA ILLUST : ALMAYNE. Azure, a lyon rampant barry (8) argent and gules, " gobbone of viij pecys."

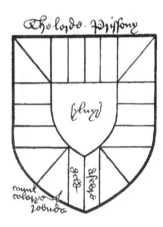

Folio 45.

1. LORD CANTLEY, OF OLDE TYME PAST. Gules, a fess vair between three leopards faces reversed jessant de lys or. CANTILUPE.

2.* THE LORDE PRISSONY. Probably per saltire or and azure, on a fess a barrulet, counter-coloured, a false escocheon argent, between in chief paly of four and in base a pale per pale all counter-coloured of the first and second.

3. TOMAS GRENFELD. Azure, three bears heads 2 and 1 couped argent, between two flaunches of the second guttée de sang.

4.* S. JOHN PECHE (LORD MAYOR 1361). Azure, a lyon rampant queue fourchée renowée ermine, crowned or.

5. WYLYAM CLYFFORD, GLOWCESTERCHYRE. Argent, three axes erect with "revyn" bill heads sable.

6. S. JOHN ROESARDE. Vert, a lyon rampant or. Called Sir Robert in L. S.

7.* JOHN PYNCHEBEK. Argent, three lyons tails fourchée sable.

8. JOHN BROWNE, LYNCOLL CHYRE. Gules, three lyons gambs bendways (couped in blason) erased argent, the first gamb on a quarter sable.

9. S. TOMAS LEWOENORE, SOWSEXCHYRE. Azure, three chevronels argent.

Folio 45b.

1. S. WYLYAM SENTGORGE, CAMBRYGE CH. Argent, a chief azure, over all a lyon rampant gules.

2. TOMAS HEWGEFORD, WARREWYK CH. Vert, on a chevron between three bucks heads cabossed or, as many mullets pierced gules.

3. S. JOHN TRAYGOSE, SOWSEX. Azure, a bar gemelle and in chief a lyon passant gardant or.

4. S. JOHN TORBOK, LANCAST CH. Or, three eagles claws à la cuisse (gules), on a chief dancettée azure, three plates.

5.* THE ARMYS OF FLORENCE. Argent, a fleur de lys gules, two stalks issuant.

6.* TOMAS SHRIGLEY (substituted for SHURLEY), CRESH. Sable, a human foot, heel to the dexter, argent.

7.* HURLESTON, CRESH. *in a later hand*, Argent four ermine spots per cross sable.

8.* HAREWELL, *in a later hand*, Azure, three hares conjoined by as many ears or, as in the illustration. See next page.

9.* JOHN SOURBY. Chequy ermine and (? ermines), a chevron or. See next page.

Folio 46.

1.* WYLYAM BOROWE. Argent, on a saltire sable, five swans of the first. See page 68.

2. Per pale or and gules, a lozenge counter-
coloured, in later hand.

3.* WARREWYK, LE HERRAWDE. Azure
a chief gules, over all a gryphon segreant or.
Tricked per fess gules and azure. JOHN
WATER, CHESTER alias WARWICK HERALD
OF ARMS, 1471, xi E. IV.

4.* "Ermyne," ermines or erminois may
be intended.

5. ROYDEN HALL, in later hand. Argent,
guttée de poix; indication of a chief undée
gules, in another hand; not in COOKE'S MS.,
L. 8, f.62b.

6. JOHN RYE (DERBESHIRE, added). Gules,
on a bend argent four rye ears (erys) sable.

7.* RYCHARD STEWKLEY. Azure, a chevron between three pears pendant or.

8.* JOHN PENK. Ermine, two greyhounds
with collars passant regardant per pale gules
and sable.

9.* TOMAS PALMER. Sable, three wolves
passant 2 and 1 argent. See page 70.

Folio 46b.

1. THE ARMYS OF LONDON; "beryth
gowlys iiij vvoyderys of sylvyr a swerde of
the felde." Also blasoned as the CROSS OF
St. George, in the first quarter a sword erect
argent.

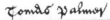

2. THE ARMYS OF YORKE; "beryth gowlys iiij lebardys of gold passant on cross goulys wt iiij vuoyderys of sylvyr." Also blasoned as the Cross of St. George charged with five lyons of England.

3. THE ARMYS OF HWLL. Azure, three crowns or, "une deseus lautyr."

4. THE ARMYS OF LEYCESTER (city, in index). Ermine, a cinquefoyle pierced gules. To Earl Bossu, is ascribed the reverse.

5. JAFFEREY YERMOWTHE. Azure, on a chevron or three escallops gules, on a chief of the third a lyon passant argent.

6. THE ARMYS OF NOTYNGHAM. Ermine, a cinquefoyle pierced ermines.

7. ———————, SOWSEX. Per pale gules and argent, a fess dancettée counter-coloured.

8. (BILLERS, in later hand). Per pale gules and sable, a lyon rampant argent, crowned or. See also No. 1, f.36б.

9.* SYMEON, LEYCESTERCHYR. Argent, three dolphins naiant embowed 2 and 1 sable.

Folio 47.

1.* ROY DE EGYPTE. Per pale or and sable, a gryphon passant gules.

fol 47 · no 2

Aymyo of the · D · portyo

fol 47 · no 6

2.* S. THOMAS FYNDARNE ("in the new bow," MS. L. 8, f.41). Azure, three arms embowed, with sword in hands conjoined argent. See also blason No. 8. A later hand adds OWEN AI EDWYN PRINCE OI INGELFEILDE, "mistaken for the he 3 hosen conjoyned."

[A beryth iij armys harneysyd wt. iij swerdys combattant joynand sayland ascure and sylvyr. This blason which is written in place of the name No. 7, refers to the fore-going blason for FYNDARNE.]

3.* THE ARMYS OF THE V PORTVS, ENG-LAND, dimidiated with, azure, three hulks in pale or.

4. ROY DE FRI[I]ESLANDE, Azure, a lyou rampant or, over all on a fess gules three fleurs de lys argent.

5. (MORTIMER?) Or, three bars sable, on a chief two palets—between as many esquires (counter-coloured); an inescocheon; gules, two bars ermine. BURGHE, K. OF THE GARTER, in later hand.

6.* Argent, two eagles legs, feathers sable talons or.

7. Azure, besantée and a lyon rampant or.

8.* S. TOMAS FYNDARNE. Argent, a chevron fracted between three crosses bo-tonnee itchée sable (illustration pp. 72, 190. Under this trick, "thys ys the trew armys as hyt schulde be wt. the iij" (rest gone). See blason No. 2.

9. GREENE (in later hand). Azure, platey 3, 2, 1, on a chief or a demy lyon rampant issuant gules.

Folio 47b.

1.* Per chevron invected or and azure, in chief an eagle displayed sable.

2.* S. TOMAS JAYE. Sable, three Midas heads proper crowned or bearded argent.

3. S. JOHN WYLSCHYRE. Per chevron azure and or, in chief six crosses formée 4, 2, of the second.

4. Sable, on a cross quarterpierced argent four martlets of the first.

5.* PYERSSE BERCHYER. Per chevron crenellée azure and or, in chief two martlets of the second.

6. TOMAS WASTNASSE. Per chevron sable and argent, three crescents counter-coloured.

7.* EDMOND AP MERY(DV)TH. Per pale gules and vert, two gryphons erect respectant argent.

8.* Per chevron sable and argent, three helmets counter-coloured.

9. CLEMENT FYSCHCOK. Gules, a chevron ermine between three portcullises 2 and 1 or.

"here I leve." A reference to L. 8.

M

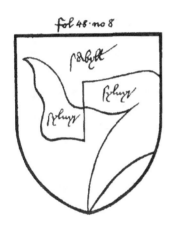

Folio 48.

1. CHAMBERLAYNE (*in later hand*). Quarterly argent and azure, over all a chevron counter-coloured.

2. JOHN LOVENEY. Per chevron invected sable and ermine.

3. TOMAS MADDOK. Azure, a bend sable between in chief three mens heads 2 and 1 couped argent, hair or, each entwined round the neck by a snake (see No. 1, f.50b), and in base as many gryphons heads erased of the fourth.

4. WELYAM BEDWELL. Per saltire ermine, and chequy or and gules.

5.* SEUAUNTE. Azure, three "ffanys" (vans) reversed 2 and 1 or. SEFTVANS. See page 73.

6. WATYR WHYTEHELL. Per pale argent and sable, a leopards face reversed or, jessant de lys counter-coloured.

7. Azure, three demy horsys courant in pale couped argent.

8.* Sable, a foot and leg fracted and embowed argent ; as engraving.

9.* S. RYCHARD PLEYS. Per pale or and gules, a lyon passant argent.

Folio 48b.

1.* S. JOHN ARCHYS. Gules, three arches with battlements and turrets, 2 and 1 argent.

2.* TOMAS LYNDE. Per chevron sable and argent, three gryphons heads erased each charged with a crescent all counter-coloured.

3.* JOHN FAWKENER. Azure, three falcons in pale each perched on a barrulet all argent.

4. BARNHAM (in later hand). Sable, a cross engrailed argent, between four crescents per pale gules and of the second.

5.* Argent, three chevrons embattled and reversed gules.

6. JOHN CROSBY. Per chevron argent and sable, three guttées 2 and 1 counter-coloured. See also No. 5, f.51b.

7.* MATHEWE REED. Per pale sable and gules guttée d'or a cross "patey" fitchée argent. See next page.

8. Quarterly ermine and sable, a lyon passant guardant quarterly of the second and argent.

9.* KILMAYNE (in late hand). Vert, three dexter hands apaumée argent, out of flames proper. Called WOLVERTON in L 8, f.63b. See next page.

Folio 49.

1. JOHN MYCHELL. Per pale argent and sable, a fess and in chief three trefoyles slipped all counter-coloured.

2. JOHN DONDUN (or DENDUN). Gules, a lyon rampaunt chequy sable and ermine, crowned or.

3. JOHN SELBYE. Per chevron sable and ermine, in chief two mullets pierced argent.

4.* VINCENT (in later hand). Per pale dancettée vert and azure, three trefoyles slipped argent. Called UNDERHYLL in L.8, f.4b.

5. GYLYS BRABAN. Sable, a fess counter embatuled argent, between three leopards faces or.

6.* ROBARD OF SETON. Gules, three passion nails meeting in base argent, a chief per pale dancettée ermine and azure.

7. Per chevron gules and or, in chief two cinquefoyles pierced of the second. BAND or BAUD in L. 8, f.4b.

8.* WYLYAM LOVVENEY. Argent, on a fess gules between three cocks sable, as many mullets pierced sable (? of the field).

9. JOHN MOURSBE (altered from MORRSBE). Sable, three false escocheons 2 and 1 argent.

Folio 49b.

1. ROY DE NORWAYE. Or, three Danish axes erect 2 and 1 sable. See also page 5.

2. TOMAS OVVYRTON. Argent, three boars heads barways couped 2 and 1 sable.

3. JOHN MARCHALL, *deleted*, POLE *also deleted*. Azure, florettée and a lyon rampant argent.

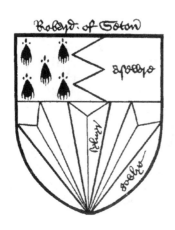

Pl. 4. S. ALEYNE DE HYNGHAM, altered to
Ingham in L. 8, f.40b. Per pale or and vert,
a cross moline gules.

5. JOHN SENKLERE. Azure, a sun of 16
rays or. SINCLAIR.

6. TOMAS LONGEVYYLE. Gules, a fess
dancettée between six crosses crosslet argent.

7. WYLYAM KYRYELL. Sable, on a fess
between three fleurs de lys argent, as many
mullets pierced of the field.

8. RYCHARD WHYTHORSSE. Gules, three
bars crenellée argent.

9. JOHN BROMEHYLL. Or, two bends
azure, on a chief of the second as many
martlets of the first.

Folio 50.

1. TOMAS FYSELYS (FITZ ELLIS?). Per
chevron argent and gules, a chevron counter-
coloured.

2. RYCHARD ESTANE. Per pale azure and
gules, three lyons rampant 2 and 1 argent,
the arms of HERBERT.

3. Per chevron gules and argent, in base a
fleur de lys sable. BATEN in L. 8, f 4b.

4. JOHN KYNGTON. Argent, guttée de poix
3. 2. 1., on a chief azure three crowns or.

5.* JOHN SPONELEY. Sable, three spoons erect handles to the base 2 and 1 or. See page 77.

6.* STOPPYNGTON. A chevron gules, between three scythe blades (? coulters) sable.

7. RONARD INGYRFELD. Barry (6) argent and gules, on a chief or a lyon passant sable.

8. TOMAS YERDE. Ermine, three saltorelies 2 and 1 gules.

9. TOMAS CORBETT. Or, two caws in pale sable.

Folio 50b.

1. VAUGHAN (*in later hand*). Gules, three mens' heads 2 and 1 argent, hair or, each entwined round the neck by a snake azure. See Maddok, No. 3, f.48.

2. MASSON (*in later hand*). Argent, a double headed lyon rampant gules.

3. JOHN LOWYS or LEWIS. Sable, a morion cap between three dice (the quatre, or **4** spot) argent.

4.* RONARD OF KYRTON. Per chevron azure and argent, three ostriches 2 and 1 those in the chief respecting each other, all countercoloured.

5.* JOHN CONNYUE (? COMYNE). Ermine, a fleur de lys ermines.

6.* TOMAS TROLLOPE.. Vert, three harts trippant 2 and 1 argent.

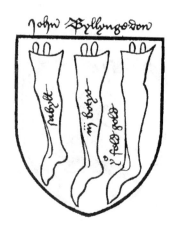

7. BARTHOLMEWE TOMASYNE. Azure, three lyons rampant per pale 2 and 1 argent and gules.

8. Argent, three bears feet conjoined at the knee "sayland" sable.

9. RYCHARD DYNTON. Sable, a pile argent.

Folio 51.

1.* JOHN BYLLYNGEDON. Or, three (boots) "botys" erect sable. THOMAS HOUSE, in MS. L. 8, f.43b.

2. WYLYAM LAGGAGE. Gules, two bars dancettée argent, on a chief azure three covered cups or—imperfectly tricked.

3. TOMAS TYLE. Per pale argent and sable, a saltire engrailed counter-coloured.

4. ROBARD HYLLE. Or, a saltire vaire azure and gules.

5.* Vert, three hands and arms embowed and conjoined "sayland" argent, each holding a mallet or, charged in the centre with a leopard's face of the last.

6. JOHN MALEMAYNE. Ermine, on a chief gules three sinister hands apaumée argent.

7. Argent, on a pale azure three eaglets displayed or. VALERE in L. 8, f.4b.

8.* JOHN LARDENER. Gules, on a fess between three boars heads couped sable, a bar undée throughout argent. See next page.

John Cordonor

John Breche

John Thornowe

9.* JOHN BRECHE. Argent, on a cross
sable five Catherine wheels of the first.

Folio 51b.

1. S. JOHN BROMWYCH. Or, a lyon rampant sable guttée d'or.
2. RYCHARD STANDELL. Argent, a chevron
between three spades, handles to the chief,
2 and 1 sable.
3. TOMAS GERVEYS. Azure, a fess dancettée argent between three crowns gules.
4.* JOHN THORNEWE. Argent, a chevron
gules between three fleurs de lys slipped sable.
5. S. ROBARD WYNTTYR (WHITNEY *added*).
Azure, a cross counter compony or and gules;
"cheeche" in blason.
6. TOMAS CROSBY (*written* GROSBY). Per
fess argent and sable, three guttées counter-
coloured. See also No. 6, f.48b.
7. TOMAS BLUNDELL. Per pale ermine and
sable, a chevron counter-coloured.

"Here I leve at the dragon not downe," a
reference no doubt to the progress of the fair
copy, L. 8. College of Arms, for which this
rough collection was the original.

8.* S. ROBARD TRENTTE (rightly BRENT).
Gules, a dragon sejant wings extended argent.
See also page 259.
9.* JOHN BROMLEY. Sable, three rakes
reversed 2 and 1 argent, handles or.

Folio 52.

1. JOHN PYELLY. Per pale or and gules, a lyon rampant sable.

2. S. RYCHARD KNYGHT. Sable, a cross gules (*sic*) between four womans heads couped argent.

3. JOHN STRETLEY. Gyronny (8) argent and sable, on a quarter gules a covered cup of the first. See No. 6, f.57*b.*

4. RYCHARD AYLEWARD. Argent, two bars between nine martlets 3. 3. 3. vert.

5. JOHN NEWPORT. Sable on a chevron between three pheons argent, as many mullets pierced or (*sic*).

6.* TOMAS XPYRSTOFFYR. Argent, a chevron indented sable between three pine cones slipped or.

7. JOHN SELOWE. Sable, on a pale gules three martlets argent.

8. JOHN SELBY. Argent, a saracen's head wreathed gules, a chief per pale or and azure.

9. JOHN METFORD. Argent, two bars dancettée sable the base blasoned azure.

Folio 52b.

1. S. TOMAS BREWNE (BRUNE). Azure, guttée de saug. a lyon rampant argent.

2.* WYLYAM ENTYRDENE. Argent, on a bend gules, three harpies of the field. TENTERDEN in L. 8, f.45.

3. S. JOHN EVVERYNGHAM. Gules, a lyon rampant vair. THOMAS in L. 8, f.45.

4. S. ROGER DE ASKEBY. Argent, a lyon rampant sable billettée or.

5.* WYLYAM BEVVER. Argent, on a chevron between three beavers paws couped sable. a cross of St. Anthony or.

6. S. JOHN NORWYCH. Per pale azure and gules, a lyon rampant ermine.

7. TOMAS WOODEHOWSE. Sable, a chevron gules guttée d'or, between three cinque-foyles pierced ermine.

8. S. JOHN HANLOW. Argent, a lyon rampant azure guttée d'or. HANDLOW in L. 8. f.45b.

9. Vert, a bend gules between six bull heads cabossed 3 and 3 argent.

Folio 53.

1. S. NYCOLL HEWVK. Gules, besantée and a lyon rampant argent.

2. NYCOLAS CARNET. Sable, three lyon-celles passant argent, between two bendlets engrailed of the second.

3. S. TOMAS TWEBYRVVYLE. Argent, billettée and a lyon rampant gules.

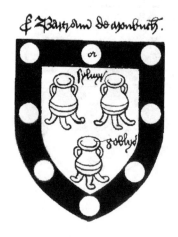

4.* S. Robard Hastynge. Gules, a chief azure, over all a lyon passant queue fourchée or. See seal in the Barons' letter, 1300. "The lyon should be rampant over all." L. 8, f.45b.

5. S. Tomas Hertforde. Argent, a lyon rampant purpure, mascully or.

6. S. Robard Boxhyll. Or, a lyon rampant azure, fretty of the field.

7. S. Rawf Stodevynt. (berle) argent, four bars azure over all three lyons rampant 2 and 1 gules.

8. S. Wylyam Felton. Gules, two lyons passant in pale argent, within a double treasure flory counterflory of the second.

9. S. John Nevvyle. Sable, a lyon rampant argent, guttée de poix.

Folio 53b.

1. Bray, *in later hand.* Gules, three bends vair.

2.* S. Bartram de Monbucher. Argent, three possenets gules, a bordure sable besantée. William in L. 8. f.46.

3. Archer, *in later hand.* Azure, six arrows 3. 2. 1. erect or.

4.* S. Rawfe Sanz Avir. Azure, crusily fitchée and three crescents 2 and 1 or.

5.* S. Tomas Fytzpayne. Argent, two wings conjoined in fess gules—"a lure" *added by later hand*

6. EDWARD COWDREY. Gules, billettée or.

7. TOMAS KOULAY. Per bend crenellée sable and argent.

8.* JOHN HYHAM. Gules, a chevron between three closed helmets argent.

9. TOMAS COSTANTVNE. Or, six fleurs de lys 3. 2. 1. sable.

Folio 54.

1. RYCHARD CHAPPYS. Gules, a fess undée between six billets argent.

2.* TOMAS WOLVVELEY. Argent, on a bend sable a wolf courant of the field.

3.* JOHN KYLVVVNGETON. Sable, a chevron between three womens heads couped argent.

4.* RYCHARD MORTON. Quarterly gules and ermine, in the first and fourth a goat's head erased argent.

5. S. (RAWFE in L. 8, f.46b.) FYTZ RAWFE. Or, three chevronels gules, on each as many fleurs de lys of the first.

6.* JOHN GAYTFORDE. Sable, three goats salient 2 and 1 argent.

7. S. HARREY NEVLLE. Gules, crusily fitchée and three leopards faces reversed jessant de lys 2 and 1 argent.

8.* S. TOMAS MOWLSOW. Ermine, on a bend sable three goats heads erased argent.

9.* JOHN CAUNDYSCH. Sable, a chevron gules (sic) between three cups argent.

Rychard Moyton

John Baytforde

S Tomelo Apeelysee.

John Colmndysch

Wylyam Collenge.

John Shypton

Nyclas Barnard

Folio 54*b.*

1.* WYLYAM COLLENGE. Quarterly ermine and azure, in the second and third a falcon (sans bells) wings elevated or.

2. Vert, on a bend gules (*sic*) three cinquefoyles pierced or.

3. S. JOHN CHAYNE. Azure, six lyoncelles rampant 3, 3, argent, a quarter ermine.

4. Vert, on a chevron argent three harts' heads cabossed gules.

5.* JOHN SHYPTON. Argent, three hand bellows 2 and 1 sable.

6. TOMAS TYMPYRLEY. Gules, a lyon rampant ermines — "ermyne Appon the sabyll."

7. JOHN OSBERNE. Argent, three fleurs de lys 2 and 1 gules.

8. NYCOLAS KENTON. Or, three lyons heads erased 2 and 1 sable.

9.* NYCOLAS BARNARD. Sable, two greyhounds erect, "dorsant," *under it* ("reversant" *in another hand*) argent. JOHN in L. 8, f.47.

Folio 55.

1.* S. JOHN ROCHE. Azure, three roach naiant in pale argent.

2. GYLBERD WAUTON. Per fess gules and argent, in chief a martlet sable.

3.* TOMAS WARRE. Azure, three dolphin naiant embowed 2 and 1 or.

fol 55b. no 2

John Bokeland

Wylyam Hautt

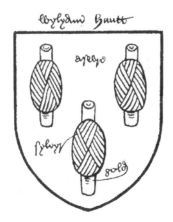

4. TOMAS WYNDHAM. Azure, guttée de
sang, a chevron between three lyons heads
erased or.

5. JOHN PELMORDA. Barry wavy (6) gules
and argent.

6. PYERSE OSSANNE. Purpure, a chevron
engrailed between three fleurs de lys or.

7. S. RAWFE DE COBHAM. Argent, a lyon
rampant chequy or and azure.

8.* TOMAS FELTON. Gules, three lyons
passant in pale ermine, crowned or; page 87.

9.* TOMAS WYSE. Argent, three wise-
men's heads 2 and 1 sable, wreathed or,
the ends flotant. See page 87.

Folio 55b.

1. Gules, four lyons rampant 2 and 2
argent, on a quarter of the last a crescent
of the first.

2.* ————a cross engrailed sable between
four hinds heads couped vert.

3.* JOHN BOKELAND. Sable, a garter *vel*
circular buckle between three square buckles
2 and 1 tongues erect.

4.* WYLYAM HOUTT (or Hunt). Azure,
three spindles 2 and 1 or, threaded argent.
HAWTE in MS. Index.

5.* WYLYAM BARNA(KE). Argent, three
barnacles (horse hames) 2 and 1 sable. See
also page 150.

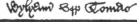

6.* TOMAS COLBY. Sable, a swan argent, gorged with a crescent or.

7.* WYLYAM VFF TOMAS. Ermine, three unicorns courant in pale gules. The uppermost spotted with ermine, erroneously in MS.

8.* Sable, a chevron between three pairs of equilateral triangles interlaced 2, 1 argent; see page 90.

9. "GLASIERS COTE" added—argent, two "grosyng eyrnes" saltireways between four "nayles," sable (corrected from malets), a chief azure (" g " later hand) in the dexter a demy lyon passant gardant couped or.

Folio 56.

"Olde lordys of tyme past."

1. LORD AMONDVVYLE. Vair.

2. LORD CANTLEY. Gules, a fess vair between three leopards faces reversed jeasant de lys. CANTELUPE. See No. 1, f.45.

3. Argent, a chief indented azure. [Fitz Ralph].

4. FITZ JOHN (added). Quarterly or and gules, a bordure vair. SIR RICHARD in L.8, f.4b.

5. Or, a bend vair and a bordure engrailed gules.

6. Azure, a bend between six martlets 3 and 3 or.

7. MARSHALL (added). Gules, a bend fusily or. EARL OF PEMBROKE in L.8, f.4b.

fol 55^b no 8

Sollyn Ednam

Symond Hoggys

("The armes of SEYNT TYBBAWTE, vj
crosseys bottonnée pychey of gold the filld
gules," in later hand). See No. 7, f.57b.

8. LONGSPEE (added). Azure, six lyoncelles rampant 3, 3. or.

9. WYLYAM COTYNGHAM. Per fess argent
and sable, a fess between six crosses formée
fitchée all counter-coloured. See No. 4, f.63b.

Folio 56b.

1.* SEVVYN EDNAM. Azure, on a bend
gules (sic) three dolphin embowed argent.
THOMAS EDMOND in L. 8, f.48.

2. MOORE (added). Argent, a fess dancettée paly (4) gules and sable, between
three mullets pierced of the last. See No. 2,
f.58b.

3. EDEMOND CHYRE ("also Pigot" added),
Sable, three picks 2 and 1 argent.

4. COUNT DE WORCESTYR. Or, a lyon
rampant azure, a label (3) gules.

5. TOMAS TORRELL. Gules, a fess engrailed
argent between three bulls heads cabossed or.

6.* SYMOND HEGGYS (HIGGS). Argent, a
chevron between three bucks lodged gules.

7.* JOHN BRESYNGHAM. Sable, a pair of
eagles wings erect and erased argent.

8. STEVVYN PERCY. Argent, two bars
undée sable, on a chief of the second a lyon
passant gardant or.

9. WYLYAM BOULL. Or, three bulls heads
cabossed 2 and 1 gules.

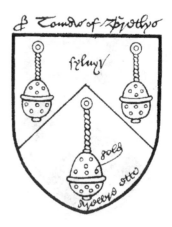

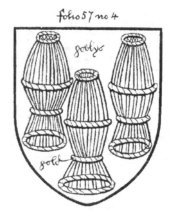

10.* S. TOMAS OF BRETLVS. Per chevron argent and azure, three pendants studded or; see page 91.

Folio 57.

1. WYLYAM OF GRANTHAM. Sable, on a fess between three covered cups argent, as many ermine spots.
2.* TOMAS CHESENALE. Argent, three crosses fitchée sable a bordure gules; page 91.
3. Vert, six lyoncelles rampant 3, 2, 1, argent. (LITTLE OF MEREFIELD in Papworth).
4.* Gules, three fish weels 2 and 1 or; page 91.
5. S. ROBARD FRAUNCYS. Argent, a chevron between three eagles displayed gules.
6. WYLYAM RYNGEBORNE. Azure, on a bend or, four mullets pierced argent (sic).
7.* WYLYAM BORTON. Sable, three open wells masoned argent.
8. S. NYCOLL DABERYCHCORT. Gules, four bars and a bordure ermine. Also blasoned as ermine, three bars humetée gules.
9.* JOHN HORSLEYE. Azure, three horses heads 2 and 1 couped or, bridled argent.

Folio 57b.

1. JOHN FLORRE. Azure, a crescent between three fleurs de lys or.
2. WYLYAM CARRANT. Argent, three roundles chevronny (6) azure and gules.
3. S. JOHN POUDSAY. Vert, a chevron between three mullets pierced or,

4.* JOHN SLYE. Gules, a chevron azure (sic) between three owls argent.

5.* WYLYAM POLE. Or, a bucks head cabossed gules.

6. JOHN STRETLEY. Gyronny (?) argent and sable, on a quarter gules a covered cup of the first. See No. 3, f.52b.

7. SEYNT TYBAWTE, KNYGHT. Gules, six crosses botonnée fitchée 3, 2, 1, or. See note on f.56.

8. HARRY DREWRY. Argent, on a chief vert, a cross of St. Anthony between two mullets pierced or.

9. JOHN ROKYS. Gules, on a fess between three chess-rooks argent, as many roses of the field.

Folio 58.

1. NYCOLAS GAWSELL. Or, three bars gules, and a quarter ermine.

2. JOHN HODY. Argent, a fess per fess dancettée throughout vert and sable, a bordure of the last.

3. WYLYAM CREDY. Or, six mascles 3, 3, sable, "but six lozenges."

4.* JOHN FAWKYS. Sable, a fess engrailed ermine between three falcons 2 and 1 argent.

5. S. WATYR TALYBOYS. Argent, a saltire gules, on a chief of the second three escallops of the first.

6.* JOHN FERBY. Sable, a fess argent, between three goats heads erased ermine.

7.* S. HARRY FENWYK. Per fess gules and argent, six martlets 3. 2. 1. counter-coloured.

8. S. JOHN CHAYNE. Gules, on a bend azure three fleurs de lys or.

9. S. GYE DE BRYAN. Azure, three piles meeting in base or.

Folio 58b.

1. S. WYLYAM BYSCHOPPYSTON. Bendy (6) or and azure, a quarter ermine.

2. ———— a fess dancettée paly (4) gules and sable, between three mullets pierced —, See No. 2, f.56b.

3.* JOHN ABBBALL. Azure, a fess between three ("orchonys") urchins *vel* hedgehogs passant or.

4. JOHN SKOOGAM. Sable, a fess dancettée between three martlets or.

5. Argent, three boars passant in pale gules; defaced. *In later hand,* "Whychecote of Lyncolneshyre beryth iij bores gules wt. a fyld of sylvyr."

6.* JOHN TREDERFFE. Or, a hart lodged azure.

7. TOMAS CHAWSERYS. Per fess gules and argent, a lyon rampant or; blasoned in a note "the tayle forche," though not so tricked.

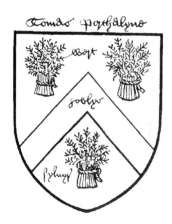

8. JOHN SAYE. Per pale vert and azure, three (6) couples close the intervening spaces counter - coloured. Evidently erroneously tricked in lieu of, 3 chevronels each surmounted of another all counter-coloured.

9. RYCHARD WORSOPPE. Gules, a dexter hand appaumée between three cinquefoyles 2 and 1 pierced argent.

Folio 59.

1. Gules, billettée 3, 2, 1, ermine. SMYTH off, in L. 8, f.59.

2.* WYLYAM BEDFORD. Burulée (12) ermine and ermines, *vel* erminois.

3. TOMAS GAMSON. WORCESTERCHYRE. Gules, a cross argent, billettée sable. "Here I leve," a reference to I. S.

4. S. RYCHARD FROGNALE. Sable, two bars or, on a chief argent a crescent of the field.

5.* TOMAS PORTHALYNE. Argent, a chevron gules between three "garbys of brome" vert. See page 105.

6. S. RYCHARD WALGRAVVE. Per pale argent and gules.

7.* JOHN HERTTLYNGTON. Sable, a chevron between three harts heads cabossed argent, attires or.

8. S. GYLBERD DELAFELD. Barry undée (6) sable and argent.

9. Argent, a false escocheon gules between nine torteaux bordurewise.

Folio 59b.

1.* AZURE, a fox salient argent, a goose
shing by the neck over his back proper.

2. WHYTFELDE, Or, a plain bend cotised
engrailed sable.

3. HARRY SOULBY, Ermine, on a chief
of two indents sable as many boars heads
couped or, armed argent. "Sandford *idem,
in later hand.*"

7.* JAMYS STANSFELDE, Sable, three goats
passant in pale argent, collared and pendant
therefrom a bell. THOMAS in L. 8, f. 51.

5. CHAUSER, Per pale argent and gules a
bend counter-coloured. Compare this with
EUCLID I. 28. 29.—See Some Feudal Coats
of Arms. page XIX.

6. CORBETT OF MARTON, Or, two "caws"
in pale sable.

7.* JOHN MARCHALL, Per chevron gules
and or, a chevron argent, in base a ("revvvn")
raven proper.

8. WYLYAM BLAUXTON, Argent, two bars
and in chief three cocks passant all gules.

9. JOHN CUNTUN or CNUTUN (NEWTON?),
Per pale argent and sable, a fess and in chief
three trefoyles all counter-coloured—defaced.
Altered to WILL CAMPTON L. 8. f. 51.

Folio 60.

1. KYNGE HARALDE, Gules, crusily argent
and two bars between six leopards faces
3. 2. 1. or—fabulous.

2.* S. WYLYAM TROUDBEKKE. Sable, three trout two saltireways heads to the base, and one in pale head to the chief argent.

3.* Ermine, three hand bellows 2 and 1 gules.

4. "The field sylvyr a vvoyde crosse of sabyll a schoychon of gold an egyll splayed of sabyll."

5.* "A beryth, asewre, a lyon passant of gold a towre pynakelyd and enbataylyd of the same."

6. "Dem——sylvyr and gowlys iiij crosse fer de molyne of the same," i.e., counter-coloured.

7. A beryth, vert, six lucies "eyronde" (hauriant) 3, 2, 1, argent.

8.* "A beryth aseure iij serpentys hedys of gold rasyd, the tongys of gold croslet-wyse." See page 98.

9.* A beryth, "a poynt sylvyr the chefe enty of asewre, v crosse forme of gold;" page 98.

Folio 60b.

1.* Argent, a chief (per fess in L. 8, f.4b) gules over all a cross moline saltireways entrailed counter-coloured; page 98.

2. CINONDE (or EMONDE) PRYORE. Azure, a bend per pale gules and or, a bordure engrailed parted per pale counter-coloured of the second and third.

3. Sable, three lilies 2 and 1 argent, a chief per pale azure and gules, in the dexter a fleur de lys, and in the sinister a lyon passant gardant both or.

4. Gules, on a chief of two indents argent three escaliops sable.

5. JOHN PASTON. Argent, florettée 3. 2. 1. azure, a chief dancettée or.

6. Gules, a chevron or between three combs 2 and 1 argent.

7.* "Demy party," i.e., per pale, or and gules, a dolphin embowed hauriant counter-coloured.

8. THE FISHMONGERS (added). Azure, three pairs of keys saltireways, 2 and 1, handles to the base argent, on a chief gules three dolphin embowed hauriant of the second. Compare with grant 19 Oct., 1512, in the ASHMOLE LIB.

9. Per pale azure and gules, a saltire counter-coloured between four crescents or.

Folio 61.

1.* Per chevron arched gules and ermine, a pale retracted of the second.

2. "Demye party," i.e., per pale and per chevron counter-coloured argent and azure, in the first and fourth a fleur de lys counter-coloured.

3.* Argent, a pale dancettée (? fusily) gules. (? Lyme.)

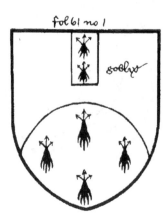

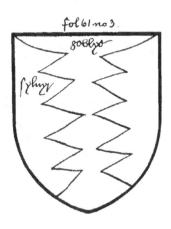

4. Per chevron crenellée sable and or, three lyoncelles rampant 2 and 1 counter-coloured.

5. VVANPAGE. Azure, an eagle displayed argent within a tressure flory of the second, usually drawn counterflory.

6. Per chevron sable and ermine, in chief two leopards faces argent.

7. "Demy," i.e., per pale or and gules, a fess between three leopards faces 2 and 1 all counter-coloured.

8. CHAPMAN (added). Per chevron gules and or, a crescent in fess point counter-coloured.

9.* [CHARLES]. Per pale ermine and ermines (vel erminois), on a chief of the first five lozenges conjoined barways gules. See page 100.

Folio 61b.

1.* COMBERTON (added). Sable, a double bodied lyon rampant gardant argent. See page 100.

2. Gules, a unicorn salient chequy argent and sable. [CLARE in L. 8. f.1]

3. Per pale ermine and azure, a fess counter-coloured.

4. LUCEY (added)). Gules, three lucies haurant between six crosses crosslet fitchée 3, 2, 1, argent. CLEREMONT in L. 8. f.1

folio 61 no 9

Combyston

fol 61 no 6

5. Per bend indented azure and argent, in chief three mullets bendways pierced gules.

6.* Argent, two piles saltireways between four demi fleurs de lys gules.

7, COTTES (added). Or, on a cross quarter pierced azure four fleurs de lys of the first, BURTON in L. 8, 15.

8. Per bend sinister gules and sable, a bend quarterly ermine and of the first and second.

9, Per pale gules and azure, a double headed eagle displayed per pale argent and or, [WANCELEYS in L. 8.]

Folio 62.

1. LES ARMYS PYECHARDE. Gules, a pale sable besantée between six crescents 2, 2, 2, ermine.

2. STONNE (added). "Demye," i.e., per pale or and azure, a lyon rampant gardant counter-coloured.

3. YONGE (added). Argent, three piles meeting in base sable, in chief as many rams' heads couped or.

4. WENLARK in L. 8, f 4. Or, florettée and a chief indented azure. (PASTON).

5, Per saltire gules and sable, a cross quarterly ermine and of the second.

6. DRAPERS' COMPANY (added). Azure, three clouds gules ("the bemys gold") radiating in base or, each crowned with triple coronets gold, surmounted of a cross pattée sable. Granted 10 March, 1439-40.

7. RYCHARD NORRYS. Azure, three mullets pierced or, a chief parted per fess crenellée argent and gules.

8. Argent, a portcullis sable.

9. Argent, on a fess dancettée sable three fish heads hauriant erased or,

Folio 62b.

1. [JASPER TUDOR, DUKE OF BEDFORD]. FRANCE AND ENGLAND, within a bordure azure charged with eight martlets or.

2. Argent, a lyon rampant queue fourchée per fess gules and sable (and renowée gules in L. 8.).

3. Per bend indented sable and or, a cross moline of the second.

4.* (WERNAM in L. 8. f. 1.) Azure, five vinres (wyres), barwise argent. See No. 2, f.64, and No. 5, f. 64b.

5.* Argent, three "crapawdys" sable. (BOTREAUX). These legendary arms of France are ascribed in L. 8. ff 1 and 90 to PHARAMOND (King of the Franks).

6. ROBARDE PRYKKE (OF BURY ST. EDMUND, SUFF.). Or, on a cross quarter pierced azure, four mascles of the first.

7.* (? CORDWELL). Three horns sable.

8. Azure, three spindles threaded 2 and 1 argent.

9. Per chevron sable and argent three crosses crosslet fitchée counter-coloured.

Folio 63.

1.* Or, three girdles 2 and 1 erect sable.

2. Quarterly argent and gules, four roses counter-coloured.

3. GIRDLERS COMPANY (added). Per fess azure and or, a pale counter-coloured, three gridirons 2 and 1 of the second.

4. Per fess sable and argent, a pale counter-coloured, three demy lyons rampant couped 2 and 1 of the second.

5. Argent, a chevron between three trivets sable.

6.* Per pale crenellée argent and sable, a Catherine wheel or.

7. Per fess azure and argent, a pale counter-coloured three cygnets 2 and 1 of the second, gorged with a coronet, chain and ring. Blasoned as " iij synettys rowsand of sylvyr crownyd and chaynyd of gold dysmembyrd wt. gowlys. ADAM GOODALE, Sergt. at Armes not soo "; see folio 66. Called FARMAN in L. 8, f. 1.

8.* JOHN OSYN. Argent, three "roys" (roes) trippant regardant 2 and 1 gules. Similar arms were granted to the Leather-sellers Company, 20 May, 1479. See next page.

9. Per bend azure and gules, a lyon rampant, regardant, queue fourchée or, holding between its fore paws a harp erect argent. The field is gules in L. 8, f. 1b.

Folio 63b.

1. (? DOLSEFEYES in L. 8, f.1b.) Quarterly sable and argent a lyon rampant counter-coloured.

2. Argent, a pale dancettée azure. See No. 5.

3. JOHN HALYS. Paly (4), per fess sable and gules counter-coloured, over all a saltire argent.

4. WYLYAM COTYNGHAM. Per fess argent and sable, a fess between six crosses formée fitchée all counter-coloured. See No. 9, f.56.

5.* HARRY HALLE. Argent, a pale dancettée gules.

6. [BLENERHASSETT]. Gules, a chevron engrailed between three dolphins hauriant and embowed argent, those in chief respecting each other. SLYTTE in L. 8, f.1b.

7.* Or, an antique ship sable, sail and pennon. NEVILL in L. 8, f.1b.

8. WYLYAM BULLE. Per fess gules and or, three bulls heads cabossed 2 and 1 counter-coloured.

9. WYLYAM BYLYNGEDON. Ermine, on a saltire sable five fleurs de lys argent.

Folio 64.

1. (OSYN in L. 8.) Azure, three bucks trippant 2 and 1 argent. See preceding page.

2.* Per pale argent and sable, a viure *eel wyre* palewise. See No. 4, f.63b, and No. 5, f.64b.

folio 64 no 3.

Sandon

John Boyd

3.* CATTESBY in L. 8, f.16. Azure, three leopards rampant 2 and 1 argent. (? FITZ-HERBERT.)

4. WYLYAM DENTTON. Argent, two bars gules, in chief three cinquefoyles pierced sable.

5. CLEMENT FFYSCHCOK (added). Gules, a chevron ermine between three portcullises or.

6. S. PYERSE DE BERESYE. Azure, a false escocheon argent, between seven crosses formée 4. 2. 1. bordurewise or.

7. TURNER (added). Ermine on a cross quarter pierced argent, four fer-du-moulines, 1, 2 and 1 sable.

8. Per fess sable and argent, a bulls head cabossed counter-coloured, horned or.

9. HEMYNEFORDE. Ermine, a chief azure besantée.

Folio 64b.

1. Gules, a lyon rampant chequy ermine and sable.

2. Ermine, a chevron and in chief three chess-rooks all sable.

3. Per bend sable and gules, three crescents in bend party of the first and argent.

4. Ermine, on a chief dancettée azure three trefoyles slipped of the first,

5.* [SANDON] Gules, a viure (vel wyre) chevron-wise argent "anewyd wt. aseure" between three bulls heads cabossed of the second horned or. See No. 4, f.62b, and No. 2, f.64.

6.* JOHN WYLD. Sable, a chevron ermine between three ("wylkys") whelk shells 2 and 1 argent.

7. JOHN HEMYNGBOURGH. Ermine, a chevron counter-battaylyd gules and in chief three ("torteys") torteaux.

8.* TOMAS PORTHELYNE. Argent, a chevron gules between three "popye bollys of vvert dessendaunte." See page 92.

9.* Or, three bars (barry of six or) and azure demi-florettée counter-coloured.

Folio 65.

1. OLEPHERNUS. Gules, a semée of trefoyles and three hawks bells 2 and 1 all or.

2. S. DEGREAVVAUNT. Azure, a saltire engrailed or, over all a double tressure flory counterflory gules. The Romance of Sir Degrevaunt. Camden Society, Vol. xx.

3.* ERMYTE. Gules, three hermits heads couped 2 and 1 argent.

4. WYVVOLDE. Per chevron crenellée gules and or, three lyons rampant 2 and 1 counter-coloured—NICHOLAS WYFOLDE, Lord Mayor, 1450.

5. Sable, a lyon rampant argent over all three bendlets gules.

folio 65.b no 4.

"The som of thys queyre of Armys ys CCCCCC, ij skore" and——

"The armys of owre lord Jesew Cryst after the forme of the passyon."

Indexed as tropheys of Christ's passion.

On a mount, see opposite page, a standing figure three-quarters, to the left, clad in the seamless "co(te) of sy(lvyr) saddely wt. gold" girt about the waist. "This is made for God's cote."

In the right hand a spear*-headed flag-staff, with banner of blue, thereon the Agnus Dei contourné with a cruciferous nimbus of gold. The sinister foot of the lamb and the staff, which terminates in a cross crosslet, are set in a golden chalice, the pennon charged with a (red) cross.

The left hand, holding a blue shield charged with the silver "Vernycle," i.e., a white cloth or handkerchief of Veronica, bearing the head of Christ, transfixed with three triple spikes, resembling a cross flory.

On a golden helmet, with rosset mantling and wreath, a golden crucifix pierced by three nails, at the top a scroll inscribed I.N.R.I., all between on the dexter a birch and on the sinister the scourge.

It will be seen that the herald painter has audaciously balanced his page by the addition of three ordinary armorial shields. See below.

_____
* The soldiers who took Jesus are usually represented by spears.

6. Per pale ermine and gules, a fess wavy counter-coloured.

7. STOKLEY. Argent, on a cross quarter pierced azure, four lyoncelles rampant 1. 2. 1. or.

8. HEWETT OF STAFF. (added). Sable, a chevron engrailed argent between three owls of the second.

9. NORMAN, Draper (of London added). Or, three bendlets gules, a chief per fess argent and ermine, charged in chief with three fleurs de lys sable. JOHN NORMAN, Lord Mayor, 1453.

Folio 65b.

"For the syetyka," then follows the recipe.

1. S. JOHN STOCTUN. Gules, a chevron vaire argent and sable between three mullets 2 and 1 pierced of the second. Lord Mayor, 1470.

2. Per bend gules and argent, a lyon rampant counter-coloured.

3. Per chevron sable and or, in chief two roses of the second.

4.* Azure, three hand bellows points meet-ing in centre or, "ye pypes sylvyr."

"For the syetyke," then follows another recipe.

1. Blanc.

2. Per pale sable and gules a leg erect couped argent.

3.* ADAM GOODALE, sergaunt of Armys, Per fess gules and argent a pale counter-coloured, three ostryches "rowsyng" (i.e., rousant) 2 and 1 (of the second ?). See full page illustration.

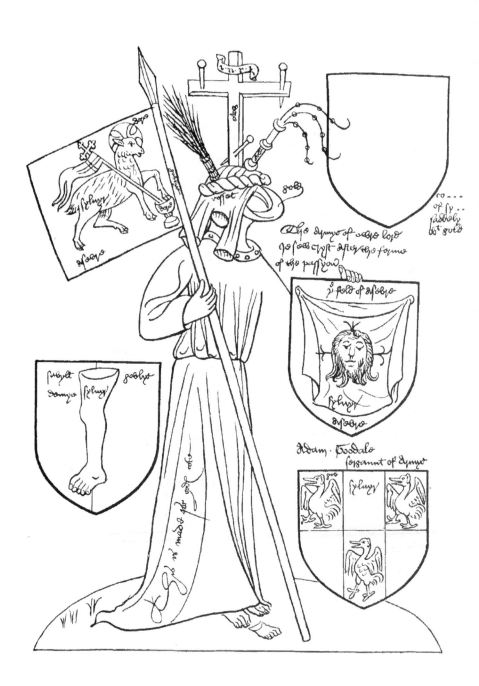

1. KYNGE OF ARRABY. Azure, a sun of 13 rays, in splendour or.

2.* ROY DE BERBERYE. Or, two serpents entwined in pale sable—defaced. A trick at the foot of this page ; or, two wyverns sans wings entwined gules. "Thys be the trewer." See illustration, page 106.

3.* ROY DE JESSE. Azure, three "eases" 2 and 1 or—fabulous. CHESSE in L.S. i.556.

4. DEWKE DE SANSON. Barry (8) or and sable, the rue crown of Saxony in bend vert.

5. THE BYSCHOPPE RYGE. Azure, florettée, on a cross or a crucified figure gules.

6. DEWKE DE HOLLONDE. Or, four lyoncelles rampant 2. 2. alternately sable and gules.

7.* DEWKE DE BAVARIE. Fusily bendy azure and argent.

8. DEWKE DE BURBUN (struck out). Azure, florettée and a bend gules ; defaced.

9. DEWKE DE OSTRYCHE (Austria). Gules, a fess argent.

There is no leaf 71 in the MS.

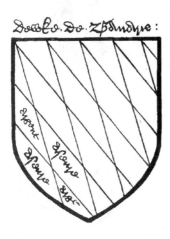

Folio 67.

" The armys of owre lorde drawe owte of the passyon."

Indexed as " Tropheys of Christ's passion."

On a mount, see page 109, a standing figure, three-quarters, to the right, clad in a loose robe, girt about the waist.

The right hand holding a quarterly shield, representing : j. The five wounds. ij. Three pots of ointment. iij. Two golden staves. iiij. The betrayer, with bag of silver round his neck.

In the left hand, a spear*-headed flagstaff with banner representing : j. The spitting. ij. The casting of lots. iij. Plucking out the hair. iiij. Cæsar or Pilate.

On a golden helmet with purple mantling and wreath, the pillar of flagellation, tied with a thong, thereon the crowing cock all between on the dexter a spear and on the sinister a reed thereon the sponge of vinegar.

It will be noticed that the herald painter has here also added two shields of arms in order to balance his page.

1. Sable, a sword in pale argent "anowyd wt. gold pomell and hyltte," between two flaunches of the second.

2. TATE. Quarterly of six pieces——incomplete. Sir Robert and Sir John Tate Lord Mayors of London 1488 and 1496 bore, per fess or and gules a pale counter-coloured, three Cornish choughs 2 and 1 proper.

* The soldiers who took Jesus are usually represented by spears.

Roy de Egypte

Roy de Caldeorum

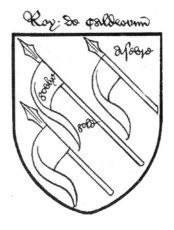

Roy de Massedonio

Roy de Assyrio

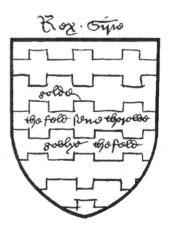

Folio 67b.

All on this page are probably fabulous.

1. THE ARMYS OF ISRAHELL. Azure, three bulls heads cabossed argent, langued gules.

2.* ROY DE EGIPTIE. Or, semée of torteanx three serpents wavy sable (? platey).

3.* ROY DE CALDEORUN. Azure, three tilting spears bendways or, pennons flotant gules.

4.* ROY DE MASSYDONIE. Or, four bars counter embattled voided gules. " the feld chewyd thorow the fecys."

5.* ROY DE AFFERYKE. Gules, a fish head and neck in fess issuant from the sinister argent, crowned or.

6.* REX DE INDIA. Or, three popinjays in pale vert. Judea in MS. index.

7.* IMPERATOR DE SALDACH. Azure on a barrulet in chief humetée a mantle all or.

8.* REX DE SIRIE. Gules, four bars (*intended*) counter embattled or. "The felde sene thorowe," *i.e.,* voided, as No. 4.

9.* REX DE PERSYA. Azure, three gryphon passant in pale, wings erect argent, armed or. See next page.

Folio 68.

All on this page are probably fabulous.—ED.

1.* SEYNT ANTONY ARMYS. Sable, the Cross of S. Antony "sylvyr anewyd wt. azure."

2. SEYNT PETYR, POPE. Gules, two keys saltireways argent.

3. DNI. PAPA DE COLUMPNE, ROME. Gules, an Ionic pillar argent, imperfect. See No. 1, f.6.

4. SCANCTUS JEREONIMUS. Azure, a cross potent fitchée at the foot or.

5. SANCTUS MAURITIUS. Vert, an eagle displayed argent.

6.* SCS. ALBYNUS, ANGLVA. Azure, a cross potent fitchée at the foot argent, between four letters A of gold.

7. SCS. MARTINUS EPISCOPUS. Azure, an escarboucle or.

8. SCS. SEBASTYANUS. Sable, three crosses crosslet fitchée or, a bordure gules entoyre of (six) pheons argent.

9. SCS. REYNOLDUS, MYLES. Per fess or and azure, over all a lyon rampant gules.

Folio 68b.

Here follow a number of Dutch coats.

1. CAMBARARYUS WORMASEN. Azure, florettée 3, 2, 1, argent, a chief dancettée or. Wormsen the chancelor.

2. DNS. DE ROTENSEYN. Per pale or and gules, a fess counter-coloured.

3.* DE MONNICH A BASEL. Argent, a monk (friar) preaching proper, book in hand gules.

4. LE S. DE ROSSENBERCH. Per fess gules and argent, paly (6) counter-coloured.

5. LE S. DE LEYEN. Azure, a pale argent.

6. LE S. DE HORST. Vert, a chief argent, over all a lyon rampant queue fourchée renowée gules.

7.* LE S. DE AYCHBERCH. Or a fess sable in base a point enarched nowy of the last.

8.* LE S. DE CHNOBIE. Gules, three fish interlaced in triangle argent.

9. MARGRAVE DE PRUSYA. Argent, on a cross formée throughout sable, a cross cornished or, thereon an escocheon—charged with an eagle displayed of the third.

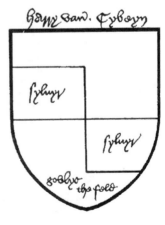

Folio 60.

("gret lorde before putt.")

1.* DEWKE DE AUREOLENSI (ORLEANS). Per bend argent and gules, a besant the edge engrailed alternate points florettée, charged with a roundle counter-coloured of the field.

2.* LE S. DE ORGENBURK. Per chevron a pile reversed throughout gules and argent, three eagles wings 2 and 1 counter-coloured.

3. S. HERRY VAN KULDVTZ. Bendy (6) or and sable, on a chief of the first, a demy-lyon rampant issuant of the second.

4. LE S. DE VAN SENTE (RYTGEN). Per bend or and gules, a mullet (8) counter-coloured.

5. LE S. DE GOTZFRYD, DOUX DE BOHEM. Barry wavy (8) argent and azure, over all a lyon rampant gules.

6.* LE S. HENRYE VAN PLESSYNGEN. Two eagles heads and necks conjoined issuant from the base.

7.* HARRY VAN CYBBYN. Gules, a fess fracted argent as No. 6, f.70

8.* REX DE VALAERIE. Or, a wing sable surmounted of a falchion azure. CALABRIA in L. 8.

9. LE SYR DE PREIAMINEN. Per bend sinister gules and argent a popinjay vert.

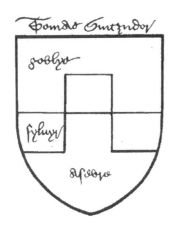

Folio 69b.

1.* HERE VAN PERGAMVVO. Argent, a winged dolphin embowed in bend gules; page 115.

2.* HERE DE HENSSCENSTEYN. Azure, a dexter hand apaumée in bend argent; page 115.

3.* DNI DE VENETIIS. Argent, the lyon of S. Mark holding in his dexter fore paw a banner, staff and pennon all gules.

4. DEWK DE GEILERN. Azure, a lyon rampant queue fourchée renowée or.

5. REX DE DALMACIE. Gules, three lyons heads 2 and 1 argent, crowned or.

6.* REX AMPULIE. Azure, a tower with flanking walls embattled and masoned in base all or.

7.* TOMAS SNITZUDOR (SNYTHINDOR, in Ms. index). Per fess gules and azure, a fess rompu argent.

8.* SEYNE ERHALT. Or, two piles embowed fretting each other sable.

9. Per chevron gules and sable, a chevron or. LE S. FFITIT in L. 8. f.58b.

Folio 70.

1. ANDREW SALBRER. Per chevron throughout gules and argent.

2.* CONRANT FYSCHBECKT. Sable, within an annulet or, a fish in bend sable (*sic*).

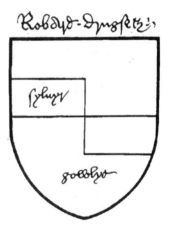

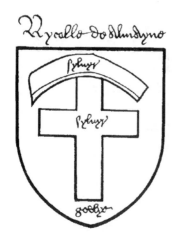

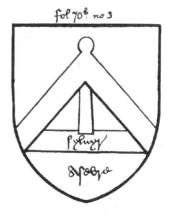

3.* CHRISTOFFYLL POTNVGER. Gules an anchor sable, double shanked saltireways or. See page 117.

4.* JESKEBBYR. Per fess gules and argent, over all two bird bolts saltireways of the second, flighted sable. See page 117.

5.* MATHEWE VAN RYSZOWE. Azure, three spoons handles to the centre argent.

6.* ROBARD DRUGSECZ. Gules, a fess fracted argent as No. 7, f.66.

7.* JWGA LANKOS. Azure, in front of a cross patriarchal fitchée at the foot argent, a horse shoe gules.

8.* PYETYR STOYSLAW. Gules, a lyons gamb issuant from the sinister argent.

9. WAULNDROFF AUGUSTINUS. Paly (6) argent and sable.

Folio 70b.

1.* NYCOLL DE ALMAYNE. Gules, a cross couped conjoined at top with the felloe of a wheel argent.

2.* PETYR DE TRONO. Bendy (6) or and gules, on a chief—three greeces gules thercout a fleur de lys.

3.* Azure, a chevron with beam and standard argent.

4.* PYERS SLANGE. Azure a serpent nowed in fess barry wavy argent and gules, crowned or.

5.* Gules, a broad arrow and sling argent.

6. Per pale dancettée argent and gules.

7. SOLIGAS DE GARBOLL, DOMINUS AWISCHA. Gules three crosses crosslet quadrate or, on a chief argent an eagle displayed sable.

8. Azure, on an ancient shield, vert, a lyon sejant tail cowed or, crowned ——.

9. Gules, two sickles addorsed argent.

Folio 71.

1, 2, 3, destroyed.

4.* Gules, on a chief argent an armed arm embowed or, holding a dagger.

5. Sable, an eagle displayed ermine.

6.* Gules, a tower masoned argent, between four mullets pierced or.

7.* FINBARNE (added). Argent, on a fess gules between three bears passant sable, muzzled of the second, as many plates on each a mullet pierced azure.

8.* OTT GUESER. Or, a beaver salient sable, claws azure. See page 122.

9. PYERS VYLZMO. Gules, a wing erect sable.

ffinis be me,

Robert Cooke,

L. 8, f.59b.

BLASONS FROM L.8 COLLEGE OF ARMS.

4b. Gules, six billets 3. 2. 1. ermine.

6. LORD HOWARD. Gules, crusily fitchée and a lyon rampant or.

——two bars within a bordure, *impaling* gules, two lyons gardant or "these leopards should be lyones," *i.e.*, passant, not gardant.

Argent, florettée and a lyon rampant sable.

Or, a lyon rampant gules.

.... two bars surmounted of a pale sable, a mullet for difference or, within a bordure gobony or and vert.

Paly (6) over all on a bend three pierced mullets—*impaling* ermine, five fusils conjoined in fess for HEBDEN.

Vaire or and azure a fess fretty or and gules.

HEBDEN. Ermine five lozenges conjoined in fess gules, *impaling* gules, on a bendlet three ears of rye, stalks sable.

Sable, three cinquefoyles pierced within a bordure engrailed, all gules.

BOWMAN (BOWSAM). Argent, three bird bolts 2 and 1 gules, headed or.

Or, a chief dancettée gules a label of three points ——.

8 (HENRY DE LANCASTER). England and a bend azure.

9. EARL OF DESMOND. Ermine, a saltire gules.

EARL OF WILTSHIRE. Paly (6) or and sable.

9b. NORMANDY. Gules two lyons passant or.

Arms of BRECKNOCK in Wales. Barry (10) argent and gules, eleven martlets 3. 3. 3. 2. 1. sable.

Arms of CORNEWALL. Ermine, a lyon rampant gules, crowned or.

BEAUFORT (Beufford). Gules, a chief sable, a bordure of the last bezantée.

12b. WILL. CLYNTON, ERLE OF HUNTINGDON, Argent, six crosses crosslet sable, on a chief azure two pierced mullets or.

13. CHETWYND. Azure, a chevron between three mullets pierced or.

23b and 35b. JAMES BEDFORD. Or, billettée and a lyon rampant sable ; ? the arms of Kychard. See page 232.

23b. SIR JOHN MYDDLETON. Argent, crusily fitchée gules three covered cups sable. A BUTLER coat.

24b. SIR NIC. STRELLEY (Sterley). Paly (6) argent and azure.

33. SIR JOHN NEWDIGATE (Nygygate),
Chyffe goge of the Kynges Bynche.
Quarterly (1) Gules, three lyons gambs
erect and erased argent. (2) Gules,
three swans argent, a canton (of
STAFFORD); argent, a chevron gules.
(3) Gules, a chevron between three
swans argent. (4) Azure, three sinister
hands apaumée argent.

34. Per chevron sable and argent in chief a
lyon passant gardant or.

36b. JOHN SUTTON. Argent, a bugle horn
stringed gules.

38. Argent, a pile gules — S. Andoyes
(? Chandos).

52b. DAVY SOLLY (Selbye ?). Per pale argent
and sable a chevron chequy of the
first and second between three hinds
heads erased counter-coloured.

SIR JOHN PESMARSH. Argent, an eagle
displayed between three crosses crosslet sable.

MAYSTER EDMOND BRUDENELL. Argent,
a chevron gules between three morion
caps azure, impaled with, argent, three
bars sable.

52b. BUSSY. Argent, three bars sable, quarterly with, gules, four fusils conjoined
in fess azure, a bordure engrailed or—
impaling gules, a chevron between ten
cinquefoyles 4, 2, 1, 2, 1, argent,

PANELL. Gules, two chevronels argent,
a bordure of the last.

COUMPERWORTHE. Chequy or and gules,
on a chief argent a lyon passant sable ;
impaling, argent, two bars engrailed
sable.

BRAYEBROGHT, struck out, LATTIMER,
in later hand. Gules, a cross botonnée
or.

53. THE ARMES OF LONDON. Per fess
argent and azure a pale counter-
coloured three lyons rampant 2 and
1 gules.

59b. HENRY OF CAMPYLL. Sable, two bars
dancettée argent.

60. WESNAM. Azure, a bend counter-em-
battled or—an untinctured roundle
added for difference.

61. Barry (6) gules and or (? HARCOURT).
Per hend argent, and bendy sinister (4)
gules and of the first ; in sinister chief
a lyon passant in bend or, sic.

63. Or, two chevronels gules, a quarter of
the second, over all a label (3) azure.

A TUDOR BOOK OF ARMS

BEING HARLEIAN MANUSCRIPT No. 6163 BLASONED BY JOSEPH FOSTER HON M.A. OXON

INTRODUCTION

~~~~~~~~~~

H ARLEIAN MANUSCRIPT No 6163 —"A curious old book in folio containing the
Arms in colours of Saints, Emperors, Kings and English Nobility and Gentry
Perhaps as early as Henry the Sixth see the Arms of the Royal Family in f 3
ard 4 , those of Hereford f 2 , of March f 3b, &c It appears to have been possessed by
Segar Garter King of Arms (1603-33), who wrote some remarks in it, and founded on it
some of his grants , see f 15b " Catalogus Librorum MSS Bibliothecæ Harleianæ

This interesting arms book contains many examples after the manner of banners, see
pages 127-142, 237-239, &c , and is in striking contrast to No 2169 Here the tricks have
been coloured, and a few of the "banners" are still in a fine state, notably Salesbury and
Devonshire, f 4b, and the royal coats on f 4, &c , &c Although the majority of the shields
are the veriest daubs, underlying many are fine examples of bold artistic delineation, some
of these are here reproduced with a little artistic help As in the former collection, so
in this, the lyons are a difficulty , a comparison with examples on pages 149, 165, 167,
210, 211, 238, 239, 256, 264, leads one to conjecture that more than one artist may have
been concerned in its reproduction

A large proportion of the shields were left unnamed by the original herald-painter, and
thus the manuscript became the sport of all sorts and conditions of arms painters and
others, those who could read the original manuscript and those who could not, principally
those who could not Many of the annotations are evidently quite obscure

The names and arms of some of the Knights of the Round Table so attributed on
pages 216 and 217 by P Le Neve, defy elucidation or identification , a rare illustration
of the Pewterers Arms 1451, appears on page 206, and the blason of the early coat of the
Haber Dalcers will be found on page 228 The arms and crest of Robert Dalby, a Douay
divine, executed in 1589, practically concludes the manuscript On page 284, the impalement
of Lloyd is somewhat puzzling, and on page 288 the marshalling for Byflete is also worthy
of notice , several instances of dimidiation will be noticed

The same difficulty arises as to origin and date of the original of this MS as in
No 2169 On the death of Peter Le Neve, Norroy, 1704-29, it probably passed out
of the possession of an officer of arms It contains many annotations by him It may
have belonged to William Flower, Norroy (1562-92), see page 221, and to William Segar
when Norroy, 1593-1602 Hence it may be inferred that this MS was one of the stock
in-trade which passed from one Norroy to another

J. F

HARLEIAN MANUSCRIPT

No. 6163.

A LATE TUDOR BOOK OF ARMS.

Presbiter Johannes

Seu Trinitas

Sca ajaria

Sanct Petir

Empe of Constantynonople

An asterisk (*) denotes a corresponding illustration.

FABULOUS COATS.

1.* PRESBITER JOHANNES. Azure, a conventional representation or; page 127. For another representation of Prester John, see Seal of Chichester Cathedral and Dict. of Illuminations, by De Gray Birch.

2.* SANCTA TRINITAS. Azure, a conventional representation of the Blessed Trinity, or. See page 127.

3.* SANCTA MARIA. Azure, a representation of the B.V.M., or.

4. SAINT GEORGE.   Argent, a cross gules.

5. SAINT DYONISE.   Gules, a cross argent.

6. SAINTE EDWARDE.   Azure, a cross patonce between five martlets, 2, 2, 1 or.

7. SEYNT EDMONDE.   Azure, three crowns 2 and 1 or.

8. "YE ARMES OF YE FAITH." Gules, a bordure argent with the device of the Trinity. See St. Michael page 11.

9. SAINT ALBON, the armes of.   Azure, a saltire or.

Folio 1.

1. SAINT THOMAS OF CANTERBURY. Argent, three beckits *vel* Cornish choughs proper, BECKETT, *impaled* on the dexter with the arms of the SEE.

2.* SAINT PETIR. Gules, a key in bend sinister argent surmounted of another in bend dexter or.

Kinge of Portingale

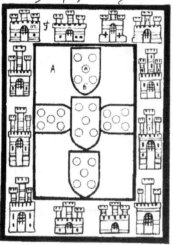

Kyng of Danmark

Kynge of Scote

3. Saint Paule. Gules, two swords saltireways hilts and pommels in base proper.

4. Jerusalem, the armes of. Argent, a
cross potent between four smaller, all or.

5. Emperour of Almaygn. Or, an eagle
displayed sable—double-headed, in Harl. MS.
437, f.48b.

6.* Emperour of Constantynenople.
Gules, a cross between four fire steels reversed
or; suggestive of the letter B reversed, the
initial of Byzantium (pages 7 and 128). See
Harl. MSS. 437, f.48b (1).

7. The Armes of Fraunce. Azure, three
fleurs de lys or.

8. The Armes of Englande and Fraunce.
France, quarterly with, England, gules, three
lyons passant gardant in pale or.

9. The King of Spaine. Gules, a castle triple-
turretted or, Castile, quarterly with, argent, a
lyon rampant purpure (? murrey). Leon.

Folio 1b.

1.* Kyng of Portingale. Argent, five
escocheons per cross azure each charged with as
many roundles saltireways, and on a bordure
(of Castile) gules, twelve towers triple turretted
or. Harl. MS. 437, f.48, gives six castles
alternately with as many fleurs de lys.

2. Kinge of Hungere. Barry (8) argent
and gules. See No. 5, f.34.

3. Kinge of Mailyorke (Malagrue in
Harl. MS. 437, f.49). Gules, four palets or.

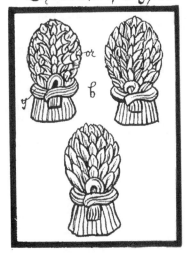

4. KING OF ERMENYE. JERUSALEM as
No. 4, f.1, *impaling*, (1) *on the dexter*, or, a
lyon rampant gules crowned (azure ?) ; (2) *on
the sinister*, azure, four bars argent oppressed
by a lyon rampant gules crowned or. Harl.
MS. 437, f.49, does not give the dexter impalement.

5. KINGE OF NAPLES. JERUSALEM as
No. 4, f.1, *impaling* (OLD) FRANCE, azure,
florettée or. In Harl. MS. 437, f.49, a label
over France.

6.* KYNG OF DANMARK. Or, semée of
human hearts gules, three lyons passant gardant
azure. See page 129.

7.* KYNGE OF SCOTTS. Or, a lyon rampant
tail inturned, within a double tressure flory
counterflory all gules. See page 129.

8.* THE ERLE OF RYCHMONDE. Chequy
azure and or, a bordure of England, over all a
quarter ermine. Probably for Arthur de Dreux.
See No. 9, f.4b.

9. ERLE OF ARTOYS. Paly (6) or and sable.

Folio 2.

1. KINGE OF ARRAGON. Quarterly; 1 and
4, or, four palets gules ; 2 and 3, paly of
three, (1) barry (6) argent and gules, (2) NAPLES
impaling (3) FRANCE as No. 5, f.1b.

2.* KINGE OF BOEME. Gules, a lyon rampant queue fourchée and renoue, argent,
crowned or. BOHEMIA.

Penenfey.   lincoln

3. KINGE OF CYPRES. Jerusalem as No. 4. f.1; *quarterly with*, barry (8 or 10) argent and azure, over all a lyon rampant gules crowned or.

4. KYNG OF NORWEY. Gules, a lyon rampant or, between the paws a Danish axe erect argent, helved azure.

5. KING OF DENMARK, SWETH, NORWEY, and LIFELAND. Quarterly; (1) Or, three lyons passant gardant azure. (2) Azure, three crowns 2 and 1 or. (3) Argent, a gryphon segreant gules. (4) Gules, a lyon rampant or, holding a Danish axe as No. 4. Over all a cross argent.

6. KYNG OF NAVERNE; OLD FRANCE azure, florettée or; *quarterly with*, gules, the Navarrese net or, over all a baston compony azure and gules (or and gules in Harl. MS. 437, ff. 48b and 68). See also No. 5, f.33b.

7.* THE ARMES OF CHESTER. Azure, three garbs or, banded gules.

8. HEREFORD. Azure, a bend argent, cotised or, between six lyoncelles rampant 3 and 3 of the last. See also No. 7, f.2b.

9. DERBY. ENGLAND, with a baston azure.

Folio 2b.

1. HENKLING. Per pale indented argent and gules. HENKLEY or HINCKLEY.

2.* PEVENSEY (a substitution). Burulée (14) argent and gules, ten martlets bordurewise sable. See also No. 5, f.3.

3. KIDWELLI (WALES added). Or, a fess dancettée gules.

4. DUC OF CORNEWARLL. Argent a lyon rampant gules crowned and langued or, a bordure sable bésantée.

5. DUC OF GUYEN. Gules, a lyon passant gardant or.

6.* LINCOLN. Or, a lyon rampant purpure.

7. NORTHAMPTON (EARLE; BOHUN, added). Azure, on a bend argent between six lyoncelles rampant or, three mullets gules. See also No. 8, f.2, and No. 5, f.4.

8. BRIGGERAK IN GUYEN. Or two eagles talons barways erased sable.

9. POUNTFREIT. Per cross or and gules, a label (5) argent. DE PONTHIEU.

Folio 3.

1. LEYCESTER (Earl of). Gules, a cinquefoyle pierced ermine.

2. PRINCE OF WALES. Argent, three lyons passant regardant tails cowed gules.

3. LANCASTER. England, and a label (3) azure.

4. BAGLES LE ROY. Per pale sable and gules, a swan argent beaked of the second, crown chain, ring and feet or. See also No. 8.

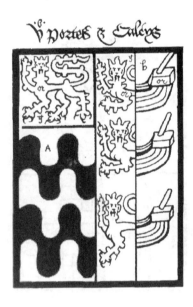

5. PEVENSAY (a town in Sussex, added). Or, au eagle displayed gules, beaked and membered azure. See also No. 2, f.2b.

6. Gules, a chief argent.

7. THE ARMES OF ESSEX. Gules, two bends the upper or, the lower argent.

8. THE KINGS BAGIES. Sable, three feathers argent, pennes and scrolls gold. See also No. 4.

9.* CALEYS AND V. PORTES. Barry undée (6) argent and sable, on a chief gules a lyon passant gardant or, impaling, gules three lyons passant gardant or, dimidiated with, azure, as many hulks of ships all or. The coats are reversed in the trick.

Folio 3b.

1. THE PRINCE. FRANCE AND ENGLAND quarterly, a label (3) argent.

2. THE DUC OF YORK. FRANCE AND ENGLAND quarterly, a label (3) argent, on each file as many torteaux.

3. MY LORD OF CLARENCE. FRANCE AND ENGLAND quarterly, a label of three argent, on each file a canton gules. See also No. 4, f.6o.

4. THE DUC OF EXCESTRE. ENGLAND, within a bordure of OLD FRANCE.

5.* THE DUC OF NORFOLK. ENGLAND, a label (3) argent.

6. THE DUC OF SOMERSET. FRANCE AND ENGLAND quarterly, a bordure gobony (16 pieces) argent and azure.

7. THE ERLE OF WARWIK. Gules, a fess between six crosses crosslet 3 and 3 or ; quarterly with, WARWICK vel NEWBURG, chequy or and azure, a chevron ermine.

8. THE ERLE OF MARCHE. Azure three bars or, a false escocheon argent, on a chief of the first two palets between as many esquires of the second; quarterly with, ? or, a cross gules. See also page 230.

9. THE LORD MOWBRAY. Gules, a lyon rampant argent.

Folio 4.

1. THE DUC OF GLOUCESTRE. FRANCE and ENGLAND quarterly, a label (3) ermine, on each file a canton gules.

2. THE DUC OF BEDFORD. FRANCE and ENGLAND quarterly, a label (5) per pale ermine and azure (the centre file azure).

3. THE DUC OF GLOUCESTRE. FRANCE and ENGLAND quarterly, a bordure argent.

4. THE DUC OF SUFFOLK. Azure, a fess between three leopards faces or ; quarterly with, argent, a chief gules, over all a lyon rampant queue fourchée or.

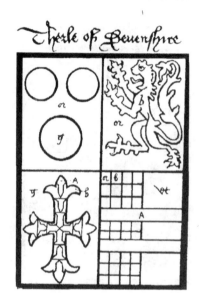

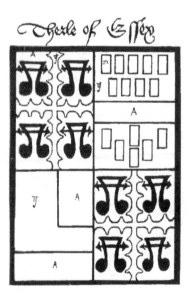

5. THE DUC OF BUKKINGHAM. Quarterly (1) FRANCE and ENGLAND quarterly, within a bordure argent. (2 and 3); azure, on a bend argent cotised or between six lyoncelles rampant, 3 and 3 of the third, three mullets gules: BOHUN. (4); or, a chevron gules, STAFFORD.

6. THE ERLE OF CAMBRIGGE. FRANCE and ENGLAND quarterly, a bordure —. Imperfect.

7. THE ERLE OF ARUNDELL. Gules, a lyon rampant or; *quarterly with*, chequy or and azure. See No. 6, f.43ᵇ.

8. THE ERLE OF WESTMORLAND. Gules, a saltire argent.

9. THE ERLE OF OXONFORD. Quarterly gules and or, a mullet argent.

Folio 4ᵇ.

1. THERLE OF STAFFORD. Or, a chevron gules.

2.* THERLE OF SALESBURY. Argent, three fusils conjoined in fess gules; *quarterly with*, or, an eagle displayed vert, beaked and membered or.

3.* THERLE OF DEVENSHIRE Quarterly (1); or, three torteaux 2 and 1. (2); or, a lyon rampant azure. REVIERS. (3); gules, a cross patonce vair. DE FORS. (4); chequy or and azure, *impaling*, vert, over all two bars argent. BARONY OF OKEHAMPTON.

Therle of Northumberland

Therle of Shrewsbury

Therle of Ormonde

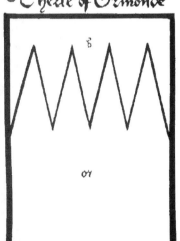

4.* THERLE OF ESSEX. Quarterly, 1 and 4; argent, a cross engrailed gules between four water bougets sable. (2); gules, billettée or and a fess argent. (3); argent, a fess and a quarter gules. See page 133.

5.* THERLE OF NORTHUMBERLAND. Or, a lyon rampant azure (as at Carlaverock 1300): *quarterly with*, gules, three lucies hauriant 2 and 1 argent.

6. LORD GRAY RUTHYN. Quarterly, 1 and 4; barry (6) argent and azure in chief three torteaux. 2 and 3; or, a maunch gules, HASTINGS, *quarterly with* VALENCE, barry (8) argent and azure, eight martlets bordurewise gules.

7. THERLE OF KENT. ENGLAND and a bordure argent.

8. LORDE FITZWAREN. Chequy or and azure.

9. THERLE OF RICHMONDE. Chequy argent and azure, a bordure of ENGLAND, over all a quarter ermine. See No. 8, f.1b.

Folio 5.

1. THE LORD MONTAGUE. Quarterly. I and IV grand quarters. 1 and 4 as Salesbury No. 2, f.4b. 2 and 3; gules, a saltire argent, a silver label (3) on each file a hurt. II and III grand quarters. (1); argent, on a quarter gules a rose or. BRADSTONE. (2); gules, a cross engrailed argent. INGLETHORPE. (3); sable a fess between three leopards faces or (? POLE). (4); argent a fess dancettée sable in each point a plate, *vel* besant.

2. THERLE OF WORCESTR. Argent, a saltire engrailed gules ; *quarterly with*, or, a lyon rampant gules.

3.* THERLE OF SHREWSBURY. Gules, a lyon rampant or, a bordure engrailed of the second ; *quarterly with*, argent two lyons passant in pale gules.

4. THERLE OF DESMONDE. Ermine, a saltire gules.

5. THERLE OF KYLDARE. Argent, a saltire gules.

6. THERLE OF PENBROCHE. Burrulée (10) argent and azure, ten martlets bordurewise gules.

7.* THERLE OF ORMONDE. Or, a chief indented azure.

8. THERLE RYVERS. Quarterly, 1 and 4 ; argent, a fess and a quarter gules. 2 and 3 ; gules an eagle displayed or ; *quarterly with*, vair ; on an escocheon of pretence, gules a gryphou segreant or.

9. LORDE MAWTREVERS. Gules, a lyon rampant or ; *quarterly with*, sable, fretty or. MALTRAVERS.

Folio 5b.

1. THE COLOURS OF LANGCASTER. Per pale argent and azure.

2. LE PRIOR HALIS. Azure, a chevron argent between three fleurs de lys or. OF HALESOWEN.

3. LORD GREY CODNOWR. Barry (6) argent and azure.

4. LORD DARCY. Azure, crusily and three cinquefoyles pierced argent ; *quarterly with*, MEYNELL, imperfectly tricked.

5.* LORD DUDLEY. Or, two lyons passant in pale azure, membered gules ; *quarterly with*, argent a cross patonce azure.

6. LORD CROMEWELLE. Argent, a chief gules : *quarterly with*, chequy or and gules, on a chief argent three ermine spots (? a chief ermine) : over all a baston azure.

7. LORD LOVELLE. Barry undée (6) or and gules ; *quarterly with*, azure, a lyon rampant gardant argent, membered gules.

8.* LORD ROOSSE. Gules, three water bougets argent.

9. LORD DE LA WARRE. Gules, crusily fitchée and a lyon rampant argent ; *quarterly with*, azure, three leopards faces reversant jessant de lys 1 and 2 (or ?).

Folio 6.

1. LORD BEAMOWT. Azure, florettée and a lyon rampant or, membered gules. BEAUMONT.

2. THE LORD GREY WILTON. Barry (6) argent and azure, a label (5) gules.

3. LORD FITZHOUGH. Azure, three chevronels interlaced in base or, a chief of the last

lord Cornolbatt

Lord 2 Bayeblen

Haftingo

4. LORD WILLEBYE. Sable, a cross engrailed or ; *quarterly with*, gules, a cross moline argent.

5. LORD HARYNGDON. Sable, fretty argent a bend gules ; *quarterly with*, per cross argent and gules, No. 2, f.8b.

6. LORD FURNEVALE. Gules, a lyon rampant or, membered azure, a bordure engrailed of the second ; *quarterly with*, argent, a bend between six martlets 3 and 3 gules.

7.* LORD CORNEWALL. Argent, a lyon rampant gules crowned or, a bordure engrailed sable bezantée.

8. LORD BURNELL. Argent, a lyon rampant sable crowned or, membered gules, a bordure azure ; *quarterly with*, or, a saltire engrailed sable.

9. LORD PONYNGIS. Barry (6) or and vert, a riband gules ; *quarterly with*, gules, three lyons passant in pale argent, a baston azure.

Folio 6b.

1. LORD SCROPE OF BOLTON. Azure, a bend or ; *quarterly with*, argent, a saltire engrailed gules.

2.* LORD BARCKLEY. Gules, crusily formée 4. 2. 1. 2. 1., and a chevron argent.

3. LORD BUGHGENY. Gules, a fess between six crosses crosslet or, a crescent sable ; *quarterly with*, argent, a bendlet sable, *quartering*, gules fretty or. See also No. 1, f.10.

4. LORD MAWLE. Or, a bend sable ; *quarterly with*, or, a lyon rampant azure, a bendlet gobony argent and gules. See also No. 2, 196.

5. LORD FERIS OF GROBY. Gules, seven mascles conjoined 3, 3, 1. or.

6. LORD FERIS OF CHARTELEY. Vaire or and gules.

7. LORD COBBHAM OF COLYNG. Gules, on a chevron or three lyons rampant sable.

8. LORD COBBHAM OF STERBURTH. Gules on a chevron or three estoyles sable.

9. LORD FUATRE (FITZWALTER, added). Or, a fess between two chevrons gules.

Folio 7.

1. LORD SEYMOUR. Or, crusily and a lyon rampant azure ; *quarterly with*, argent two chevrons gules.

2. LORD HASTYNGS (of ELSING in NORFOLK, added). Or, a maunch gules ; *quarterly with*, gules, a bend argent. (FOLIOT of ELSING, added). See also page 311.

3.* LORD CHAMBRELAYNE (HASTINGS). Argent a maunch sable.

4. LORD FERRERS. Argent, six fers-de-cheval 3, 2, 1. sable.

5. LORD COBBHAM. Gules, on a chevron or three crosses crosslet sable.

6. LORD COBBHAM. Gules, on a chevron or three fleurs de lys sable.

7. LORD SEYNTAMOUNT. Or, fretty sable, on a chief of the second three besants. See page 183.

8.* LORD OF KYME. Gules, crusily patonce and a cinquefoyle pierced or.

9. LORD DEYNCOURT. Azure, billettée and a fess dancettée or.

Folio 7b.

1. LORD ROOSSE. Gules, three water bougets argent ; *quarterly with*, argent, a fess double cotised gules, on an escocheon of pretence, azure a wheel or.

2. LORD MOLENOE. Paly wavy (6) or and gules. MOLINES.

3.* LORD STRANGE. Gules, two lyons passant in pale argent membered azure.

4.* LORD LATEMERE. Gules, a cross patonce or. See page 138.

5. LORD OF SEYNT JOHN. Argent, on a chief gules two mullets pierced or.

6. LORD CAMEUX. Or, on a chief gules three plates. CAMOYS.

7. BAR(O)NE OF CAROW. Or, three lyons passant in pale sable membered or.

8. THE ARMES OF GLOUCESTER. Or, three chevrons gules. CLARE, EARL of GLOUCESTER.

9. LORD ZOUCHE. Gules, besantée and a quarter ermine.

Lord Lutomore

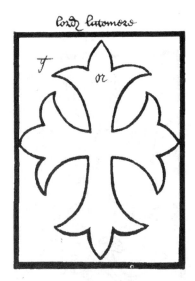

Lord Daboy

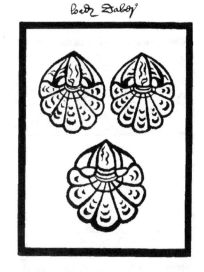

Lord Morley

Folio 8.

1.* LORD DAKER. Gules, three escallops 2 and 1 argent.

2.* LORD MORLEY. Argent, a lyon rampant sable crowned or, membered gules.

3.* TWENG. Argent, a fess gules between three popinjays proper, *i.e.*, vert, beaked and membered gules.

4.* LORD LUCE. Gules, crusily and three lucies hauriant 2 and 1 or.

5. LORD CLIFFORD. Chequy or and azure, a fess gules.

6. LORD ECHYNGHAM. Azure fretty argent.

7. LORD MONE. Or, a cross engrailed vert. MOHUN.

8.* BARON OF WHEME. Sable, a cross moline ermine. WEMME.

9. BARON OF HELTON. Argent, two bars azure.

Folio 8b.

1.* BARON OF HILTON—? HUTTON—(an error for GREYSTOCK). Barry (8) argent and azure, three chaplets 2 and 1 gules ; *quarterly with*, REDMAN, gules, three cushions argent tasselled or. See page 140.

2. HARYNGTON. Same as No. 5, f.6.

3. LORD HUNGERFORD. Sable, two bars argent in chief three plates.

4. LORD BEAMOWNT OF DEVONSHER. Barry (6) ermine and gules.

5. LORD BASSET. Or, three piles meeting in base gules, a quarter ermine.

Cweng

lord luco

6. LORD CLYNTON. Argent, on a chief azure, two mullets pierced or ; *quarterly with*, per cross or and gules.

7. LORD STANLEY. Argent, on a bend azure three bucks heads cabossed or ; *quarterly with*, or, on a chief dancettée azure three plates. LATHOM.

8. LORD HARYNGTON. Sable, fretty argent ; *quarterly with*, argent, a cross patonce sable.

9. LORD COBHAM (OLDCASTLE, added). Argent, a castle triple turretted sable ; *quarterly with*, gules on a chevron or, three lyons rampant sable. for COBHAM.

Folio 9.

1. MY LORD OF ARUNDEL and my lady his wife ; FITZALAN and WARREN quarterly as No. 7 f.4., and a label (3) argent ; an escocheon of pretence, sable fretty or ; *impaling* WIDVILE quarterly of six, (1) ; argent, a fess and a quarter gules. (2) ; gules, a gryphon segreant or. (3) ; argent, a lyon rampant gules. (4) ; gules, an estoyle argent. (5) ; gules, an eagle displayed or. (6) ; vair. See also RYVERS No. 8. f.5.

2. MY LORD OF ESSEX (rightly VISCOUNT BOURCHIER, *o.v.p.*) and my lady his wife ; argent, a cross engrailed gules between four water bougets sable ; *quarterly with*, gules, billettée and a fess or ; over all a label (3) argent ; *impaling* WIDVILE as in the preceding.

2Barn of wygsmo

Baron of Hilton

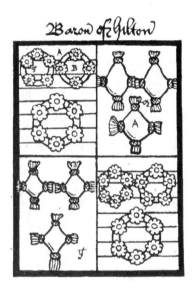

Vevers

Lord Bardolfe

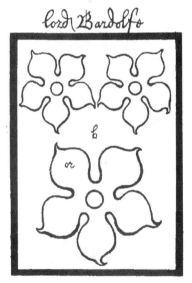

3. My Lord of Kente and my lady his wife
(Visctss. Bourchier), Lord Grey de Ruthyn,
as No. 6, f.4b, impaling as Nos. 1 and 2.

4. Ser Richard Wydevile (Wodefeld).
An estoile or, for difference and 5; Master
John. A mullet or, for difference; quarterly of
six, as impalement No. 1, each with impalement
blanc.

6. (Bluntte.) Quarterly (1); argent, two
wolves passant in pale sable, a bordure or, entoyre of saltorelles gules. (2); or, a tower
triple turretted azure. (3); sable, three bars
undée or. (4); vair.

7. Prewes. Gules, an eagle displayed or.
8. Beachame. Vair.
9.* Revers. Gules, a gryphon segreant or.

Folio 9b.

1. Lord Darcy. Azure, crusily and three
cinquefoyles pierced argent.

2. Le S. Mawle. Or, a bend sable.
(Mauley). See also No. 4, f.6b.

3.* Lord Bardolfe. Azure, three cinquefoyles pierced or.

4. S. John Fastolfe. Quarterly or and
azure, on a bend gules three crosses crosslet of
the first.

5. Lord Leukexor. Azure, three chevronels
argent.

6. S. John Tipto(ft). Ermine, a saltire engrailed gules a label (3) azure.

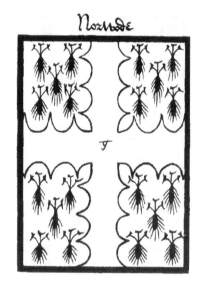

7. S. GERARD USFLETE. Argent, on a fess azure three fleurs de lys or ; *quarterly with*, or, a bend between six martlets gules.

8. LORD VESSE. Or, a cross sable.

9. TAYLBOYS. Argent, a saltire gules, on a chief of the second three escallops of the first.

Folio 10.

1. LORD BURHGENY. Gules, on a fess between three crosses crosslet or, a crescent for difference sable. BEAUCHAMP. See also No. 3, f.6b.

2. LORD STOURTON. Sable, a bend or between six plates (fountains were probably intended). See also No. 1, f.127.

3.* LORD WENLOKE. Argent, a chevron sable between three blackamoors heads erased proper.

4.* NORWODE. Ermine, a cross engrailed gules.

5.* S. JOHN HAWERD. Gules, a bend between six crosses crosslet fitchée argent.

6. S. THOMAS MONGOMERE. Gules, a chevron ermine between three fleurs de lys or.

7. LORD OGLE. Argent, a fess between three crescents gules.

8. LORD BONVILE. Sable, six mullets 3. 2. 1. argent, pierced gules ; *quarterly with*, gules, three lyoncelles rampant 2 and 1 or.

9. LORD BUTTELER. Gules, a fess counter-compony argent and sable between six crosses formée fitchée at the feet or ; *quarterly with* SUDLEY ; or, two bends gules.

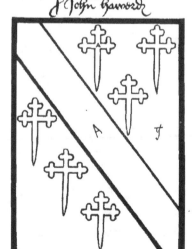

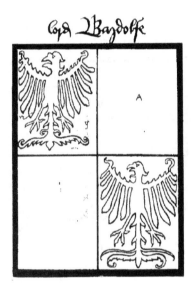

1. LORD BOURCHIER (BARNES added). Quarterly I and IV as No. 2, f.9.; II and III, per cross or and vert; over all a label (3) azure.

2. SYR HUMFHREY BOURCHIER (added). Quarterly as No. 2, f.9, without the label; impaling, quarterly per fess indented argent and gules; *quarterly with*, argent, two bends undée sable.

3. (GLE) GOWDWYN, ERLE OF KYNTT. Armys —gules seven lozenges conjoined 3. 3. 1. vair. HUBERT DE BURGH.

4. LORD SAYE. Quarterly or and gules.

5. LE S. FELTON. Gules, three lyons passant gardant argent.

6. LORD CAMFERE *sic*. Sable, a fess argent. WEERE.

7. BECHAM BYSSCHOPPE OF SALISBERY, (RICHARD). Quarterly 1 and 4; gules, a fess or between six martlets 3 and 3 argent, a bordure of the third (pellettée?). (2); gules, two lyons passant in pale argent. (3) azure, gone.

8. LORD FACONBYGG (FAUCONBRIDGE). Gules, on a saltire argent, a mullet of the first; *quarterly with*, argent, a lyon rampant azure.

9.* BRYAN TALBOT. Argent, three lyons rampant 2 and 1 purpure. See also No. 8, f.14, and No. 6, f.2b.

1. LORD BASSETT. Azure, three piles meeting in base or, a quarter ermine.

2. LORD CLINTON (added). Argent, six crosses crosslet fitchée 3. 2. 1. sable, on a chief azure two mullets or pierced gules.

3. LORD ROBBESERD. Vert, a lyon rampant or, vulned on the shoulder proper; *quarterly with*, BOURCHIER, argent, a cross engrailed gules between four water bougets sable.

4. LORD SPENCER. Or, three chevronels gules; *quarterly with*, per cross argent, a riband sable, and gules fretty or.

5. LORD MOVERANT, *sic*. (? MORANT.) Or, three pallets gules, a bordure azure besantée.

6. BYRMENCHAM. Per pale indented azure and or.

7.* LORD BARDOLFE (PHELIP, added). Per cross gules and (blanc), in the first and fourth quarters an eagle displayed or.

8. DUKE OF LANSUM. Azure, three fleurs de lys 2 and 1 or, a bordure gules besantée.

9. LORD OF HOFFORD AND DE NORWICH (UFFORD, SUFF., added). Sable, a cross engrailed or; *quarterly with*, per pale dancettée argent and gules; over all an escocheon of pretence, gules platey 3. 2. 1.

End of the banners, see also pages 237-239.

Folio 11b.

1. S. UMFREY STAFFORD. Or, a chevron gules, a bordure sable.

2. S. JOHN CHEYNYE. Chequy or and azure, a fess gules fretty ermine : *quarterly with*, or, a lyon rampant per fess sable and gules.

3.* SIR WILLIAM CHENYE. Gules, four fusils conjoined in fess argent, each charged with an escallop sable ; *quarterly with*, azure, a cross pattée formée florettée or.

4.* SIR ARNOLDE SAVAGE. Argent, six lyoncelles rampant sable.

5. SIR JOHN DALYNGRIGE. Argent, a cross engrailed gules.

6. SIR JOHN FOGGE. Argent, on a fess between three annulets sable as many mullets pierced of the first.

7. SIR ROLAND LENTHALE (and Jhon Stanley, added, see also No. 2, f.22). Sable, five lozenges in bend argent ; *quarterly with*, argent on a bend sable cotised or three mullets of the last.

8.* SIR WILLIAM PORTEUR. Sable, three bells pendant 2 and 1 argent, clappers of the first, on the second the letters "war.

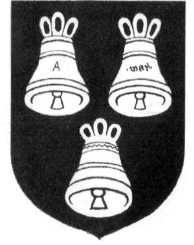

Sir nicholas mongomery

Sir thomõ Erpynghm

Sir Nicoll Hawte

9.* SIR NICHOLAS MONGOMERY. Gules, a false escocheon ermine, between eight horseshoes bordurewise or; *quarterly with*, or, an eagle displayed azure, beaked and membered gules.

Folio 12.

1. SIR JOHN BABETHORPE. Sable, a chevron or between three crescents ermine.

2.* SIR THOMAS ERPYNGHAM. Vert, a false escocheon between eight martlets bordurewise all argent.

3. SIR SYMOUND FELBREGGE. Or, a lyon "embelif" gules, membered azure.

4.* SIR NICOLL HAWTE. Argent, on a bend azure three lyoncelles passant or.

5. SIR THOMAS CULPEPER. Argent, a bend engrailed gules.

6.* SIR MORIS BROYNE (or BRUNE). Azure, a cross recercelée or; *quarterly with*, lozengy argent and gules. ROCKELE added.

7.* SIR NICOLL PECCHE. Sable, an eagle wings elevated argent, crown beak and talons or.

8.* SIR JOHN ROTHENALE. Sable, a chevron between three conies heads erased argent.

9. SIR PHILIP LECHE. Ermine, a chief dancettée gules, on each point a coronet or.

Folio 12b.

1. SIR JOHN STEWARD. Per chevron gules and azure, a chevron between three lyons heads erased or.

Syr Morus Draymo

Syj Nicoll Peccho

Syz John Gothenalo

Syj hugh Cotorell

Sr̃ Osmond Hoboby Ebr

8 Nicoll colfox

Sr̃ porcalo Lynley

2.* SIR HUGH LOTERELL. Or, a bend between six martletts 3 and 3 sable. See page 145,

3. SIR JOHN CORBONELL (CARBONELL). Gules. a cross argent, a bordure engrailed or ; *quarterly with*, gules. a chevron argent between three eagles displayed of the second, beaked and membered for. (or CASTON of Caston in Norfolk.)

4. SIR JOHN ASHTON (LANC., added). Argent, a mullet pierced sable.

5.* SIR THOMAS ROKEBY (EBOR., added). Argent, a chevron sable *between* three rooks proper.

6.* SIR NICOLL COLFOX. Argent, on a chief azure three foxes heads erased or.

SIR RAUFE BRASEBRYGE. Vaire argent and sable a fess gules.

8. SIR WILLIAM BOWES (DUNELM). Ermine, three bows strung gules.

9.* SIR PERCIVALE LYNLEY. Argent, on a chief sable three storks heads erased of the first.

Folio 13.

1. SIR JOHN BEAUCHAMP. Gules, a fess between six billets or ; *quarterly with*, gules, a lyon rampant queue (? fourchée) renowée argent.

2. SIR WILLIAM MOWNTENEY. Azure, a bend between six martlets or.

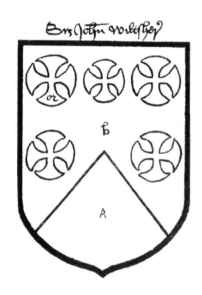

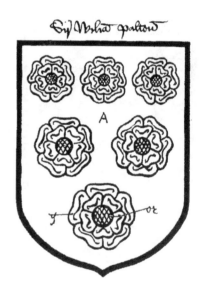

3. SIR ROBERT CHALONS. Gules, two bars between eight martlets 3, 2, 3, argent, on the sovereign bar a besant ; *quarterly with*, vair.

4. SIR PERS DUTTON (CHESHIRE, added). Per cross argent and gules fretty or.

5. SIR THOMAS CHAWORTH. Azure, two chevrons or ; *quarterly with*, argent, a false escocheon within eight cinquefoyles bordurewise pierced sable.

6. SIR THOMAS GENEY. Azure, a false escocheon within eight martlets bordurewise all or.

7. SIR JOHN COLVILL. Or, three chess rooks 2 and 1 gules ; *quarterly with*, azure, a lyon rampant argent, a label (3) gules.

8. SIR JOHN COPILDIKE (LINC. added). Argent, a chevron between three crosses crosslet gules ; *quarterly with*, lozengy ermine and gules.

9. SIR JOHN CLYFTON OF BOKENHAM, NORFOLK. Chequy or and azure, a bend ermine.

Folio 13b.

1.* SIR JOHN WILTSHER (ESSEX, added). Per chevron azure and argent, in chief five crosses formée convexed 3 and 2 or.

2. SIR THOMAS GRYSLEY (DERBY added). Vaire argent and gules ; *quarterly with*, sable, a lyon rampant argent a crescent for difference gules.

3.* SIR WILIAM PALTON. Argent, six roses 3, 2, 1, gules.

Sir Nichas full thorpe

Sr George Carew

Sir Trompyngton

4. SIR THOMAS MORDRED (MAREDREDE). Azure, a fess argent between three cinquefoyles pierced or.

5. SIR THOMAS BARRE. Gules, three bars company argent and sable, *quarterly with*, barry (6) or and azure, a baston gules.

6.* SIR JOHN HORSLEY (Somerset, added). Azure, three horses heads couped or, bridled purpure. See page 147.

7. SIR JOHN RADCLIFFE (LANC., added). Argent, a bend engrailed sable, a crescent of the first for difference.

8.* SIR WILIAM FULLTHORPE. Ermine, a cross moline sable.

9. SIR HERRY INGLOSE (NORFOLK, added). Gules, six barrulets or, on a quarter argent, five billets saltirewise sable.

Folio 14.

1. SIR ROB. OF CLIFTON (NORFF., added). Gules, five bendlets argent; *quarterly with*, chequy or and gules on a bend ermine a plain cross of the second.

2.* A patent to SIR GEORGE CAREW. Quarterly. (1); azure, a lyon rampant or, crowned argent, membered gules. (2); sable, three lyons passant in pale or. (3); sable, six lyoncelles rampant or. (4); argent, a bendlet undée between two plain bendlets gules; *quarterly with*, argent a gurges gules.

lord Barkley

braytofto

3.* SIR (———) TROMPYNGTON, CANTABR. Azure, crusily and two trumpets saltirewise or.

4. MABANK. Barry undée (8) argent and gules a saltire or.

5. SIR THOMAS FIZPAYNE. Argent, a pair of wings conjoined gules.

6. SIR WILIA GRAUNTSUM. Paly (6) argent and azure, on a bend gules three round buckles or. GRANDISON.

7. SIR RAUFE GRENE. Chequy or and azure, a bordure gules ; *quarterly with*, argent, a cross engrailed gules.

8. LEWKENORE (SUSSEX, added). Azure, three chevronels argent.

9. SIR JOHN DE KYRKYNGTON. Gules, three bars ermine.

Folio 14b.

1. LORD BEAUMONT OF DEVONSHIRE. Barry (6) ermine and gules.

2. LORD DYNHAM. Gules, four lozenges in fess ermine.

3. LORD GOLDISBOURTH. Azure, a cross patonce argent ; *quarterly with*, argent, three chevronels sable.

4. SIR ADAM FRANCEIS. Per bend sinister sable and or a lyon rampant counter coloured.

5. S. THOMAS GRAY. Argent, on a bend cotised azure three gryphons passant or ; *quarterly with*, gules, three bars argent.

6. SIR JOHN KOKIRHAM. Argent, on a bend sable three leopards faces or. COCKERHAM.

7. SIR FYLYP BECHAM. Gules, a fess between six martlets or.

8. SYR RAF PAYLE. Purpure (see also No. 9, f.10b) a lyon rampant or.

9. SYR (———) DREWRY. Argent, on a chief vert, a cross tau between two mullets pierced or. See page 271.

Folio 15.

1.* LORD BARKLEY. Gules, crusily formée and a chevron argent, within a bordure of the last.

2. LORD RAMESTON. Argent, a chevron and in dexter chief point a cinquefoyle pierced sable. REMFSTON or RAMPSTON.

3. SIR JOHN DAUTRE. Sable, five fusils in fess argent.

4. SIR JOHN STRELLEY (NOTTS., added). Paly (6) argent and azure, a quarter gules.

5.* BRAYTOFTE. Azure, crusily (as illustration), and a lyon rampant gardant argent.

6. TRUSSELL (STAFF., added). Argent, fretty gules, besantée at the joints.

7. SYR LENARD OF RESTON (SR. LEONARD DE KERDESTON NORFF.) Gules, a saltire engrailed argent.

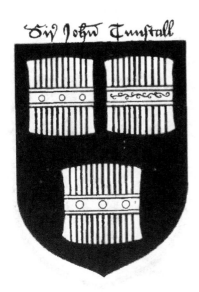

Sir John Tunstall

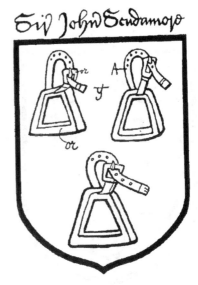

Sir John Scudamoro

Sir John Pellam

8.* Sir John Dunstall (Tunstall). Sable, three combs 2 and 1 argent.

9.* Sir John Seycmor (Scudamore, Heref., added). Gules, three stirrups 2 and 1 or, leathers argent.

Folio 15b.

1.* Sir John Pellam (Sussex, added). Azure, three pelicans argent, beaks and legs gules, vulning themselves proper.

2. *Syr Watyr Walcotte. Azure, a false escocheon between eight martlets bordurewise argent.

3.* Wyllm Barnake. Argent, three barnacles 2 and 1 sable. See also page 88.

4.* Robert Mauley. Or, on a bend sable three eagles displayed argent.

5. S. Edmond (Yorpe), Thorpe of Norfolk, added. Azure, three crescents argent.

6.* Thomas Kok. Gules, fretty argent, over all a fess sable. Cock.

7. Shyrley. Gules, a chevron chequy sable and argent between three fleurs de lys or; a marginal note by P. le Neve adds, this coat was granted by Segar, Garter to Robert Shirley citizen of London 10 of Sept. 1609; see my book of Grants f.465 blotted. The coat was confirmed and a crest granted by Segar.

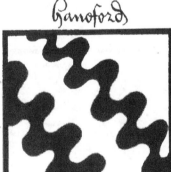

8. ROGER POWTRELL (or S. AMYS POULET, knyght, added). Argent, a fess between three cinquefoyles pierced gules.

9.* JOHN BROWNFLETE, BROMFLETE (LORD VESEY, added). Sable, a bend cotised flory counterflory or.

Folio 16.

1.* S. WYLYAM ARCHE. Gules, a double arche in chief and a single arch in base argent, the turrets or.

2. S. JOHN DE POPPHAM. Argent, on a chief gules two bucks heads cabossed or, a besant for difference ; *quarterly with*, gules, besantée and a chevron argent.

3. Or, a cross patonce gules ; *quarterly with*, or, three bendlets azure.

4. WYLLIAM DAMPORT (DAVENPORT, CHESH., added). Argent, a chevron between three crosses botonnée fitchée sable, a bordure engrailed gules.

5.* HANEFORD. Argent, two bends undée sable.

6.* WYLBURRY. Sable, crusily fitchée or, three lyons rampant 2 and 1 argent.

7. SIR WYLLAM BOWET, NORFF. Argent, three reindeers heads cabossed sable.

8. SIR WILYE SANDYS (HANTS., added). Argent, a cross ragulée sable.

9.* S. WYLLAM BRENTE. Gules, a wyvern sejant tail nowed argent. See also pp. 86, 259.

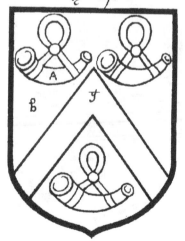

Folio 16b.

1. RECHEMOND. Per fess gules and argent, a cross patonce between four mullets all counter coloured.

2. KYLNEY. Azure, a cross moline or.

3. SYR ROBRET SCHOTYSBROK. Ermine, on a chief per pale dancettée or and gules, a cinque-foyle pierced of the last. See also No. 2, f.44, and No. 4, f.86.

4. SYR PERS TYLYOLL. Paly (6) or and gules, a chief ermine.

5. S. JOHN CURSUNE OF FELTON. Gules, two lyons passant argent, FELTON; *quarterly with,* CURSON, ermine, a bend counter compony argent and sable.

6. NORWODE (KENT, added). Ermine, a cross engrailed gules.

7. S. (————) COYTYFE. Azure, a chevron between three crescents or.

8. BABTHORP. Sable, a fess between three crescents argent.

9. SIR JOHN BOHUN. Or, a cross azure.

Folio 17.

1.* WYTTEHEDE. Azure, a chevron gules (? or) between three bugles argent.

2. SIR THOMAS WODEVILE. Argent, two bars and a quarter gules.

Y

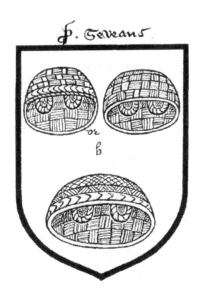

3. SENT QEYNTON. Or, a chevron gules, a chief vair.

4. BRAYBROKE. Argent, seven mascles conjoined 3. 3. 1. gules.

5.* S. SEVEANS (SEPTVANS, KENT, added). Azure, three vans reversed 2 and 1 or.

6.* SYR THOMAS SEYNCCLER (ST. CLAIR). Azure, an estoyle of 16 points or. SINCLAIR.

7. SIR (———) SAKEVYLL. Quarterly or and gules, a bend vair.

8. SIR WILLM. WALEYS. Gules, a fess ermine.

9.* SIR WYLLM. COGGSCHALE. Sable, a cross between four escallops argent.

Folio 17b.

1. SIR ALEN BUXHYLL. Or, a lyon rampant azure, fretty argent.

2.* SIR ALEX GOLDYNGHAM. Argent, a bend undée gules.

3. SIR COSTANTYN MARTYN. Gules, two bars and in chief three mullets pierced all argent.

4. SIR ROBT. LOWTHER (WESTMORLD., added). Or, six annulets 3. 2. 1. sable.

5. SIR (———) BECHAMP OF SOMERSET. Gules, a fess between six martlets 3 and 3 or.

6.* SIR JOHN TRUSTHELL. Argent, a cross pattée florettée gules. See No. 4, f.18, for " a nodyr TRUSSELL."

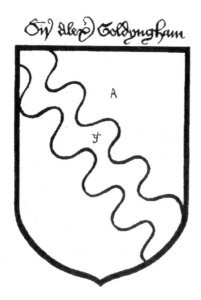

Sir Alexr Goldyngham

Sir John Trufhell

7. SIR JOHN SWYNBORNE. Gules, crusily and three swine heads couped paleways 2 and 1 argent; *quarterly with*, or, on a saltire engrailed sable an annulet of the first for difference.

8. SYR WYLLAM BERDEWELL (of WEST HARLYNG, NORFOLK, added). Quarterly 1 and 4; gules, a goat enbelif argent, horns or. 2 and 3; per cross or and gules in the first quarter an eagle displayed vert. PAKENHAM.

9. SIR ANDREW BOTTELER. Argent, three covered cups in bend sable between two bendlets gules; *quarterly with*, gules, a cross argent, a bordure engrailed or. See No. 3, f.12b.

Folio 18.

1. SIR ROBT. ALESBURY. Azure, a cross argent.

2. S. RYCHARD WALGRAVE. Per pale argent and gules.

3. SYR JOHN TREBETT. Sable, three chevronels ermine.

4. A NODYR TRUSSELL. Argent, a cross pattée florettée gules, an annulet of the first; *quarterly with*, argent, five lozenges 3 and 2 gules.

5.* SIR WYLLAM GASCON (GASCOYNE, added). Sable, three lucies heads erect 2 and 1 or.

6. SIR LAURENCE OF MERYBER. Coat cut away. MERBURY.

Sir Wyll Gaston

Sir   Sotynley

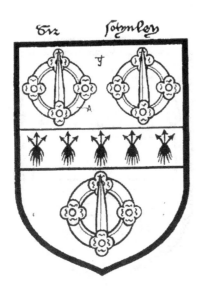

Sir Bryan Stapylton

Sir John Schellyng

7. Sir Wyllam Hoo. Quarterly sable and argent.

8. Sir Edward Parene or Parerre (Perrers). Quarterly, argent and sable.

9.* Sir (————) Sotynley. Gules, a fess ermine between three round buckles, tongues to the chief, argent.

Folio 18b.

1. Sir Herry Huse. Ermine, three bars gules.

2. Sir John Kynghley. Argent, a fess sable.

3. Pers Osanne. Purpure, a chevron engrailed between three fleurs de lys or.

4. Sir Thomas Borton. Coat cut away. See No. 1, f.21b.

5.* Sir Bryan or Stapylton (Ebor, added). Argent, a lyon rampant sable, on the shoulder a mullet of the first. Bryan Stapylton. See No. 8, f.20.

6. Sir (————) Maleverer (Ebor, added). Gules, three levriers courant in pale argent, collared or.

7. Syr John Downfrest (Dowynffrezst.) Gules, on a bend cotised argent, three eagles displayed vert, beaked and legged of the first.

8.* Sir John Schellyng. Azure, a chevron engrailed between three martlets argent. Nichell Hunt, erased.

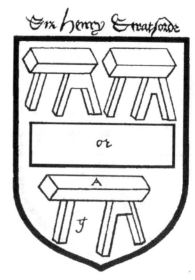

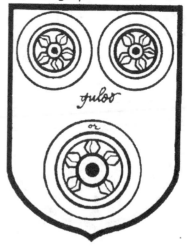

9. SIR FF. . . FEW WAREN (FitzWarren). quarterly per fess indented ermine and gules.

Folio 19.

1.* RYCHARD WODHERTTON. Gules, a chevron argent between three lyons gambs erect and erased sable.

2. ROBBES or ROWES. Lozengy argent and gules, on a bend azure two annulets interlaced of the first.

3.* SIR HENRY STRATFORDE VPON AVON. Gules, a fess humettée or between three threstles 2 and 1 argent.

4. SIR (————) BASKYRVELL. Argent, a chevron gules between three fountains.

5.* SWYNFORD. Gules, three wheels 2 and 1 or. Query! Sir Payne Roet, father of that Swinforde. See also No. 7, f.19*b*.

6. SIR WATER CLOPTON (SUFF., added). Sable, on a bend argent cotised dancettée or, an amulet of the first. See No. 3, f.22.

7. SIR RYCHARD NEVELL. Gules, three leopards faces jessant de lys argent.

8. SIR HARY HARCOURT. Gules, two bars or.

9. SIR THOMAS BLOUNT. Quarterly argent and gules, on a bend sable three eagles displayed or.

Folio 19b.

1. THOMAS COLVILE. Or, on a fess gules three lyons rampant argent.

2.* S. Lewes John (after called Fitz Lewis of Essex, added). Sable, a chevron between three trefoyles slipped argent.

3.* Sir John Pecche. Azure, a lyon rampant queue fourchée renowée ermine, crowned or.

4. Sir ———— Etton (rather Ecton). Barry (8) or and azure, on a quarter gules a cross patonce argent.

5. Sir John Ecton. Burulée (14) argent and gules, on a quarter sable a cross patonce or.

6. Godfrey Hylton. Argent, two bars azure ; *quarterly with*, Lassells, argent, three chaplets 2 and 1 gules.

7.* Swynford. Argent, on a chevron sable three boars heads paleways couped of the field, a label of (3)——. See No. 5, f.19.

8.* Sir Thomas Thorell (Essex, added). Gules, a fess engrailed argent between three bulls heads couped or.

9. S. de Seynt John. Argent, a bend gules, on a chief of the second two mullets vert.

Folio 20.

1.* Cavvndishe. Gules, three piles wavy meeting in base argent. Gernon of Cavendish, Suff., added.

2. Shelton. Azure, a cross or, written over it Malbby. Norfolk added.

Sir thomas thorolt

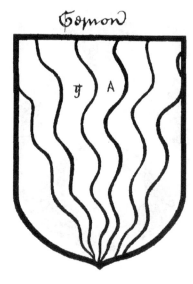

Gomon

3. PHILIP DEVEROS. Argent, a fess gules in chief three torteaux. DEVEREUX.

4. ROSE OF KENDAL now WILM PARRE. Or, three water bougets 2 and 1 sable.

5.* SENT MARTENS, ARMYS. Gules, a wheel or.

6. JOHN MORTEMERE. Ermine, on a fess azure three crosses sarcelly or, a label (3) gules. See No. 4 f.42b.

7. WYLLM. BRYTTE. Argent, crusily fitchée and a lyon rampant gules.

8. SIR BRYAN STAPILTON (EBOR., added). Argent, a lyon rampant sable, on the shoulder a mullet gules; *quarterly with*, gules, a lyon rampant argent. See No. 5, f.188.

9. BRERETON, CHESHIRE. Argent, two bars sable.

Folio 20b.

1. SIR JOHN BVERICHE (BEVERIDGE.) Per pale gules and vert, a lyon rampant argent.

2. SIR PHILIP THORNBURY (written Chornbury). Azure, crusily or and three crescents 2 and 1 argent.

3. SIR RICHARDE VERNON. Argent, fretty sable, a quarter gules.

4.* REYNFORD. Gules, a chevron engrailed argent between three fleurs de lys of the last; *quarterly with*, gules, six eagles displayed or. See page 160.

Sent Marten

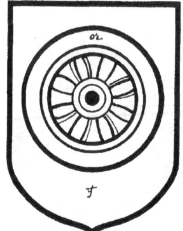

Reymfors

Sy John wolfe

John Veyney.

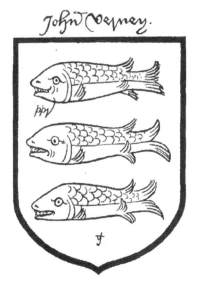

5. SYR WYLLM TEMPEST. Argent, a bend engrailed between six martlets all sable.

6. JOHN HALIS. Sable, on a chevron between three lyons rampant argent, a crown gules.

7. SIR JOHN KESAL. Per pale or and azure a fess counter-coloured. A CUSACK Coat.

8. DE LA BERE (HEREF., added.) Azure, a bend double cotised or, between six martlets 3. 3. argent.

9. SYR THOMAS TERELL (Essex, added). Argent, two chevrons azure a bordure engrailed gules.

Folio 21.

1. SIR JOHN COKAYNE OF DERBY. Vert, two bars or.

2.* SIR JOHN WOLFE. Argent, a chevron sable between three wolf heads erased of the second, each gorged with a coronet or. See page 276.

3. JOHN STAFFORD. Or, a chevron gules, and a quarter ermine; *quarterly with*, gules, a chief azure over all a lyon rampant or.

4. SYR (———) PORTER. Argent, a saltire engrailed gules.

5. LILLE. Sable, a fess between two chevrons or.

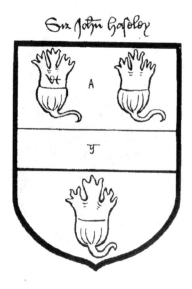

6. GRAY (TALBOT, VISCOUNT LILE, added).
Gules, a lyon rampant argent, a label (3) azure,
a bordure engrailed of the second, *impaling*
BEAUCHAMP (with a crescent sable) *quartering,*
NEVILL.

7.* JOHN VERNEY. Gules, three (lucies?)
naiant in pale proper.

8.* SIR JOHN HASELEY. Argent, a fess gules
between three hasel nuts slipped vert.

9. SYR RYCHARD ATTE LEES. Gules, a cross
crosslet ermine.

Folio 21b.

1. SYR WYLLAM BORTON. Gules, a pile
argent, a crescent for difference or.

2. SIR DAVYD ROUCLYFF (EBOR., added).
Argent, on a chevron between three lyons heads
erased gules, a chess-rook or.

3. ROOS OF INGMANTHORP. Azure, three
water bougets 2 and 1 or.

4. GRAY. Barry (6) argent and azure, in
chief three torteaux.

5. GRAY. Barry (6) argent, and azure, on a
bend gules three leopards faces reversed jessant
de lys or.

6. GRAY. Barry (6) argent and azure, on a
bend gules three martlets or.

7. GRAY. Barry (6) argent and azure, a
label (3) gules.

8. SIR (......) WATERTON (EBOR., added)
Barry (6) argent and gules, three crescents 2
and 1 sable.

9.* SIR PERCYVVALL (SANDON) SOWDAN.
Paly wavy (6) argent and sable; *quarterly with,*
gules, a Sowdan's head argent. See also page 31.

Folio 22.

1. SIR RAFF ROCHEFORD. Per cross or and
gules, a bordure sable; *quarterly with,* gules, an
eagle displayed or.

2. JOHN STANLEY (see No. 7, f.11b.) Argent,
on a bend azure three bucks heads cabossed or;
quarterly with, argent, on a bend azure three
mullets or.

3. SIR WAT CLOPTON (SUFF., added). Sable,
on a bend argent, cotised dancettée or, an
annulet of the field. See No. 6, f.19.

4. GRANTSON. Paly (6) argent and azure, on
a bend gules three mullets or.

5. GRANTSON. Paly (6) argent and azure, on
a bend gules, three eagles displayed or.

6. GRAY. Barry (6) argent and azure, a bend
compony or and gules.

7. SIR WILLIAM WYSAM. Sable, a fess between six martlets 3 and 3 argent.

8.* STANDYSCH (LANC., added). Azure,
three standing dishes 2 and 1 argent, a label (3)
or. See page 162.

z

Standyfch

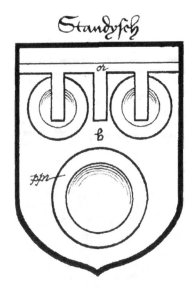

Sir John Trelott

Osbayrn

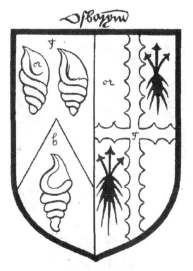

9.* SIR JOHN TREVVETT (TRIVET, added). Argent, a trivet sable.

Folio 22b.

1. SIR JOHN CURSON. Ermine, a bend counter-compony argent and sable.

2. ROBERT CURSON. Gules, billettée or, on a bend of the second three escallops sable.

3. JOHN HORE (or Here). Sable, three cinquefoyles argent, pierced gules.

4. WAKEHURST. Argent, a pale azure, impaling, SCELES otherwise called JOYNOUR; gules, on a chevron engrailed argent between three falcons of the second membered or, a trefoyle azure, a bordure engrailed of the second.

5. WAKEHURST quartering JOYNOUR as the last, but without the trefoyle.

6.* OSBARYNE. Per chevron gules and azure three whelk shells 2 and 1 or; impaling, quarterly or and ermine a cross engrailed gules.

7. CHAMBYRLAN. Argent, a chevron between three leopards' faces gules.

8.* HOLLTT. Argent, three fleurs de lys azure.

9. KELCY (BRAKELEY, added). Chequy argent and gules, on a bend azure three billets or.

Folio 23.

1. JOHN HERON. Gules, a chevron engrailed argent, between three herons of the last.

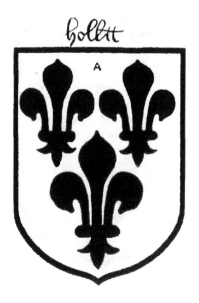

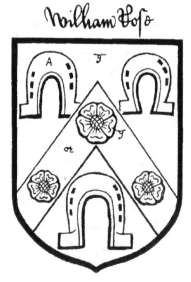

2.* WILLIAM ROSE, Merchaunt. Gules, on a chevron or, between three horse shoes argent, as many roses of the field; and ys wyffe, viz. :—

3. Paly (6) argent and sable, on a bend or, three broad arrows reversed azure. (Hatheway bore pheons azure).

4. JOHN MAHON (MOHUN, added). Ermine, a maunch gules.

ᶠ 5. SYR WILLM. FYLOLL, WILTS. Vair, and a quarter gules.

6. HERRY TRENCHARDE (SOMERSETSHIRE, added). Azure; *impaling*, paly (6) sable and argent. Probably a mistake for per pale argent and azure, in the first three palets sable.

7. S. J. GYFORDE. Gules, three lyons passant (? gardant) argent. iij. lybards passant sylver.

8.* JOHN T[AR]LETON. Sable, a saltire or between four crosses formée argent.

9. TONGRA. Or, three broad arrows azure; *quarterly with*, argent, on a bend azure three lyons rampant or, all within a bordure sable.

Folio 23b.

1. SENT PETER OF EXETER. Gules, a sword erect proper surmounted of two keys in saltire or. See Tanner's Notitia.

2.* YE ABBOT OF HARTLAND (DEVON, added). Argent, a buck's head cabossed azure, attires gules, enfiled by a crosier erect or. (Page 164.) See Tanner's Notitia.

y° Abbot of Haylland .

y° Abbot of Bokfastlay

Barlowe

3.* YE ABBOT OF BOKFASTCLAY. Azure, a bucks head cabossed proper, attires argent, enfiled by a crosier or. See Tanner.

4. MASTR. BORTON. Or, a cross quarter pierced azure.

5. COP(LE)STON OF DEFNSCHYR. Argent, a chevron engrailed gules between three leopards faces sable.

6. TYRGKHAM (q. KIRKHAM, added). Azure, a saltire engrailed argent.

7. TRUSSBUT. Azure, three water bougets or. Quartered by Ros.

8. PETERBOROUGH MONASTERY. Gules, two keys in saltire or.

9.* WILLIAM BARLOWE. Argent, on a bend engrailed azure, three greyhounds heads erased of the field, the first collared and garnished with an annulet or. See Nos. 7 and 8, f.24.

Folio 24.

1. YE ABBOT OF BELAND (BYLAND, EBOR., added). Quarterly argent and gules, a crosier in bend or. See Tanner's Notitia.

2. RICHARD BYFLETE OF HAMSHIRE. Azure, two swords in saltire proper, between four fleurs de lys or ; *quarterly with*, gules, a chevron between three hawk's lures or ; *impaling*, argent a chevron azure, on a chief of the second two mullets pierced of the first. See No. 1, f.49b, and No. 4, f.102b.

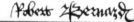

3. SPYLMAN OF WALDEN in Essex. Sable, two bars argent between as many mullets in chief, and in base an annulet, all or.

4. DAVVYLLE (now TYRINGHAM, added). Azure, fretty or.

5. PAPENHAM. (nowe TYRINGHAM, BUCKS., added). Barry (6) argent and azure, on a bend gules three mullets pierced of the first. PAKEN-HAM.

6.* CATTESBY. Argent, two lyons passant in pale sable, crowned or.

7. SENT. ASAFFE, the SEE. Azure, a key surmounted of a crosier in saltire both or ; *impaled on the dexter by* BARLOWE. NO. 9, f.23b.

8. ARMYS OF ROCHESTER, the SEE. Azure, on a saltire gules an escallop or ; *impaled on the dexter by* BARLOWE, NO. 9, f.23b.

Note by Peter Le Neve : (Nos. 7 and 8 :) qre. St. DAVIDS or Lontaff or St. Asaph rather all three altered now, but is S. Asaph, for William Barlow was Bishop of St. Asaph in the 27th year of King Henry 8, after of St. Davids same year and after of Rochester, and after of Lincoln.

9. LANGHAM OF KEBERLE IN NORFOLK (Kimberley). Argent, three chevronels gules, on the second an annulet or. Qre. of Langham in Suff. and Tanfeld in Essex, added. See No. 9, f.26b.

Folio 24b.

1. JOHN PURY and MORE. Argent, on a fess between three martlets sable as many mullets pierced of the first ; *quarterly with,* MORE (1st wife) gules, a chevron or between three martlets sable.

2.* JOHN PURY OF BARKSHIRE. Argent, on a fess between three martlets sable as many mullets pierced of the first. See next page for the arms of his 3rd wife.

3.* SWANNE (2nd wife of John Pury). In a shield in the MS. ; azure, a fess wavy or between three cygnets proper, membered gules.

4. PILKYNGTON. Argent, a cross patonce voided gules.

5. Sable, a lyon rampant argent.

6. Paly (6) argent and gules, on a bend sable three mullets or.

7.* ROBERT BERNARD. Sable, two grey-hounds addorsed respectant argent, in the centre chief point a bulls head cabossed of the second. See page 165.

8.* WUS. WHYTEHELL. Per pale argent and sable, a leopards face or, jessant de lys counter-coloured. See page 165.

9.* THOMAS COSYN. Azure, a lyon rampant queue forchée renowée or, guttée de sang, crowned argent.

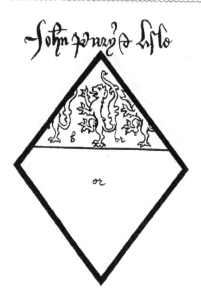

Folio 25.

1.* LISLE (3rd wife of John Pury, No. 2, f.24b). In a shield in the MS.; or, on a chief azure three lyoncelles rampant of the first.

2. MICHELL CARVANELL. Argent, on a fess azure three crosses patée of the first, in chief as many leopards faces gules, the base fretty of the last, *sic*.

3. Per pale azure and sable, a lyon rampant argent, membered gules; *impaling*, sable, three spear heads erect 2 and 1 argent.

4. SIR PIERS ARDERN, knyght of Yorkshire. Paly (6) or and sable, on a chief argent three lozenges of the second, on the centre lozenge a chess-rook of the first.

5. DAUNAY in Com. Ebor (COWICK, added). Argent, on a bend cotised sable three annulets of the first.

6. THOMAS DELELOWND. Azure, four bars argent, a crescent for difference of the first.

7. ROBT. INGILTON. Argent, crusily fitchée (5) and a chevron sable, between three gryphons heads erased azure; *quarterly with* (BALL?) argent, a chevron sable between three fire balls proper.

8. Paly (6) argent and azure, a mullet of the first for difference; *quarterly with*, STRELLEY (Qre. Shaw), gules, a chevron between three mascles all ermine; on an escocheon of pretence. ARUNDELL, azure, six hirondelles (or martlets) 3. 2. 1. argent.

9. BEKE. Gules, a cross moline ermine.

Folio 25b.

1. COORTE (Courte). Quarterly, 1 and 4; paly (6) or and vert, on a chief of the first an eagle displayed sable. 2 and 3; per cross gules and or, a mullet argent, *quarterly with*, or a fess between two chevrons gules.

2. SIR HENRY STONARD, knyght of Cornwall in Edward the secunde hys tyme. Sable, a chevron argent between three plates; *quarterly with* (MICHELSTOWE), sable three wings 2 and 1 argent.

3. SIR JOHN BROCAS. Sable, a lyon rampant gardant or; *quarterly with*, WARREN, chequy or and azure.

4.* MONS. BARNARD BROCAS, M. de Buk-hounds Rx. Sable, a lyon rampant gardant or; *quarterly with*, sable, two lyons couchant gardant, cowed argent, membered gules.

5. SIR JOHN STONARD, chief justice in the daies of King Edward the third: fader to Harry Stonard (see No. 2). Azure, a fess dancettée and a chief or.

6. IYNGGYLTHORP (NORF., added). Gules, a cross engrailed argent; *quarterly with*, argent, on a fess dancettée sable three besants. INGLE-THORP.

7. Argent, a fess sable, between three lozenges azure.

Reede

Brampton

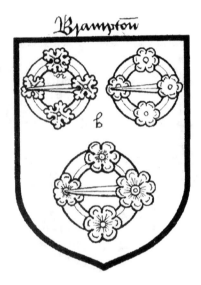

folio 26 no 4

8. Per fess or and argent, over all a lyon rampant azure, debruised of a bar gemelles gules.

9.* REEDE (added). Azure, a gryphon segreant or, a mullet argent.

Folio 26.

1.* BRAMPTON. Azure, three round buckles tongues to the dexter, or. See No. 9, f.82.

2. WYLLIAM BURTON. Ermine, a fess sable, a chief counter compony or and of the second.

3. S.(——)KYNARDYSLY. Vert, a chevron sable (sic) between three leopards faces or.

4.* Azure, three (herring?) naiant in pale argent, a bordure ermine. "Vatter is Erin," added; ? intended for Walter Herring.

5. Paly (6) sable and argent, on a chevron gules, a cross crosslet or.

6. HYDE OF ESSEX. Argent, a chevron gules between two mullets in chief sable and in base a cinquefoyle pierced of the second.

7. Argent a fess gules between three bucks heads cabossed sable.

8. Argent, crusily and three roses 2 and 1 gules.

9. (ARCHDEACON, DEVON, added). Argent, three chevronels sable, on the first a crescent gold. Richard larchedeken also added.

Folio 26b.

1. Per fess argent and gules, a martlet for difference sable.

folio 26^b no 2

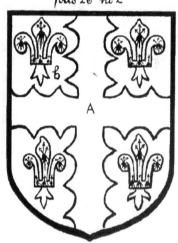

f John Wroth

Danyell

2.* Azure, a cross engrailed argent, between four fleurs de lys ermine.

3.* S. JOHN WROTH. Gules, three lyons rampant argent, a quarter sable fretty or.

4. CODYNGTON. Gules, a cross argent fretty azure.

5. Argent, three bars wavy azure.

6. Argent, a chevron sable between three rooks proper.

7. Argent, a fess double cotised gules; *quarterly with*, azure, a chevron argent between three doves proper beaked and legged gules.

8. SANTCLO. Argent, on a bend sable three annulets or, a label (3) gules.

9. LANGHAM. Argent, three chevronels gules, an annulet or; *impaling* BARDOLLFE, argent, on a chevron between three fleurs de lys sable, a mullet of the first. See No. 9, f.24.

Folio 27.

1. ROBERT KEYNES. Vair, three bars gules.

2. HARCORT. Argent, on a chevron sable three escallops of the first.

3. WAKE. Or, a fess gules in chief three torteaux.

4.* DANYELL (CHESSHYRE, added). Argent, a pale fusily sable.

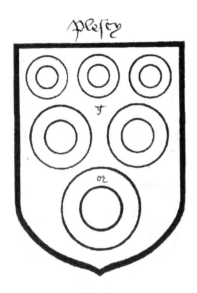

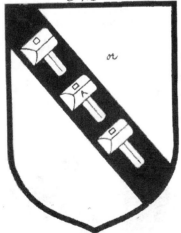

5. JOHN WELASONE (WOLASTON, added) of Lelande. Argent, on a bend sable three pheons 2 and 1 of the first ; *quarterly with*, NEWTON, azure, two shin bones saltireways argent.

6. DABRICHCOURT. Barry (6) gules and ermine, a bordure of the second. Sometimes blasoned ermine three bars humettée gules.

7. CHYDEOKE. Gules, a false escocheon between eight martlets bordurewise argent.

8.* PLESCY. Gules, six annulets 3. 2. 1. or.

9. CHANDOS. Or, a pile gules.

Folio 27b.

1.* SYMKYN EYYR. Gules, a porcupine saliant argent, quills barry of the second and sable, collar ring and chain or. Lord Mayor of London, 1445.

2.* BETYLSSGATE. Or, on a bend sable three mallets argent.

3.* BREKNOCKE. Argent, a chevron sable between three ——— of the second, guttée d'eau ; *impaling*, azure, two bars gemelles and a chief or.

4. LONDON. Argent, three cinquefoyles 2 and 1 pierced sable.

5. BRACAYS. Chequy argent and azure, on a fess of the first three lyons passant sable.

6.* Vert, a fess flory counterflory or. (RICHARD FRANCEYS.)

7. Argent, on a bend azure three annulets or.

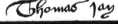

8. Per fess sable and gules, paly (4) counter coloured, over all a saltire argent.

9.* Ermine a cross formée throughout gules. See page 171.

Folio 28.

1. WELLYNGTON. Ermine three bendlets azure.

2. WALLYNGTON. Paly wavy (6) meeting in point argent and sable, on a chief gules a saltire or.

3. BOKYNGHAM. Azure, on a chevron gules, three crescents argent, in chief a dolphin naiant embowed of the last.

4.* Per chevron argent and sable three guttées d'or (sic) 2 and 1. See page 171.

5. Argent, a gryphon segreant azure, membered or.

6.* CORBET. Or, two "caws" in pale sable.

7. LECHE. Ermine, on a chief dancettée gules, three crowns or, a bordure sable.

8. NEWTON. Sable, two shin bones in saltire argent.

9. FYNCHEHAM. Sable, three bars ermine.

Folio 28b.

1.* THOMAS JAY. Sable, three Midas heads 2 and 1 argent, crowned or.

2.* DUFFELD. Sable, a chevron argent between three doves proper beaked and legged argent.

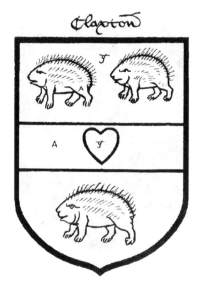

Claxton

f Richart Corbot

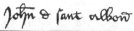

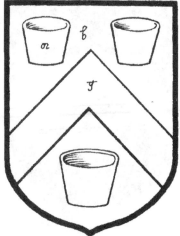

John de sant albon

3. HARPELEY. Barry (10) argent and or, over all three chevronels engrailed sable.

4.* CLAXTON. Gules, on a fess between three hedgehogs passant argent, an ace of hearts of the first.

5.* S. RICHARD CORBET. Or, a caw sable.

6. WYLLIAM HAWT. Or, a cross engrailed gules ; quarterly with, per pale azure and gules, a lyon rampant queue forchée argent, guttée de poix.

7. ASPALLE (SUFF., added). Azure, three chevronels or.

8. ROSSE. Argent, three bars gules, a bend engrailed sable.

9. TYLNEY (of Boston, Lincs., added). Argent a chevron between three gryphons heads erased gules.

Folio 29.

1. RAYNES. Chequy or and gules, a quarter ermine.

2.* JOHN DE SANT. ALBON. Azure, a chevron gules (? or) between three loving cups or.

3. SIMON FRANCES. Gules, a saltire between four crosses botonnée or.

4. BOSELEY. Argent, three torteaux, a label (3) azure.

5.* METFORD. Azure, a chevron argent between three moles (? proper *vel* argent). See page 174.

Metford

Golofjo

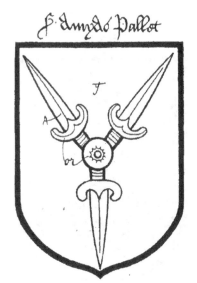

S. Amyas Pallot

6.* Le Sr. Golofre. Barry undée (6) argent and gules, on a bend sable three bezants.

7. Thorp. Azure, three crescents 2 and 1 argent " of Ashwellthorp in Norff. *quartered by* Tylney of Boston," added.

8. Hyllary (*quartered by* Tylney, added). Argent, crusily fitchée and three fleurs de lys 2 and 1 sable, a bordure of the last.

9. Banyarde. Sable, a fess between two chevrons or.

Folio 29b.

1. Garnyshe. Argent, a chevron azure, between three escallops sable.

2.* S. Amyas Pallet. Gules, three swords conjoined in fess, points to the dexter and sinister chief and base proper.

3. Gules, a lyon rampant gardant or, collared azure, over all a bendlet of the last.

4. Wylliam Morreys. Barry undée (8) ermines and argent.

5.* Thomas Chambers. Sable, three goats courant in pale within a bordure engrailed, all argent.

6. Burghhepe. Argent, a chevron azure.

7. John Terell. Argent, two chevrons azure and a bordure engrailed (of the last ?).

8. John Terell. Gules, on a chevron engrailed argent, three dolphin naiant embowed azure.

9.* JOHN MONPYSSON. Argent, a lyon rampant sable.

Folio 30.

1. MONCHENSY. Or, three false escocheons 2 and 1, barry (6) gules and vair.

2. ROBT. OF CLYDERHAWE (Cletheroe). Gules, a saltire or, a label (3) argent.

3. JOHN BAWD. Gules, three chevronels argent.

4. JOHN FRANCES. Ermine, three bars sable.

5. JOHN FEEW. Argent, on a chevron sable, an escallop of the first. The name perhaps Jues, or Ives.

6. ALEN CAWTHORPP. Argent, a fess between three escallops gules.

7. S. THOMAS BOROWGH, knyght, lord of Gaynsburgh. Azure, three fleurs de lys 2 and 1 ermine ; *quarterly with*, or, a lyon rampant azure, *quartering*, or, three pallets sable.

8. WYLLM. PEPE (POPE). Argent, two chevronels gules, on a quarter of the second an escallop or, all within a bordure gold.

9. PURCELL. Argent, two bars undée gules over all on a bend sable three boars heads couped of the first ; *quarterly with*, argent, three bends azure, on a quarter sable, a lyon passant of the first.

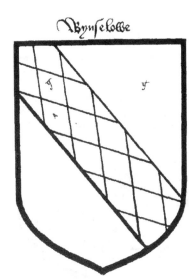

Folio 30b.

1. AMERLE LE H. (? lt). Barry (6) azure and argent guttées de sang, a bordure of the second: might be blasoned, argent guttées de sang, three bars humettée azure.

2. JOHN HUNTE. A cross patonce a bordure gules, besantée. Imperfect.

3.* WYLLY. Argent, three gryphons passant in pale sable, semée of trefoyles slipped vert. See page 176.

4.* WYNSELOWE OF CEZ HECHE. Gules, a bend lozengy argent and of the first.

5.* BAWDEWYNNE TUTESBERY. Per bend argent and sable, five fusils in bend or, between six lyoncelles counter-coloured of the field.

6. THOMAS PALMER. Or, two bars gules, on a bend of the second three trefoyles slipped sable (*sic*).

7.* THOMAS CHAMBYR. Argent, on a chief indented gules a lyon passant or.

8. WYLLM. BURNS. Quarterly ermine and gules.

9. RYCHARD ROOS. Sable, on a bend argent three sixefoyles or (*sic*).

Folio 31.

1.* JOHN DURANT. Argent, on a chevron azure between three bugle horns sable, leathered of the second, garnished or, a mullet gules (A note by le Neve ? if not Forester of Rutland see Wright).

2.* WALTER HAKE. Azure, three [hake hauriant 2 and 1 argent ; *quarterly with*, argent, three boars heads fessways erased or.

3.* WYLLSI. PAKYNHAM. Sable, crusily fitchée and a stork passant argent, beak and legs or.

4. THOMAS CLERVAUX (EBOR., added). Sable, on a saltire or a cinquefoyle pierced of the field.

5.* THOMAS DUNNE. Azure, a double headed eagle displayed argent, charged on the breast with an escocheon gules thereon a leopards face or ; all within a bordure of the last. See page 178.

6. HALSTHALE. Argent, three dragons heads 2 and 1 erased azure ; *quarterly with*, gules, three unicorns heads couped 2 and 1 or.

7. VENABLES (CHESHIRE, added). Azure, two bars argent.

8. JOHN DUNHED. Argent, a lyon rampant within a bordure engrailed all gules.

9. GEFERY CURTES. Per fess azure and gules, a fess dancettée argent, between three dueal crowns 2 and 1 or.

Folio 31b.

1. WETNALE (CHESHIRE, added). Vert, a cross engrailed ermine.

2. BREWYS. Argent, a bend gules, a bordure counter-compony or and azure ; *quarterly with*, azure, crusily and a lyon rampant or.

Thomas Dune

Barker

Akastir

3. ¶ KOKYSSEYE (COKESAY). Argent, on a bend azure three cinquefoyles or, pierced gules.

4. ALEN. Sable, three lozenges 2 and 1 or.

5. CLYFFORD. Chequy or and azure, a fess gules, a bordure of the first.

6.* BARKER. Gules, a cross patonce or, over all a chevron argent, charged with five annulets sable.

7.* AKASTIR. Argent, on a chevron azure three acorns erect slipped or.

8.* ARMES OF CLAREL. Gules, six martlets 3. 2. 1. argent.

9.* HERTOPT (? Hartup, added). Sable, three fish heads erect and erased 2 and 1 argent. ⁙

Folio 32.

1.* FYNEUX (FYNEWYS.) Vert, a chevron between three crowned eagles displayed or.

2.* MYNET. Azure, three escallops 2 and 1 or.

3.* DODDYNGSELL (D'ODDINGSELL). Argent, four fusils conjoined in pale gules, a bordure sable bezantée. See page 180.

4. LE CONESSTABLE DE HULDERNESSE (EBOR., added). Barry (6) or and azure.

5. MUSGRAVE LE S. R. (WESTMORLAND. added). Azure, six annulets 3. 2. 1. or.

Armes of Clarel

heytopt

Fynowye

Mynot

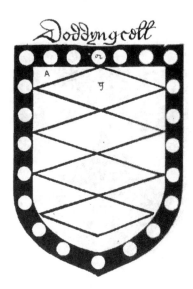

6. SABYLTON, LE S. Argent, three swords conjoined at the hilt points to the dexter and sinister chief and base gules. STAPLETON.

7.* PEWPE. Gules a leg in armour erect argent, garnished or. See No. 2, f.82b.

8. PEWPE. Azure, two bars and in chief three roses all argent.

9.* PEWPE. Argent, three horses heads couped sable, gorged with a collar wreathy or and sable.

Folio 32b.

1. Per cross or and gules, in the first and fourth a fleur de lys sable, a bordure of the third besantée.

2.* CLERKE, JUSTYS. Argent, a chevron vert between three lilies (? columbines) azure, slipped of the second; *impaled with*, azure, billettée and a cross argent. Probably for STANGRAVE.

3.* Name erased. Sable, a chevron engrailed or between three butterflies argent. See another, No. 4, f.57b.

4.* BOULONQUE (FRANCE, added). Or, a (———) gules. See Add. MS. 35,346, f.19, borne by Baudoyer le connestable, a chevalier of the round table.

5.* SANT POL (FRANCE, added). Gules, three palets vair, on a chief or, a label (5) of the first.

Lembourgo

Artoys

6. BOURBON, FRANCE. Azure, florettée or, and a baston gules.

7. FLANDRES (COUNTY, added). Or, a lyon rampant sable.

8. HAYNAU(L)I (COUNTY, added). Per cross or, four lyons rampant, the first and fourth gules, the second and third sable.

9. ATHANAS (? ATHENS.) Gules, a cross quarter pierced ermine.

Folio 33.

1. LUXEMBOURGH (FRANCE, added). Burulée (12) argent and azure, over all a lyon rampant gules.

2.* LEMBOURE. Argent, a lyon rampant queue forchée gules, crowned or.

3. FRESNES. Argent, a lyon rampant sable, armed gules.

4. BRETAYGNE (Earl, Duke, FRANCE, added). Ermine.

5.* ARTOYS, County or city. Azure, florettée or, a label (3) gules on each file two castles of the second.

6. ENGHIEN. Gyronny (10) argent and sable, on each of the second, three crosses crosslet or.

7. ANIO (ANJOU, FRANCE, added). Azure, florettée or, a bordure gules.

8. ROCHELI. Cut out.

9. BRIENNE. Azure, billettée and a lyon rampant or.

Folio 33b.

1. SAINT SIEURIN (Severin). Argent, a fess gules. Austria, the reverse, see No. 6, f.34.

2. ARDERE (FRANCE, added). Gules, a mullet of sixteen points argent.

3. LUMESIN (FRANCE, added). Azure, three lyons rampant 2 and 1 or.

4. CASTYLL. Argent, a lyon rampant purpure (LEON); quarterly with, CASTILE, gules, a castle triple turretted or.

5. NAVARE. Gules, the Navarrese net or; quarterly with, BOURBON, azure, florettée or, over all a baston gobony argent and gules. See also No. 6, f.z.

6. TARENNE (TORANTO, ITALY, added). ARDERE as No. 2; quarterly with, or, a bugle, leathered azure, over all on a lozenge, bendy (6) in base argent and gules, a fess or, on a chief argent a cinquefoyle pierced gules. But see URSINO, No. 8, f.34.

7. GENEVE (COUNTY, added). Or, a cross quarter pierced azure.

8. LE DUC WYET, S. de BUSLAU (BRESLAU). Cut out.

9. LE DUC DE SABRON. Gules, a lyon rampant argent. SABRAN.

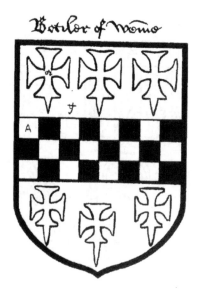

Folio 34.

1. LESUAUX. As ARDERE, No. 2, f.33*b* ; *Quarterly with*, OLD FRANCE, azure, florettée or,

2. FOYS, COUNT, added—(FOIX). Or, three palets gules ; *quarterly with*, or, two bulls couchant in pale gules.

3. MESESIN. Or, a lyon rampant gules, semée of mullets of the second, a bordure of the first (*sic*) powdered also with mullets alternately, or and azure, all of eight points ——estoyles may be intended. MESSINA.

4. BAVIARE (DUC her. added). Barry bendy (6) argent and azure.

5. HONGUERIE (KINGDOM OF HUNGARY, added). Burulée (12) argent and gules. See No. 2, f.1*b*.

6. OSTRREE (AUSTRIA. added). Gules, a fess argent.

7. SAVOYE (DUC, added). Gules a cross argent.

8. URSINO (ITALY, added). Argent, in base three bendlets gules, in the chief per fess of the first and or, a cinquefoyle of the second pierced gold ; see lozenge in No. 6, f.33*b*. An alternate blazon, or on a chief argent a cinquefoyle pierced gules, *dimidiated in base with*, argent, three bendlets gules.

9. LANGLE. Quarterly per fess indented or and azure.

Folio 34*b*.

1. BOYDON. Gules, fretty or *quarterly with*, ermine.

2.* WEMME (BOTILER of WEMME, added). Gules, a fess chequy argent and sable between six crosses formée fitchée at the feet or.

3. Sr. TH. COLVVLL of NORTHPOYS. Or, on a fess gules three lyoncelles rampant argent.

4. TAVRNEER, added (TAVERNER). Argent, on a cross engrailed gules five crescents or. See also No. 7, f.43.

5. BRAYBROKE. Or, fretty sable, on a chief of the second three bezants, SAINT AMAND ; *quarterly with*, BRAYBROKE, argent, seven mascles conjoined 3. 3. 1. gules.

6. WAT HALYSNAKYS. Argent, a chevron sable, between three trefoyles slipped vert ; *quarterly with*, argent, two lyons passant in pale sable. Halvax, No. 2, f.40*b*.

7.* YEVELTONE. Argent, two bars undée sable, a crescent for difference.

8. YEVELTONE. Argent, two bars undée sable, a crescent for difference.

9. MORE. Barry (6) argent and azure ; *quarterly with*, azure fretty argent.

Folio 35.

1. MASTYR HALYS. Gules, two bars wavy argent between seven torteaux 3. 3. 1. on a quarter azure, a stag's head couped at the neck or.

2.* WYMOUR. Argent, a chevron between three (hinds ?) heads erased all gules.

3. DICCON (DICTON). Sable, a pile argent, over all a chevronel gules.

4.* THOMAS MOUNDZ. Argent, a wing erect sable, over all a baston or.

5. JOHN ESMON. Ermine, a saltire engrailed sable. (Estmond).

6.* JOHN ALLINGHAM. Per chevron gules and sable, three eagles heads erased argent, beaked or.

7.* JOHN BOLNROWN. Sable, on a chief argent a cross flory of the first.

8.* MAYSTON. Argent, a chevron or (? gules) between three hedgehogs passant sable. MAYNSTON.

9. WHATTON. Ermine, on a fess gules three escallops sable (sic).

Folio 35b.

1. CLAYPOLL. Ermine, a chief bendy (4) or and azure, an annulet for difference sable.

2. DEVEROSE. Argent, a fess gules in chief three torteaux.

3. LE FYZ JOHN. Quarterly or and gules, a
bordure vair.

4. SENT JOHN. Argent on a chief indented
gules, two mullets or.

5.* THOMAS WYSE. Argent, three wise men's
heads sable, wreathed or.

6. GRAUMFORD (of SUSSEX, added). Gules,
a lyon rampant argent, a bordure engrailed
sable. See also page 10.

7. EVERARD. Azure, on a bend argent three
crosses crosslet fitchée gules, a crescent of the
last.

8. TANFELD OF GAYTON (NORTHANTS.,
added). Argent, two chevronels between three
martlets 2 and 1 all sable, an annulet of the
first. See No. 7, f.41.

9. WHYNTON. Gules, a fess counter-compony or and azure; *quarterly with*, argent, a
chevron azure between three lyons heads erased
or.

Folio 36.

1. FUA SINS AVER (Hue sans Aver). Azure,
crusily and three crescents 2 and 1 or.

2. S. HOLYE (OLIVER) BURDET. Azure, two
bars or. See No. 6, f.102b.

3. WILLIAM NORWICH. Ermine, a fess engrailed azure: "q're if not the judge, see the
baronets' pedigree" added by Le Neve.

folio 36ᵇ no 2

4. S. JOHN DEFNECHIS (Devenish). Vert, on a saltire engrailed argent between four crosses crosslet fitchée of the second, a fleur de lys or.

5.* THORLE (? Charles) SQUYER. Argent, on a bend flory counterflory sable, three mullets (6) pierced of the field.

6.* FARWEYE. Sable, a chevron between three escallops argent.

7. BORTON. Ermine, a fess counter-compony or and azure. The coat of ARDEN.

8. TRYSTLOW. Sable, three escallops 2 and 1 argent.

9. HENRY [ELME]DEN. Argent, on a bend sable three crescents of the field.

Folio 36b.

1. Sable, a fess between three escallops a bordure engrailed, all argent.

2.* Sable, three tortoise enbelif or, a bordure argent entoyre of martlets of the first.

3. Sable, six fleurs de lys 3. 2. 1. or, a bordure engrailed argent.

4. Per fess azure and or, a lyon rampant counter-coloured.

5. THROGMORTON. Gules, on a chevron argent three bars gemelles sable.

6. Vert, a chevron between three martlets argent.

7.* JOHN FFE JOHN (Fitz John). Azure, on
a bend sable between three heads couped at the
bust each encircled at the neck by a serpent all
argent, in chief, and in base as many gryphons
heads erased or, an annulet of the last.

8. ISELEY (KENT, added). Ermine, a bend
gules.

9. Sable, a cross between four martlets argent.

Folio 37.

1. Argent, fretty gules, on a chief of the
second, a crescent of the first.

2. Gules, on a fess crenellée (on the top)
argent, three trefoyles slipped vert.

3. Gules, a fess vaire argent and sable
between three boars heads 2 and 1 barways of
the third.

4. ENDERBY. Argent, six chevronels conjoined 2, 2, 2, sable, in the centre chief point
three ermine spots 2 and 1. This trick is probably intended for, argent three bars danceltée
sable, in chief a pale ermine.

5. Azure, two bars or, a demy lyon rampant
issuant from the first gules (sic).

6.* CHARLTON, WALES. Argent, a chevron
engrailed sable, between three gryphons heads
erased of the second.

7.* COSON. Azure, three roses 2 and 1 or,
leaved vert.

8. Argent, a fess between four martlets 3 and 1 gules.

9. Azure, a bendlet gobony sable and gules, between six escallops argent.

Folio 37b.

1.* GENEVVYL. Azure, three barnacles open or, on a chief ermine a demy lyon rampant issuant gules. See No. 7, f.66.

2. Argent, a chevron between three annulets azure.

3.* Ermine, a fess or between three tortoise embelif sable. [REPLEY.]

4. HILTON. Argent, two bars azure ; *quarterly with*, argent, three chaplets 2 and 1 gules ; for LASCELLS, q're GREYSTOKE.

5. Lozengy sable and argent, a label (3) ermine.

6.* FITZJAMYS. Azure, a dolphin embowed argent.

7. Ros. Or, three water bougets 2 and 1 sable.

8. JOHN RYPON, Serjeaunt at Armys, of Barks. Chequy or and azure, on a fess argent three birds sable ; *quarterly with*, sable, on a saltire between four fleurs de lys or, five roses gules ; *impaling*, argent, on a chevron between three crosses crosslet fitchée sable, as many leopards faces or.

Ardern

John Stanley of Wyver

9.* ARDERNE. Gules, three crosses crosslet fitchée or, a chief of the second, all within a bordure ermine.

Folio 38.

1. Azure, a chevron between three roses argent.

2. NYCOLAS CORNWELL. Azure, on a bend sable (*sic*), three cinquefoyles pierced argent.

3. Sable, a lyon rampant argent, over all a bendlet gobonny or and gules.

4. Ermine, on a fess azure, three crosses moline or, a label (3) gules.

5. Argent, a fess sable between three crescents or (? gules) a bordure engrailed of the second.

6.* JOHN STANLEY OF WYVER. Sable, a fess et demi argent, on the sinister a garb or, banded gules. See also page 272.

7.* S. ROBERTE WARPECUPE (WARCUP, WEST-MORLAND, added). Sable, three covered cups 2 and 1 argent.

8. Azure, a lyon rampant argent, billettée gules.

9. Argent, on a chevron between three stags lodged gules, a bugle stringed vert.

S Roberte Warpecupe

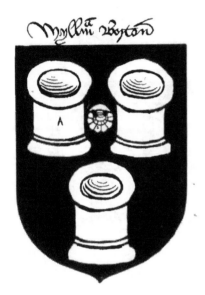

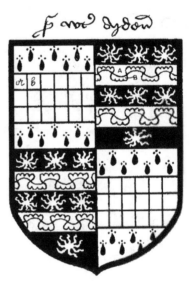

Folio 38b.

1. RYCHARD WORSOP. Gules, a dexter hand apaumée argent, between three cinquefoyles 2 and 1 pierced of the last.

2. RYCHARD (MARTEN). Gules, a chevron ermine of three spots, in base a rose or.

3. WATR. DAUNDESEYE. Per pale or and argent, two bars undée gules.

4.* WYLLM. BORTON. Sable, three drinking troughs 2 and 1 argent, an escallop of the last for difference.

5. TOCHET. Ermine, a chevron gules.

6. TOTEHYLL. Azure, two bars argent, in the cantel a leopards face of the last.

7. EDMOND AP MERE(DI)TH. Per pale gules and sable, two gryphons segreant respecting each other argent. See also page 72.

8. SHYRLEY. Gules, on a bend argent three eagles talons sable.

9.* S. Wt. ARDEN. Ermine, a fess chequy or and azure; *quarterly with*, sable, two viures barways argent, all between seven estoyles 3, 3, 1 or.

Folio 39.

1. TRESAWELL. Argent, a boars head in fess sable, between three mullets 2 and 1 gules.

2.* ASLAK, ROBT. (NORFOLK, added). Gules, a chevron ermine, between three Catherine wheels sable (sic).

3. JOHN WELL. Per pale gules and sable, a bend argent.

4.* THOMAS STYKLEVEYE. Argent, three asses passant 2 and 1 sable. (? STEWKLEY.)

5.* JOHN STRATON. Argent, a — sable, as in the illustration.

6. CAWESTON. Azure, three crescents or; quarterly with, sable, a cross engrailed ermine; perhaps the cross argent and guttée de poix.

7. PERNELL (Peynell). Chequy argent and gules, on a chief of the first three mullets sable.

8. JOHN BLESBY. Argent, three mullets (6) pierced or, a crescent for difference sable.

9. RAHER MAUNDHAM. Argent, on a quarter sable, a trefoyle or; a mullet of the last for difference. (Coat similar to that of Agmondi-sham.)

Folio 39b.

1.* NYCH. BURSER. Vert, three boars heads erect and erased 2 and 1 or, a riband sable.

2. ROBERT LANGTON. Quarterly azure and or, a baston gules.

3. RYCHARD HARYSON. Argent, a chevron between three escallops, a bordure engrailed, all sable.

4. CANTHYN. Gules, a chevron ermine between three pheons argent.

5. HENYNG LAWKYN. Sable, three mullets argent, on a chief of the second, a demy lyon rampant issuant gules.

6. PREWYS. Per saltire azure and gules, a cross potent or.

7.* ROBERT EVERTON. Argent, a chevron sable, between three pears pendant or (? gules) a crescent of the last for difference.

8. S. WAT. GOLDYNGHAM. Barry undée (9) gules and ermine, perhaps intended for gules, three bars undée ermine.

9.* CLEMENT FYCHECOKE. Gules, a chevron ermine, between three portcullises or.

Folio 40.

1. JOHN TALBOT. Argent, a lyon rampant gules.

2. GILBERT. Argent, a fess sable, in the cantel a round buckle tongue pendant gules.

3. THOMAS NEWDYKE. Paly (4) argent and sable, on a bend gules five besants.

4.* HARRY KYRKTON. Argent, three martlets 2 and 1 or (*sic*).

5. ROB. SYMEON. Gules, a fess or, between three lyons passant 2 and 1 argent.

6.* JOHN SEFFELLE. ("Qy. Seyvile," now Savile). Argent, on a bend sable, three owls of the field, a label (3) gules.

7. JOHN WYBERY. Sable, crusily bottonnée fitchée or, and two lyons passant in pale argent ; *impaling*, argent, a chevron sable between three round buckles, tongues to the dexter, or. See page 152.

8. MARTYN. Ermine, a cross gules.

9. WARBURTON (WAYBORTON). Lozengy or and sable.

Folio 40b.

1. JOHN OKE. Argent, on a cross engrailed gules five water bougets sable (*sic*).

2.* WYLL HALYAX. Argent, a chevron sable between three trefoyles slipped 2 and 1 vert. See also No. 6, f.34b.

3. MAST. ROBT. HUNTE. Vert, on a chevron or, three bugles unstrung gules ; the tinctures of the chevron and bugles reversed in trick.

4.* WYLL. PYTY. Sable, a chevron between three shovellers 2 and 1 argent.

5.* WYLL. CONSTABYLL. Sable, crusily and a cinquefoyle pierced or. See page 194.

6. KOKYSSEY (Cokesay). Argent, on a plain bend azure, cotised dancettée gules, three cinquefoyles or, pierced of the third.

vyll conftabyll

Robert Aelworth

Jothn Barondye

7.* ROBERT ACWORTH. Argent, a gryphon segreant sable, beaked or.

8. HORME OF KENT (HORNE). Gules, three bugle horns leathered sable (sic); *quarterly with*, gules, crusily fitchée a chevron between three garbs, all argent.

9. DEDERYK FOYS (Leys). Azure, six plates 3. 2. 1, on a chief argent a demy lyon rampant issuant gules.

Folio 41.

1. MORESBY. Sable, on a cross argent, an annulet of the first, in the cantel a cinquefoyle pierced of the second.

2. BYNLYTON. Argent, a chevron or (sic) between three mullets sable (? Kinnerton).

3. WYLL FEYCE. Argent, four barrulets azure.

4. MAYNWARON (CHESHIRE, added). Argent, two bars gules.

5. *JOHN BARONDYE. Azure, a chevron between three (does ?) heads couped argent.

6. S. PHILIP THORNBURY. Azure, crusily or and three crescents 2 and 1 argent.

7. ROBT. TANFELD OF GAYTON. Argent, two chevrons between three martlets 2 and 1 sable; *quarterly with*, argent, a chevron sable between three lyons heads erased gules. See also No. 8, f.35b.

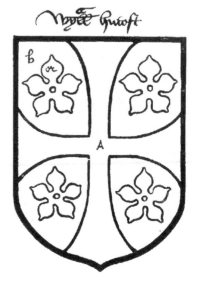

8. BRERETON, (CHESHIRE added). Argent, two bars sable.

9. JOHN POOLE. Azure, a fess or, in chief three leopards faces of the last.

Folio 41b.

1. WALSCHE. Argent, a fess between six martlets 3 and 3 all sable.

2.* STA(N)SUM. Argent, a unicorn passant gules, horned or.

3.* BERTRAM MOUNBOCHIER. Argent, three possenets 2 and 1 gules, a bordure sable besantée.

4. SYR DE GREY, Northumberland. Gules, a lyon rampant argent, a bordure engrailed of the last.

5. RAYNOLD CURTES. Argent, a chevron sable between three bulls heads cabossed gules ; *quarterly with*, gules, a chevron vair, a chief or.

6. JOHN HAMPTON. Argent, on a chevron gules, between three cinquefoyles pierced azure, as many besants.

7.* WYLL HUTOFT. Azure, a cross formée throughout between four cinquefoyles pierced or.

8.* FYNDERNE (DERB., added). Argent, a chevron fracted sable, between three crosses botonnée fitchée of the last. See pages 72 and 196.

9. PENSTHON. Per bend sable and argent, three roundles counter-coloured; "?if not born by Pynchion of Writtle and Honychurche in Essex." P. Le Neve.

Folio 42.

1.* MORLEY. Sable, a leopards face or jessant de lys argent.

2.* WYTHE (NORFOLK, added). Azure, three gryphons passant or.

3.* BRESSYNGHAM. Sable, two wings addorsed argent.

4.* THOMAS ARBLASTER (of WYCHINGHAM, NORFOLK, added). Ermine, an arquebus gules.

5. THOMAS PRESTON. Sable, a cross ermine between four leopards faces or.

6. JOHN LONYE. Per chevron engrailed sable and ermine. See LOVENEY, page 74.

7. BYTTEYNNE. Cut out.

8. JOHN CORKE. Gules, three estoyles chevronwise argent between as many cinquefoyles pierced 2 and 1 or.

9.* S. WYLLYAM TEMPEST. Argent, a bend engrailed sable, between six martlets vel storm finches of the last.

Folio 42b.

1. NYCHOLAS HERVY. Barry undée (4) argent and sable, on a chief azure three crosses formée fitchée or.

Haſylfote

Willm Gaſcoyne

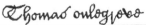

Thomas oulegroo

2. SKYLLYNG. Argent, a chevron gules, on a chief sable three besants.

3.* WYLLYAM GASCOYNE (of WELLES added). Azure, a fess undée ermine between three crosses formée fitchée 2 and 1 or. See page 197 and below.

4. MORTEMER OF NORTHAMPTONSHIRE (in a later hand). Ermine, a chevron and a chief sable ; a crescent argent for difference ; quarterly with, ermine, on a fess azure two crosses moline or. See No. 6, f.20.

5.* HASYLFOTE. Argent, three trevets 2 and 1, sable.

6.* WILLIAM GASCOYNE OF WELLS (in another hand). Argent, a chevron azure between three bulls heads cabossed gules. See No. 3.

7. Argent, a fess between three mascles gules.

8.* THOMAS OULEGREVE. Azure, a fess engrailed argent, between three owls of the last.

9. HERT——— Cut out.

Folio 43.

1. RAUFF SEYNT LEGERE (Kent. added). Azure, fretty argent, a chief gules (*sic*).

2. HERRY COLK (COCK). Vaire or and azure, a bend ermine ; quarterly with, or (gules) on a bend argent, cotised sable, three fusils of the first, *i.e.*, gules.

3.* (1) DYLA SUWYLL ; (2) MORYS AP DAVID
AP JEVAN ; (3) MORES AS AP DAVID. Sable,
three spear heads erect 2 and 1 argent, staves
eradicated or, between as many crescents 1 and
2 of the last.

4.* WACYS OF WAYNFLETE. Azure, a chevron between three garbs or.

5. T. LYTTYLBURY alias dict. HORNE (LINC.,
added). Quarterly, (1); gules, three lyons
passant argent. (2); argent, a chevron gules
between three nails sable, SEYNTCLOWE. See
No. 9 below. (3); gules, a gryphon segreant or,
BATTELL. (4); argent, billettée and a chevron
sable. LELHOME.

6. MORE DE LA MORE. Argent, a fess
dancettée paly (6) sable and gules, between
three mullets pierced of the second ; quarterly
with, CHALERE, argent, a fess between three
annulets gules.

7. TAVERNER. Quarterly 1 and 4 ; argent,
on a cross engrailed gules, five crescents or. 2
and 3 ; argent, three chevronels gules an annulet or, for difference ; quarterly with, argent, on a
chevron between three fleurs de lys sable, a
like fleur de lys for difference of the first.

8. COOKE OF ESSEX. Or, a chevron counter-
compony azure and gules, between three cinquefoyles pierced of the second.

9.* T. LYTILBURY. Impaling SAINT LOWE as
in No. 5. See also page 239.

Trotte

Hauff Arundell

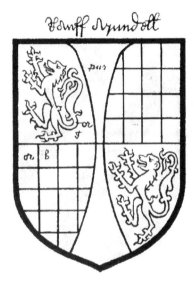

yakney

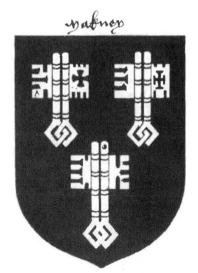

1. W. WYSETOWE. Sable, three rams 2 and 1 argent; *quarterly with*, lozengy argent and sable.

2. HORNE (KENT, added). Argent, on a chevron gules, between three bugle horns stringed sable, as many estoyles or.

3.* SCOTTE (KENT, added). Argent, three Catherine wheels 2 and 1 sable, a bordure engrailed gules.

4. MANSTON (MAR. struck out). Gules, a fess ermine between three mullets or.

5. VALANS. Paly wavy (4) or and gules.

6.* RAUFF ARUNDELL, qy if not a bastard of FITZALAN. FITZALAN *quartering* WARREN (W. Colyngrygge, struck out). Murrey, two flaunches, the dexter per fess ARUNDEL and WARREN, the sinister per fess WARREN and ARUNDEL, as No. 7, f.4. For murrey or purpure see also No. 8, f.14*b*.

7. JOHN GRYGGE. Argent three fleurs de lys and a bordure engrailed azure.

8.* MAKNEY. Sable, six keys 2. 2. 2 addorsed 2 and 1 argent.

9. ELKESFELD. Barry undée (6) argent and sable.

1.* ESTBURY. Barry wavy (5) argent and sable.

2. SHOTESBROKE (BERKS., added). Ermine, a chief per pale dancettée or and gules. See No. 3, f.16b. and No. 4, f.86b.

3. Vaire argent and sable; impaling, azure, florettée and a lyon rampant argent.

4.* THOMAS DEURYSSE. Argent, a chevron between three bulls heads cabossed gules; impaling, argent, a bend cotised sable a bordure engrailed of the last. (IPRES or CURTIS.)

5.* GEORGE BROWNE. Sable, three lyoncelles rampant in bend argent, between two bendlets engrailed of the last.

6. JOHN BOKENHAM. Vert, a cross patonce counter-compony argent and gules.

7. KNYVET OF BOKENHAM, Norfolk. Argent, a bend within a bordure engrailed all sable; quarterly with, CLYFFTON, chequy or and gules, a bend ermine.

8. KNYVET OF WELDON, Northants. Argent, a bend within a bordure engrailed all sable; quarterly with, BASSETT, or, three palets gules a bordure azure bezantée.

9. KNYVET OF WELDON. Argent, a bend within a bordure engrailed all sable; quarterly with, FITZ OTES of MENDLESHAM, SUFFOLK, bendy (6) or and azure, a quarter ermine.

Folio 44b.

1.* DAWNAY, in Com. EBOR. Argent, on a
bend cotised sable three annulets of the first ;
quarterly with, gules, a Sowdan's head wreathed
argent, etc.

2. WESTON. Ermine, on a chief azure five
besants barways.

3. DRYWARD. Ermine, on a chevron sable
three crescents or.

4.* GEFFERAY WARTON. Argent, on a chief
gules a kingfisher of the first.

5. PERS BOTTLER. Sable, three covered cups
2 and 1 argent, a bordure or ; *quarterly with,*
sable a chevron engrailed or, between three
butterflies 2 and 1 argent.

6. THOMAS BOWHYTT (BOOTH). Argent three
boars heads 2 and 1 erect and erased sable, a
Catherine wheel of the last.

7.* RICHARD BERD. Argent, on a bend sable
three cross tau's of the first.

8. RANDAL OF BRERETON (CHESHIRE, added).
Argent, two bars sable, a crescent of the last for
difference ; *quarterly with,* argent, a fess between
three crescents gules.

9. DE LA MARE OF ALDERMARSTON (BERKS.,
added). Gules, two lyons passant in pale
argent ; *quarterly with,* ACHARD, or, a bend
fusily sable.

No folios 45 and 45b.

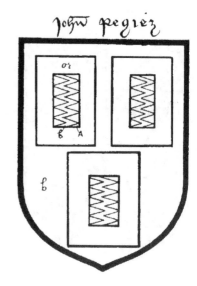

Folio 46.

1. FFYZ-RAUFF. Argent, on a cross gules five escallops or.

2. Argent, a fess between six martlets 3 and 3 gules.

3. Per saltire argent and azure.

4. Azure, three lyons passant in pale or.

5. BEAUCHAMP OF HATCH. Gules, a fess between six martlets 3 and 3 or.

6.* KENERDEWE OF CORNEWALL. Sable, three lamp holders pendant argent.

7. MASTER BARGANE (BERGAVENNY). Quarterly 1 WARREN, 2 NEVILLE, 3 CLARE quartering AUDLEY (4) BEAUCHAMP; rudely tricked. No colours indicated.

8. SR. JOHN SAY. Per pale azure and gules, three chevrons argent voided of the field.

9. SULYARD. Argent, a chevron gules between three pheons reversed 2 and 1 sable.

Folio 46b.

1. BACON, added (WATON originally in MS.). Gules, on a chief argent two mullets pierced sable.

2. GLAUMVYLE. Gules, a chevron azure (sic) between three lyons rampant 2 and 1 argent.

3. BARYNGTON. Argent, three chevronels gules.

4. HUNGATE (EBOR., added). Gules, a chevron engrailed argent between three hounds (talbots) erect of the second.

5. ANDREWS. Argent, on a bend sable three mullets of the first.

6. THOMAS TALBOT DE MOLAHIDE. A lyon rampant, a bordure gobony azure and or.

7. S. ROGER TOKETT. Arms not drawn.

8. JOHN EUSTACE. Arms not drawn.

9.* JOHN PEGIEZ. Azure, three billets or, voided argent (sic), each charged with a pale indented of the first. Combs are perhaps meant.

Folio 47.

1. FELDE. A lyon rampant, on his shoulder a mullet (no tinctures), a bordure azure.

2. MASTER ANNE. Argent, on a bend sable three martlets of the first; quarterly with, argent, three ermine spots between two chevronels azure, all enclosed by three crosses patée quadrat quarter pierced gules (this doubtful); impaling, gules, three lyons passant in pale argent.

3. Argent, three fleurs de lys 2 and 1 gules, a label (3) azure; impaling, sable, a chevron ermine between three escallops argent.

4. MELESFORD. Gules, a fess and in chief three martlets; quarterly with, a lyon rampant imperfectly indicated, and untinctured.

5. FROWYK (LONDON, added). Azure, a chevron between three leopards faces or.

6. JOHN ESTON. Azure, a chevron between three mullets or.

7. MASTER DE LA HYDDE. Argent, three bars gules, a bend azure.

8.* DUNSTABYLL. Sable, a chevron ermine between three dun-staples argent.

9. MASTER MEDYLTON. A cross formée; quartering and impalement imperfect, and untinctured.

Folio 47b.

1. ROBERT HYDYNGHAM (HEADINGHAM). Ermine, a bend engrailed argent (sic) guttée de sang, on a chief azure a hart's head couped or, attires argent.

2.* CHEYNEW. Argent, on a chevron gules two chevronels couched dexter and sinister or.

3. COLBROND. Gules, a cross argent, between four swords erect proper.

4. CLYDAROW (LANC., added). Argent, on a chevron between three covered cups sable, a mullet or.

5. CHEYNEW. Gules, on a chevron argent, a mullet or (sic) on a chief azure three leopards faces of the third.

6.* WODE. Argent, a wolf salient sable, collared or, langued gules.

7. TURBOCK (LANC., added). Argent, an eagle's talon crased gules, on a chief dancettée azure three plates. TORBOCK.

8. POWER. Gules, on a chief argent, three mullets sable.

9.* WHYTEWELL. Gules, a chevron between three buckets 2 and 1 or.

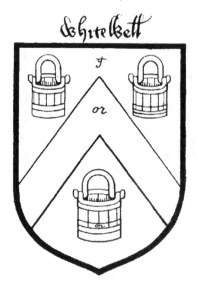

Folio 48.

1.* SNAYTH. Argent, a chevron sable, between three rooks heads erased proper, beaked gules.

2.* S. JOHN DETTLYNG (KENT, added). Azure, six lyoncelles rampant 3. 3 argent.

3. CHEYNE (KENT, added). Azure, six lyoncelles rampant 3 and 3 argent, in the dexter chief point a billet ermine (five spots).

4. WATTON. Argent, a lyon rampant gules, over all on a bend sable, three crosses botonnée fitchée of the first.

5. TOWNE. Argent, on a chevron sable, three crosses crosslet ermine.

6. ARDERNE, no colours. Guttée (? ermine) a fess chequy between three crescents.

7. SEYLBY. Ermine, on a fess gules three fleurs de lys or.

8.* CROSHOLME. Argent, a cross botonnée gules. See page 206.

9. GASCOYN. Argent, on a pale gules, a lucies head erect or.

Folio 48b.

1. Z. YERLONDE (IRELAND, LANC., added). gules, six fleurs de lys 3. 2. 1 argent.

2. R. LEE. Azure, on a fess cotised or three leopards faces gules.

3. WESTBROK. Gules, a leopards face jessant de lys or ; *quarterly with*, sable, a fess dancettée or between three fish naiant argent ; *impaling*, argent, a chevron gules between three mullets pierced sable.

4. WYNGEFELD (SUFFOLK, added). Argent, on a bend gules cotised sable, three pairs of wings conjoined of the first.

5. NIGHTINGALE OF CAMBRIDGESHIRE from Essex, all added. Per pale ermine and gules, a rose counter-coloured, seeded or.

6. AMCOTTS. Argent, a castle triple turretted between three covered cups azure ; *impaling*, HAWBOROUGH, gules, guttée d'eau and a castle triple turretted or.

7. ROKELYS. Gules, two barrulets sable (*sic*) between three annulets 2 and 1 argent.

8.* CROWNER (KENT, added). Argent, a chevron engrailed sable between three crows proper.

9. CANTILOW. Ermine, on a chevron gules, three leopards faces jessant de lys or.

Folio 49.

1. RO. LYLLYNG. Gules, three salmon naiant proper, a bordure engrailed argent.

2. B. MALORY. Argent, a demy lyon rampant couped gules.

3. GE. BASSYNGBORNE. Gules, three piles wavy argent.

4. THOMAS GARNETT. Azure, three gryphons heads erased or, a martlet for difference argent; *quarterly with*, azure, a lyon rampant argent. crowned or ; *impaling*, gules, crusily and three boars heads couped barwise 2 and 1 argent ; *quarterly with*, or, a saltire engrailed sable.

5. S. ROBERD CHAMBERLEYNE. Argent, two chevronels interlaced sable, on a chief of the second three plates.

6. RYCHARD GARNET. In pencil only.

7. STRATTON. Argent, on a cross sable five besants.

8. EDEWARD BANBRYG. Azure, two battle-axes erect or, a bordure engrailed of the second ; *quarterly with*, gules, a boar saliant or, on a chief of the second two mullets of the first. The boar has a squirrels tail and an apple in his mouth !

9.* THE PEWTTARARS ARMS. Gules, on a chevron sable (sic, for silver) between three lily pots argent. four straks of tynne (limbecks) proper, in the poynt of the chevron two angels in clouds holding up our lady of gold, crowned under the hands of her blessed fader in a cloud ; " vj angels " in the confirmation of 13 August 1451 29 Hen. VI, by Clarenceux, King of Arms of the South Marches of England. This record was unknown to the editor of the *History of the Pewterers Company*, 1903.

Folio 49b.

1. BYFLETE. Azure, two swords saltireways, points to the base proper, between four fleurs de lys or. See also No. 2, f.24 and No. 4, f.102b.

2. WYNGEHAM. Gules, a chevron between three hawks lures or ; these seem to have been originally intended for pairs of wings. the lines argent having been added.

3. BASYNG. Argent, a chevron azure, on a chief of the second two mullets pierced of the first.

4.* WODE. Gules, a fess argent between three woodmen of the second, each holding over his sinister shoulder a club ragulée or ; *quarterly with*, BENELEYGH, argent, a pelican in its piety sable.

5. OSBERN-CLARELL. Quarterly ; imperfect.

6. Per fess gules and sable.

7.* Argent, a chevron sable between three pine cones slipped or (sic).

8. DODDE. Ermine. a chief counter compony azure and or.

9. S. W. CRAVENE (of SUFFOLK, added). Argent, a fess quarterly or and gules between four crosses crosslet 3 and 1 of the third.

Folio 50.

1. SER MORYS WYTHE. Sable, a bordure argent.

2. DRAYTON. Argent, a bend sable ; *impaling*, WYNNE, per bend sable and argent.

John Sweny

John ffletham

John Peny

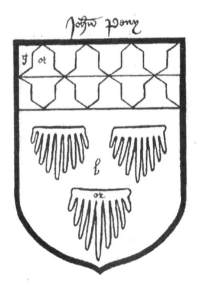

3. MOMFORD. Quarterly (1) ; a lyon rampant. (2) ; argent, a chief azure. (3) : or, three bendlets azure. (4) ; sable, a pale argent.

4. S. JOHN BARRE. Gules, three bars gobonated sable and argent.

5. HEW CROSSE. Per pale sable and argent, on the sinister a chief gules, *vel.* sable ; *impaled with* argent, a chief gules.

6. HENRY BEUFLOWYR. Gules, on a chief sable three crosses crosslet or. (? BOUTFLOWER.)

7. The arms cut out.

8.* JOHN SWENY (Thaytys, ? Thwayts). Argent, a chevron engrailed between three swine passant sable, crined tusked and unguled or.

9. JOHN CHECHYS (CHICHE). Azure, three lyons rampant 2 and 1 argent.

Folio 50b.

1. JOHN MARTYN cu. kann (altered to cit. kann). Argent, on a chevron gules three talbots passant of the first ; *quarterly with.* RAYNES or CHEYNEY ; azure, six lyoncelles rampant 3 and 3 or, on a canton of the second (sylver, added in a note), a mullet of the first,

2. WILLIAM GRACE. Per chevron gules and or, three gem rings counter-coloured.

3.* JOHN FLETHAM. Or, an eagle displayed vert, membered gules.

4.* JOHN PENY. Azure, three rays 2 and 1 or, a chief vaire gules and of the second.

John Googe

mulso

Waller

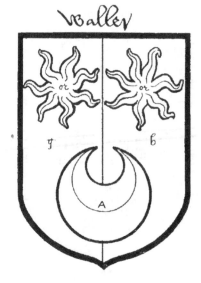

5. HOWGHTON. Argent, on a bend sable, three eagles displayed or, membered gules; *quarterly with*, argent, on a chevron sable, three mullets pierced of the first.

6. WALLES. Per chevron grady gules and azure, three whales heads couped and erect or.

7. SHAMBROKE. Argent, a chevron between three congers heads barways 2 and 1 couped gules, a crescent or.

8.* JOHN GOORGE. Argent, a chevron between three cocks passant sable. (GOOGE.)

9. The Arms cut out.

Folio 51.

1.* MOWSHOLE (MULSO, NORTHAMPTON, added). Ermine, on a bend sable three goats heads erased argent, horns and beard or.

2. Gules, a chevron between three fleurs de lys argent, an annulet for difference sable.

3. Gules, on a fess argent cotised or, three martlets sable, qr. Fitz Williams, Ireland; of Milton, after com. Northt. added.

4. Sable, a fess dancettée argent.

5. Argent, a fess sable between three crescents gules, each charged with another of the first.

6.* (WALLER). Per pale gules and azure, in chief two estoyles or, in base a crescent argent.

7. CHAMPERNOND. Gules, billettée or, a saltire vair; *impaling* BECNBERY, or, an eagle displayed sable, membered gules.

2 F

8. FERRERS. Or, on a bend sable, three fers-du-cheval argent.

9. BEELSCHAMVYR (BELCHAMBER). Sable, three hawks bells 2 and 1 or ; *impaling* KOWEFOLLD, or, three bulls heads cabossed 2 and 1 gules.

Folio 51b.

1. CALCOTE. Per pale or and azure, a chief gules.

2. HOPTON. Argent, a chevron azure, a label 3) ermine ; *quarterly with* SWILLINGTON, argent, a gryphon segreant gules.

3. GRYFFYTH. Azure, a fess between three lozenges argent.

4. GRYFFYTH. Sable, on a fess dancettée argent, three martlets of the first.

5. CLAYTON. Gules, on a bend argent, three roses of the field, seeded or, a crescent for difference of the second.

6. ROBERD MYCHELL. Argent, a fess between three lozenges ermines.

7. HERRY TURNER (SUFF., added). Ermines, on a cross quarter pierced argent, four fers-de-moline sable.

8. SIR GILBERT PECCHE. Quarterly (1) ; argent, a fess between two chevronels gules. (2) SIRE THOMAS, NOTEBEME ; gules, a fess dancettée argent. (3) HYNKELE ; azure, a chevron engrailed argent. (4)? CALDEBEK ;

argent, on a chevron between three martlets sable, as many roses of the first. Quartered by TURNER of Great Bradley Suff. and Bladwell of Swannington Norfolk. P. Le Neve.

9. ARMYS OF YE BREWERS OF LONDON. Azure, on a chevron gules (*sic*), between three garbs banded or, as many tuns barways argent.

Folio 52.

1. Azure, a saltire between four crosses formée fitchée or.

2. Sable, three bars wavy argent, on a chief gules a bull passant or.

3. SANT AUSTEN. Sable, a cross argent. Fictitious coat for ST. AUGUSTINE, added by Le Neve.

4. YE ARMYS OF YORKE CITY. Argent, on a cross of St. George, five lyoncelles of England.

5. KYNG HACHELBERD (KING ETHELRED YE SAXON, added). Gules, three besants 2 and 1, on the first a lyou rampant argent, on the second a wyvern passant nowed silver, on the third a demi King crowned and robed, cape ermine, in dexter hand the sword of justice in the sinister the sceptre, all argent. *Fabulous*.

6. WELYE HYLLE, mercer of London. Argent, a double headed eagle sable, on a chief of the second three roses of the first, seeded or.

7.* SR. JOHN HERVYLLE. Argent, three lyons passant 2 and 1 sable.

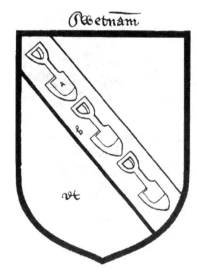

8. DODYNGSEALE. Argent, a fess and in chief two mullets gules.

9.* WALDYF. Or, three leopards faces 2 and 1 erased sable, eared, etc., gules.

Folio 52b.

1. "Kingdom of Powys in Wales," added. CHARLETON, LORD POWYS. Or, a lyon rampant gules.

2. BEAWPRE (Piers Beaupre added). Gules, a leg in armour erect couped at the thigh argent, garnished or. See also No. 7, f.32.

3. Gules, two lyons passant gardant or, a bordure engrailed sable.

4. Sable, three grey hounds courant in pale argent, collared gules ringed and studded or.

5. Or, two chevrons ermine.

6. Sable, three owls 2 and 1 argent, legged gules.

7. Argent, three hinds heads sable, couped gules.

8. Azure, two bars and in chief three roses argent.

9. Or, three lyons gambs erased and erect 2 and 1 gules.

Folio 53.

1. Argent, three boars heads barways 2 and 1 couped sable, tusked or.

2. Be MARIE LINCOLNENSIS (Arma sedi-Episcopalis). Gules, three lyons passant gardant or, on a chief azure, the Virgin and child argent.

3.* S. T. DYMMOK OF SCRIVELSBY com. LINC. Argent, two lyons passant gardant sable, crowned or, membered gules.

4. MORDAUNT OF TURVEY (BEDS., added). Argent, a chevron between three estoyles sable ; *quarterly with* FROWYCK, azure, a chevron between three leopards faces or.

5. MARMYON (quartered by DYMOCK, added). Vair, a fess lozengy gules and or.

6. RICHARD LEE. Azure, on a fess entised or three leopards faces gules.

7. BAGSSHAM (? BOLTSHAM). Gules, three bird bolts erect 2 and 1 argent. See also page 121.

8. WADHULL (" or Wodhull of Bedf." added). Quarterly (1) ; gules, three crescents 2 and 1 or. (2) ; argent, a lyon rampant gules. (3) ; per cross argent and gules, four crosses patée counter-coloured, for CHETWODE. (4) ; argent, two bars counter-compony gules and or, in chief three leopards faces azure.

9.* SWETENHAM, CHESHIRE. Vert, on a bend azure, three spades argent. Rightly, argent, on a bend sable, three spades of the first.

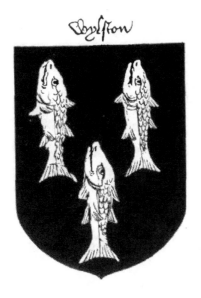

Wylston

Olney

Grene

Folio 53*b*.

1. GREY. Barry (8) argent and azure, a bend gobony or and gules.

2.* WYLSTON. Sable, three fish hauriant 2 and 1 argent.

3. MANNTELL (KENT, added). Quarterly (1); argent, a cross engrailed sable. (2); gules, a maunch or. (3); barry undée (8) or and gules, on a bend sable three besants. (4); argent, on a bend gules four lozenges or; *impaling*, ermine, a bend chevronelly (6) gules and or.

4. HUDLYSTON Cumbr. (CANTBR., added). Gules, fretty argent; *quarterly with*, argent, a bend sable between two mullets pierced of the last.

5. COTYS. Ermine, on a fess azure, three escallops or.

6. THROGMORTON. Gules, on a chevron argent three bars gemelles sable, *impaling* OLNEY, argent, on a fess crenellée (on top) between six crosses crosslet fitchée gules three crescents of the field.

7.* OLNEY (BUCKS., added). As impalement in last coat.

8.* GRENE. Azure, three bucks trippant 2 and 1 or; *impaling*, Throgmorton as No. 6.

9. THORLEY. Vert, nine escallops 3. 3. 2. 1 argent; *impaling* ST. LEGER, azure, fretty argent a chief of the last.

Folio 54.

1. BOUTON (THORLEY, a mistake for ST LEGER). Sable, three crescents 2 and 1 argent on the third an annulet sable ; *impaling* ST LEGER as in preceding.

2. STERBORGH. Argent, two bars sable, in chief three roses gules ; *impaling* ST. LEGER as in the preceding.

3. VVEERE. Argent, a cross gules.

4. TRUSSELL. Argent, fretty gules bezantée at the joints; *impaling* GRENE as No. 8, f.53*b*.

5. HAROWDON (of NORTHT., added). Gules, two bars, the lower argent the upper one ermine, a quarter of the last ; *impaling*, argent, two lyons passant in pale sable.

6. SWYMERTON. Sable, six wings conjoined 2. 2. 2 argent ; *impaling*, HARROWDEN No. 5.

7. SPREGE. Chequy or and azure, a fess ermine. SPRIGG.

8. BYRMYNGHAM "Warr. LORD BERMINGHAM in Ireland" added. Per pale dancettée argent and sable.

9. RUSSELL (of STRENSHAM, Wygorn, added). Argent, a chevron between three crosses crosslet fitchée sable.

Folio 54b.

1.* TERRYNGHAM (BUCKS., added). Azure a saltire engrailed argent a label (3) gules ; *impaling*, argent, two lyons passant in pale sable, crowned or.

2. HAVERSHAM. Azure, a fess between six crosses patée 3 and 3 argent.

3.* DE LA PLANKE. Argent, billettée and a lyon rampant sable.

4. ARMENTYRE. Azure, three swords paleways, the points of the second upwards all proper.

5. DE LA SOWCH. Gules, a fess ermine between six bezants.

6. KYME. Or, two chevronels sable.

7. ARDERNE. Ermine, a fess chequy or and azure.

8. SERVNGHVIL (? Teringham). Azure, a saltire engrailed argent.

9. WOBRVE (? WOLF). Argent, two bars and in chief three wolves heads couped gules.

Folio 55.

1. Argent, a fess crenellée (on top) gules.

2. LUFVON. Argent, a lyon rampant gules, over all a bendlet gobony or and of the second.

3. GOULOFER. Azure, a bucks head cabossed or.

4.* RICHARD WYLLY. Argent, on a chevron sable, between three lobster creels vert, as many ermine spots argent.

5. BUTLER OF YORKSHYRE. Gules, a chevron between three covered cups or; *quarterly with,* argent, a chevron between three fleurs de lys sable; on an escocheon of pretence; argent, a fess gules between three eagles displayed sable.

6.* TWYNYHO. Argent, a chevron between three lapwings sable.

7. SOLERS. Argent, a chevron gules between three cinquefoyles azure. RICHARD SCLERYS.

8.* STOKIS. Sable, florettée argent, fretty or.

9. The arms cut out.

Folio 55b.

1. LORD STRA(N)GE. Quarterly (1); azure, six lyoncelles passant 2, 1, 2, 1, argent. (2); chequy or and azure. (3); or, a lyon rampant gules. (4); or, a cross engrailed sable. (5); barry undée (6) gules and or. (6); gules, on a chevron or three estoyles sable. On an escocheon of pretence; gules, two lyons passant argent; for LE STRANGE.

2. Sable, six fleurs de lys 3. 2. 1 argent.

3. Gules, on a cross moline argent, five escallops of the field.

4.* WYDIMER. Vert, on a fess argent between two gryphons passant argent, three barrulets wavy azure.

5. LEGGEY. Azure, a stags head cabossed or, a chief scaly argent. The coat borne by Ley Earl of Dartmouth, made from this. P. Le Neve.

6. ROBARD DERANT. Azure, three (lucies?) naiant in pale argent. DYRANT.

7. The arms cut away.

8. THOMAS WARNER. Per bend indented argent and sable; *quarterly with*, azure, a fleur de lys gules (sic).

9.* MORTON OF GLOWER (GLOUCESTER). Per fess sable and argent a pale counter-coloured, three rams saliant 2 and 1 of the second.

Folio 56.

1. YE ARMYS OF YE FYNTTENERS. Sable, a chevron between three butts ("tuns") argent. "Vintiners company of London," added.

2. DERWENTWATER. Argent, two bars gules, on a quarter of the second, a cinquefoyle pierced of the first.

3. TOMAS STOCTON. Argent, on a saltire gules, between four staples sable, an annulet or.

4. MYDDYLMOR. Argent, a chevron between three birch-brooms sable; *quarterly with*, per chevron argent and sable, in chief two (moor cocks proper).

5.* BYONNE (or Brome ?). Argent, a chevron between three birch-brooms sable, as in the preceding. See illustration, page 220.

6. TOTTOFET OF BOSSTONE (LINC., added). Ermine, on a chief indented gules, three crosses tau argent.

7. JOHN REDY. Azure, three crosses botonnée 2 and 1 argent, on a chief gules, a lyon passant or.

8. J. WADHAM OF SOM'SETSHIRE. Gules, a chevron argent, between three roses of the second, seeded or.

9. SHIRLEY. Azure, three palets argent, a quarter ermine; *quarterly with*, gules, crusily or and a lyon rampant of the second, crowned azure.

Folio 56b.

1. HARRI STACMBER (STANBERY). Per pale azure and or, a lyon rampant per fess gules and sable (sic).

2. MIDDYLMORE OF EGGEBASTON (WARW., added). Per chevron argent and sable, in chief two (moor cocks proper as No. 4, f.56; *quarterly with*, per pale indented argent and sable.

Coppeaulx

Baynago Oloftracu

Coto malbtally

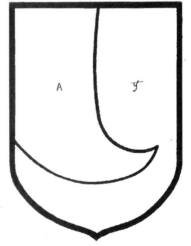

3 CHIKE (CHEKE). Ermine, on a chief argent, three lozenges gules.

4. J. ETON (? ESTONNE). Sable, a cross flory argent ; *quarterly with*, argent, on a fess sable three bezants.

5. S. ROBARD GRENE OF ESSEX. Azure, a chevron argent, between three bucks trippant or ; *quarterly with*, sable, a fess ermine.

6. MAL LERRE (Mallory). Ermine, a chevron gules, a bordure engrailed sable ; *quarterly with*, or, three lyons passant in pale sable.

7. THURLAND. Ermine, on a chief gules three crosses tau argent. PRIFET or PROSETT in Papworth.

8. Per fess argent and or, a fess vert, over all a lyon rampant gules.

9.* SERGFAULX. Argent, a saltire sable between 32 cheries slipped proper.

Folio 57.

Knights of King Arthur's Round Table. i to vij, added by P. Le Neve fabulous. See also Lansdowne MS. 865 and 882, Add. 35,346.

1. S. LAWNCELOT DE LAKE (i). Argent, three bends gules. "Two red bends" in Mallory.

2. S. MODERET (MODRED) (ii). Argent, an eagle displayed sable, membered gules.

3. S. NOWEN (iii). Argent, a cross pattée gules. (? MORVEN.)

Low

war' Tho Bodrygean

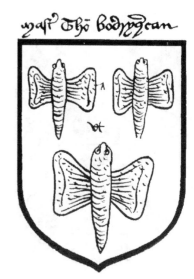

4. S. TRISTRAM (iv). Argent, a lyon rampant sable.

5.* BARNAGO ELESTRACU(M) (v). Argent, three (? lizard, crocodile, or badger) passant in pale, tails nowed, vert. (? BADERNAGUS.)

6. Sable, a wolf saliant or.

7. TYWLODES (vi). Argent, a chevron sable, between three boars heads barways 2 and 1 couped gules.

8.* COTE MAWTALLE (Sir La Cote-Male-tailé) (vij). Gyronny of three "Arondia" argent and gules.

9. TROWRO. Argent, a bend azure.

Folio 57b.

1.* LOW. Gules, a fess or between three birds argent.

2. (? WESTCOTE, added). Argent, a chevron between three escallops azure.

3. RODNEY (Randoney). Or, three eagles displayed 2 and 1 purpure.

4.* MASTR. THOMAS BODRYGAN. Vert, three butterflies 2 and 1 argent.

5.* (LOWE). Argent, three wolves passant in pale azure, langued gules.

6.* ARONDELL. Sable, six hirondelles 3. 2. 1 argent. See page 218.

7. CARMENOW. Azure, a bend or.

Lobbe

Arondell

Bulstrode

Speke

8. HENRY BUTLER OF LONDON, skynner. Gyronny (12) azure and ermine.

9. Argent, six crosses pattée 3. 2. 1 gules.

Folio 58.

1.* BOTSTROSTP, over it BOLSTRODE (BUCKS., added). Sable, a bucks head cabossed argent, between the attires or, a cross pattée of the third, through the nostrils an arrow fessways or, flighted of the second; *quarterly with*, argent, a chevron between three squirrels sejant cracking a nut gules.

2. NORE(Y)S. Argent, a chevron sable between three ravens heads erased proper.

3. Azure, on a cross or, five martlets gules.

4. Per fess nebulée argent and sable, two barrulets one in chief and the other in base counter-coloured.

5. HOWNTT (Hunt). Azure, on a bend between six leopards faces or, three water bougets sable.

6. JOHN GAY OF FOWWEY, CORNWALL. Ermine, on a chief gules, three cinquefoyles pierced argent.

7. Argent, two triangles interlaced gules, on a chief or, three lozenges of the second; *impaled with*, sable, a chevron between three (foxes ?) heads erased ermine.

Treelond

Welye Babham

8.* SPEKE OF SOMERSET & DEVINCHER. Azure, a fess gules over all a double headed eagle displayed or. See also No. 1, f.129.

9.* TREELOND (TRELAWNY) of Cornwall. Argent, a chevron gules between three oak leaves slipped vert, a crescent for difference of the first.

Folio 58b.

1. CLOO—indistinct. Azure, a chevron or between three bezants. HOTFT or OTOFT.

2. RESTON. Azure, a fess ermine between three leopards faces argent; *quarterly with,* argent, three bugle horns stringed sable garnished or.

3. Azure three boars heads 2 and 1 barways argent, tusked or; *quarterly with,* gules, three piles wavy meeting in base argent.

4.* WELYE BABHAM. Sable, on a chevron between three eagles wings argent, as many torteaux.

5. ARMYS DE DYERSE. Sable, a chevron engrailed argent, between three madder bags of the second, corded or. The Dyers Company.

6.* WYLLYSLEY. Argent, a lyon sable, holding between his paws a baston azure.

7. NEH(A)M. Chequy or and azure, a chief of the first.

8. YNKPEN. Gules, two barrulets or, a chief invected ermine.

Wyllysley

Byonne

Robt Follman

* BYONNE, blazon. See No. 5, page 215.
9. HALTUN. Gules, a lyon rampant or, a bend ermine.

Folio 59.

1. WATR. HARNEYS. Argent, on a chevron sable three guttées d'or; *impaled with*, argent, a fess and in chief a lyon passant gardant sable
2. HERRY HARNEYS bore No. 1. quarterly.
3. TELYNG OFF MOLAWAFFE. Quarterly per fess indented argent and gules.
4. RAYNE. Gules, a pair of wings ermine. P. Le Neve adds "borne by Sir Jo. Rayney Baronet."
5. BANASTER. Argent, a manuch sable.
6. MAYST JOHN FOST(ER). Sable, a chevron ermine between three broad arrows 2 and 1 or, an annulet for difference.
7. WILLIAM SAYE (and SIR JOHN SAYE, added). Per pale azure and gules, three chevronels humettée argent, voided of the field, *i.e.*, counter-coloured.
8. FYCHETT. Gules, a saltire vair, between four mullets pierced or.
9. S. GILBERT DEBEN(HA)M. Sable, a bend between two crescents or; *impaling*, BEAUCHAMP, gules, crusily and a fess or. See also page 281.

Folio 59b.

1.* ROBART FOLLMAN. Argent, a chevron sable between three crowns 2 and 1 of the second, jewelled gules.
2. LORD FEU(FITZ) WARREN. Quarterly I and IV; argent, a cross engrailed gules between four water bougets sable, BOURCHIER; *impaled with* LOVEYN, gules, billettée and a fess, or. II. and III. gules, a chief dancettée argent. FITZWARREN.
3. BOTELER OF WILTESHIRE. Argent, a bend between six covered cups sable; *quarterly with*, or, three leopards faces sable.
4. CURSON OF MASSALL. Or, on a bend argent (*sic*), three martlets sable.
5. CRAFFORD. Or, on a chevron azure, three hawks heads erased argent.
6. RAF. GAMAGE (of COYTY, GLAMORGAN, added). Argent, three lozenges in bend gules, on a chief azure three escallops or; *quarterly with*, chequy or and gules a fess ermine.
7. Sable, a chevron ermine between three doves proper, membered gules.
8. Gules, a chevron between three lyons rampant argent; *quarterly with*, No. 7.
9. No. 8 *impaled with*, vaire argent and sable, a fess gules. (? BRACEBRIDGE.)

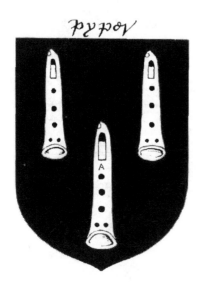

1. (? CLOPTON, added). Argent, a bend between two cotises indented sable, a martlet of the second for difference.

2. CLOPTON. As No. 1 ; without the martlet.

3.* ROB PYP(ER). "Blason" sable, three pipes erect 2 and 1 argent.

4. MY LORD OF CLARANS. FRANCE and ENGLAND quarterly, a label (3) argent, on each file a canton gules ; *impaling*, quarterly of seven, 1 ; chequy or and gules a chevron ermine. 2 ; argent, a fess and in chief a maunch gules, in base a lyon rampant azure. 3 ; Montacute. 4 ; Monthermer. 5 ; Nevill with a label. (6) ; azure, a lyon rampant argent, over all a riband gules. 7 ; per cross argent and gules fretty or, over all a riband sable. See also No. 3, f.3*b.*

5. DREWE LYSLE. Or, a fess between two chevronels sable ; LYSLE, added ; *impaling* DREWE, or, a bend cotised sable between three boars heads erased bendways 2 and 1 of the second.

6. HATTON. Argent, a bend barry (4) indented or and gules.

7. Arms as No. 9, f.59*b. The impalement quarterly with*, gules, two bars or.

8. ARMYS MARBELER. Paly (6) ermine and sable, a chevron counter-coloured. STONE-CUTTERS of LONDON. P. Le Neve.

9. DE HARMIS OF CHALCERRS (CHALCETRIS, added). Argent, three pairs of glazing irons saltireways 2 and 1 sable, on a chief gules a demi lyon passant gardant or. "Md. 4 nails added sable between the three" glazing *vel* grazing irons. I find it to be the arms of the Glaziers Company of London. FL. Norrey (*i.e.*, Flower). Note by P. Le Neve.

1. BELLERS, Leic. Per pale gules and sable, a lyon rampant argent. See No. 3, f.65.

2. VYLLERS, Leic. Argent, on a cross gules five escallops or.

3. SUTHYLL (EBOR, added). Gules, an eagle displayed argent.

4. VYLLERS AND SESSYS ; sable, a fess between three roses argent.

5. PAYNELL. Gules, a cross patonce argent.

6. PAYNELL. Ermine, on a fess azure, three crosses moline or.

7.* W. APPULBY. Azure, three stags lodged 2 and 1 or.

8. W. APPULBY (LEIC., added). Sable, six martlets 3. 2. 1 argent.

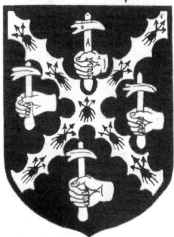

9.* W. APPULBY. Argent, on a bend sable, three apples gules, slipped vert (sic).

Folio 61.

1. LE S. THOMAS BOUGCHER, originally written Boccer (Bourchier). Per fess, in chief FRANCE and ENGLAND quarterly, and in base Bourchier and Loveyne quarterly as No. 2, f.59b; *impaled with*, quarterly (1); or, a chevron engrailed gules. (2); barry (6) gules and sable, billettée 3. 2. 3 argent, on the sable. (3); barry (6) or and azure, a bend gules. (4); sable, three lucies (?) heads erect and erased 2 and 1 argent.

2. HERUI. Gules, on a bend argent, three trefoyles slipped vert. HERVY.

3. BOTTELLER OF CHANC (? CO. LANC.). Argent, a fess between three escallops 2 and 1 sable; *impaling*, gules, two bars ermine, a cinquefoyle pierced sable (sic).

4. LOWYS (LEWIS). Sable, a chevron between three trefoyles slipped argent, a bordure engrailed of the second; *impaled with* DENESTON, barry (6) argent and azure, on a chief gules, a lyon passant gardant or.

5.* LAMKYN. Per bend argent and sable, a bordure azure; *quarterly with* LAMKYN, gules, a stags head and neck couped or.

6. LOMNNOR (LOMENOUR, NORFF., added). Sable, on a bend argent, cotised ermine, three escallops gules.

7. BETHUM. Or, three fleurs de lys azure; *quarterly with*, argent, a chief indented azure.

8. W. BEREDE. Sable, on a cross argent five mullets pierced or.

9. CARESWELL. Lozengy gules and or, a fess ermine.

Folio 61b.

1. MASTYR CAYMES OF DEFNSCHYR. Gules, a cross ermine.

2. CAPYS OF GLOWSETSHYR. Argent, a chevron between three trefoyles slipped sable.

3. THOMAS PLESSETZ. Argent, a chevron gules between three mullets sable; *quarterly with*, lozengy ermine and gules; *impaled with*, barry (8) gules and argent, on a bend sable three escallops or.

4. PLESSETZ. Quarterly. (1); argent, a chevron gules between three mullets sable. (2); argent, three falcons close 2 and 1 purpure, belled and membered or, (3) as impalement in the preceding, (4) lozengy ermine and gules.

5. JOHN BARETT. Gules, three chevronels ermine.

6. SIR JOHN HARLWYN. Azure, florettée 3, 3, 3 argent; *quarterly with*, gules, a bend or, a label (5) argent.

7.* EDMUND TANCARDE. Sable, a saltire engrailed ermine between four dexter hands couped, each holding a hammer with claws erect all argent.

8. WENTWORTH. Quarterly. (1); argent, on a bend sable, a mullet of the first; *quarterly with*, lozengy gules and or. (2); argent, a saltire engrailed gules. (3); gules, on a bend argent three escallops sable. (4); azure, three bars or, a canton ermine.

9.* OWYN. Argent, a chevron couched from the sinister sable, between three rooks proper.

Folio 62.

1. SYR BAWDWEN HOWNFREUYLLE (UMFREVILLE). Or, a cross patonce gules, between five lozenges vert.

2. WONFREUYLL (UMFREVILLE). Gules, an orle ermine.

3. MORTON. Per cross gules and ermine, in the first and fourth a goat's head erased argent horned or.

4. TURBREVYLE. Argent, a lyon rampant gules, crowned or.

5. *SPROT. Argent, a chevron sable between three sprats 2 and 1 naiant proper.

Chelworth

Pynchepole.

Bryan

6. JON MORTON. Per fess argent and sable, a fess azure voided or, between in chief two roses gules and in base a rose of the first.

7.* CHELWORTH. Gules, on a fess sable (sic) between three stags heads erased or, a rose argent.

8.* PYNCHEPOLE OF ESSEX. Argent, a bugle unstrung sable, garnished or, between three trefoyles slipped of the second.

9. HONFREUYLL (UMFREVILE). Argent, crusily patée 3. 3. 2. 1 gules.

Folio 62b.

1. MI LORD LE (FERRERS DE GROBY, added). Gules, seven mascles conjoined 3. 3. 1 or; *quarterly with* ASTLEY, azure, a cinquefoyle pierced ermine.

2. JON WYLLYAMSON. Argent, three crosses humettée 2 and 1 sable.

3. COKKYNG (Hertfordshire). Per pale argent and sable, a fess undée counter-coloured.

4. BRYAN OF BOKYNGH'MCHYRE. Per cross argent and gules, in the first and fourth, on a bend of the second a handcuff (manacle) or.

5.* BRYAN. Azure, three (sic) birds 2 and 1 or, membered gules.

6. BRYAN. Vair, three mascles 2 and 1 gules.

7. WILLIAM SHIRLEY. Azure, three besants in fess between two bars ermine.

8. COLLAY. Azure, a fess counter-compony of the first and per bend sinister gules and argent, six fleurs de lys 3 and 3 or.

9.* LLANDAFF (BISHOPS, added). Sable, two keys endorsed in bend sinister argent, bows interlaced or, a sword interposed in bend dexter proper, the grip gules; on a chief azure three mitres of the second garnished of the third, riband and lined of the fourth.

Folio 63.

1.* Argent, on a bend sable between two lyons of the second, a dragon passant of the first.

2. Argent, a cross moline gules, *quarterly with*, azure fretty or.

3. Arms as No. 2, *impaling* sable, a lyon rampant or.

4. Arms as No. 2 *quarterly with*, sable, on a bend argent, three mullets pierced or.

5. Arms as No. 2, *quarterly with*, gules, a lyon rampant argent.

6. Argent, a cross moline gules; *quarterly with*, gules a bend vair.

7. COMPTON. Quarterly or and gules, in the first and fourth a water bouget ermine, in the second and third, a crescent ermine, all within a bordure engrailed of the third.

2 H

loebol

hoso

Gamston

8. SELENGER (St. Leger). Azure, fretty argent, a chief or.

9. NEWPORT OF ESSEX. Argent, a fess between three crescents sable.

Folio 63b.

1.* RICHARD BRAY. Argent, a chevron between three eagles legs erased sable. See page 225.

2.* LOWEL. Sable, three padlocks 2 and 1 argent.

3. Per chevron azure and argent, in chief two lyons combatant and in base a fleur de lys counter-coloured.

4.* HOSE. Or, three men's hose 2 and 1 sable.

5.* GAMSTON. Ermine, a castle triple turretted sable. ? SAMPSON.

6. FLORYE WULLEY, bishope of Cloucher (Clogher) in Ireland. Or, on a chief azure, three fleurs de lys argent. The name of this prelate does not occur. CHICHESTER is added.

7. BOTLYR. Gules, a chevron between three covered cups or; *quarterly with*, argent, a chevron between three fleurs de lys sable; *on an escocheon of pretence*, argent, a fess gules between three eagles displayed sable.

8. LE CONYAS OF YE NORTHE. Azure, a maunch or; *quarterly with*, or, a chevron gules, a chief vair.

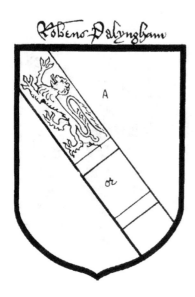

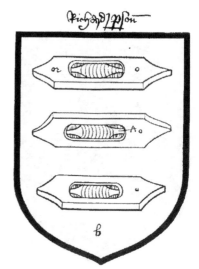

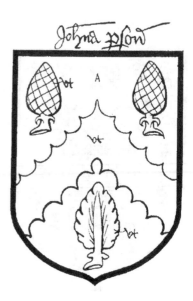

9. CONYAS, KENT. Or, a maunch azure.
CONVERS.

Folio 64.

1. ROCHFORD (LINC., added). Per cross or
and gules, a bordure sable; *quarterly with,*
azure, a fess wavy between two talbots passant
argent.

2.* ROBERTUS PALYNGHAM. Argent (*sic*) on
a bend or, a lyon passant gules and two
barrulets of the last.

3. JOHN APSLE. Argent, three bars gules, a
quarter ermine.

4.* RICHARD P'SON. Azure, three shuttles
barways or, furnished argent.

5.* JOHN P'SON. Argent, a chevron engrailed
between two pine cones in chief and an oak leaf
in base, all vert.

6. RICHARD WETHYLLE. Per fess azure and
or, a pale counter-coloured, three lyons rampant 2 and 1 of the second.

7. CONYAR Knt. Or, a maunch sable.

8. POLE. Per pale or and sable, a saltire
counter-coloured; all within a bordure of the
second.

Uothorham

Syr John Cloy

9. LE LERDES BOWSER (BERNERS, added).
Quarterly. (1); per cross azure and gules.
(2); argent, a cross engrailed gules between four
bousers (water bougets) sable, BOURCHIER.
(3); gules, billettée or, a fess argent, and a label
(3) of the last, on each file three roundles,
LOVEYN. (4); argent, a bend azure and a chief
gules, CROMWELL; quarterly with TATESHALL,
chequy or and gules, a chief ermine.

Folio 64b.

1. WYLLYAM LOVELAS. Gules, on a chief
dancettée argent, three martlets of the first.

2. LOVELAS. Azure, on a saltire engrailed
argent, five martlets sable.

3.* (? ROTHERHAM, ARCHB. OF YORK, added).
Vert, three bucks trippant 2 and 1 argent.

4. (? 1 TIRWYT OF Linc. or 2 PENISTON).
Gules, three tyrwhits (or lapwings) 2 and 1
argent ; *impaled with*, quarterly 1 and 4 ; gules,
bezantée and a quarter ermine, ZOUCHE. 2 and
3 ; or, a lyon rampant azure, *quartering*, argent,
two chevrons gules.

5. BARENTYNE. Azure, three eagles displayed 2 and 1 argent.

6. THOMAS GIBON. Or, a chevron gules between three leopards faces purpure.

7. HABER DALCER (Haberdashers Company,
anciently called "Hurrers and Milaners").
Argent, on a chevron azure between three
fan-brushes gules, as many cartwheels or. See
also page 300.

8. LE S. BURNEL. Argent, a lyon rampant
queue fourchée azure, guttée d'or, crowned of
the last.

9. RICHARD MAYL. Argent on a chevron
sable three cinquefoyles pierced of the first.

Folio 65.

1. GAYE. Gules, a chevron between three
oak leaves erect or ; *quarterly with*, sable, three
leopards faces or, jessant de lys azure.

2. GAYE. Gules, on a bend azure (*sic*)
three mullets or, a crescent of the last for
difference.

3. BELLERS. Per pale gules and sable, a
lyon rampant queue fourchée argent, crowned
or (see No. 1, f.60b) *impaled with*, gules, fretty
ermine.

4. Sable a chevron between three gryphons
heads erased argent, a crescent of the first for
difference ; *impaled with*, argent, a chief
dancettée azure.

5. ROCHES. Sable, two lyons passant gardant in pale argent.

6.* SYR JOHN CLEY. Argent, three wolves
two in chief combatant one in base passant
sable ; *quarterly with* THWENG, argent, a fess
vert, between three popinjays proper, *impaled
with* ASTLEY quartering HARCOURT, 1 and 4
azure, a cinquefoyle pierced ermine ; 2 and 3
gules two bars or.

Robertt Latymer

Johnd ffetylton

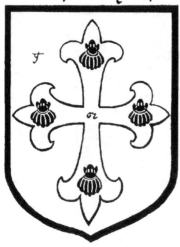

7. ROBERTT BOURTON. Or, on a cross quarter pierced azure, four fleurs de lys of the first.

8.* ROBERTT LATYMER. Gules, on a cross flory or, four escallops sable.

9.* JOHN FETTYLTON. Gules, a chevron sable (*sic*), between three goats heads erased argent.

Folio 65b.

1. GYGGES, NORFOLK. Sable, fretty ermine, a chief counter compony argent and of the first.

2.* MAUNDEFYLDE. Per cross or and azure four caps counter-coloured, as in the illustration.

3. THE DUKE OF BOKYNGHAM (THOMAS of WODESTOKE). FRANCE and ENGLAND quarterly and a bordure argent. See No. 5, f.4.

4. THE ERLE WARYN. Chequy or and azure.

5. THE ERLE OF KENT. ENGLAND, and a bordure argent.

6. THE LORD CLARE. Argent, a quarter gules.

7. S. GILBERT DE CLARE. ERLE OF GLOU'C. Or, three chevronels gules.

8. DAME MAUDE LONGSPEE. ENGLAND, over all a sword erect proper, grip gules.

9. THE LORD VERDON. Or, fretty gules.

Folio 66.

1. CADWALLADER, King of Britain. Azure, a cross patée fitchée or—fabulous.

mavnde fylde

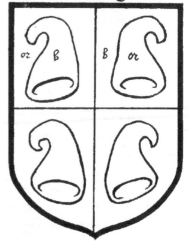

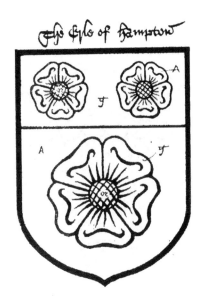

2. DUKE OF YORKE. FRANCE and ENGLAND quarterly, a label (3) argent, on each file as many torteaux.

3.* GLADIUS, the Prynce of Wales doughter. Per cross or and gules four lyons passant counter-coloured.

4. REX HISPANIE. Per cross argent and gules, in the first and fourth a lyon rampant purpure, in the second and third a tower triple turretted or.

5. THE ERLE OF MARCHE. Azure, three bars or, on a chief of the first two palets between as many esquires of the second, over all a false escocheon argent. See also page 132.

6. THE ERLE OF ULCESTRE (IRELAND, added). Or, a cross gules.

7. DAME JANE GYENUYLE (GENEVILE). Azure three barnacles open or, on a chief argent, a demy lyon rampant issuant gules. See No. 1, f.37b.

8. LACY. Or, a fess gules; impaled with BATYLSMER, barulée (14) gules and argent, BADLESMERE.

9.* THE ERLE OF HAMPTON (SIR BEVIS). Argent, a chief gules, three roses 2 and 1 counter-coloured.

Folio 66b.

1. (FISHEAD, erased). Argent, a chevron between three millrinds sable.

f 66ᵇ no 7.

folio 67 no 1

2. (? FULFORD or TULFORD). Gules, a chevron or. See No. 8.

3. SPE STR WYFFE (? of the preceding). Argent, a saltire gules; the field is bedaubed with indications of crusily or. (See DENNY, page 293.)

4. POLLARD (DEVONSHIRE, added). Argent, a chevron sable between three mullets pierced gules.

5.* JOHN BLAKE OF YE (WALYS ?). Argent, a lyon rampant sable.

6. ? HAYDOCK, Lancr. Argent, a cross sable, a fleur de lys of the last. See No. 8, f.70.

7.* Azure, a fess engrailed ermine between three eagles displayed or.

8. FULFORD. Gules, a chevron argent.

9. BELSTON. Or, on a bend gules three millrinds argent. Borne also by SPECCOTT.

Folio 67.

1.* Sable, a lyon with two bodies argent, crowned or, as illustration. See John of Northampton, page 56.

2. Ermine, on a quarter sable a covered cup or.

3. Sable, a bend argent.

4. Gules, on a chevron sable (sic), three leopards faces or.

5.* CALDWALL. Argent, on a fess dancettée azure, three whales heads erect and erased or.

Caldwall

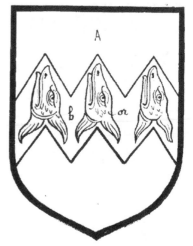

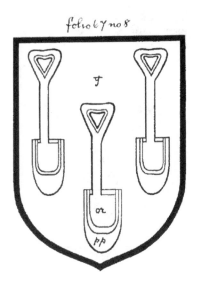

folio 67 no 8

Banaster

Chorley

6. SYR RICHARD CHARLETON. Azure, a chevron or, between three cygnets, wings elevated, argent, membered gules ; *quarterly with*, azure a chevron between three escallops or, on a chief gules a lyon passant gardant of the second.

7. JOHN FORSSE. Ermine, a chevron sable, ARRAS.

8.* Gules, three spades erect 2 and 1 or, shoes argent. [BECTUN.]

9.* BANASTER. Argent, a cross flory sable ; *quarterly with*, gules, a crown or. See No. 4, f.69.

Folio 67b.

1. UMFREVILE Earl of Anegos. Gules, a cinquefoyle pierced or within nine crosses pattée bordurewise of the last.

2. MOUBARAY (MOWDRAY). Gules, a lyon rampant argent.

3. KYCHARD. Or, billettée sable and a lyon rampant azure.

4. DEVENECHER (COURTNEY, EARL of DEVONSHIRE, added). Or, three torteaux, a label (3) azure.

5. WYNDISSOR. Sable, a saltire argent.

6.* CALVERLEY. Argent, a fess gules between three cats passant sable. Probably in error for calves.

7.* FULTUN. Gules, two lyons passant gardant in pale argent, crowned or.

8. KNOLLYS. Gules, on a chevron argent, three roses of the second seeded or.

9. SULLY. Ermine, three chevronels gules.

Folio 68.

1. RAFFE FERES. Gules, six mascles 3. 2. 1 or, a bordure engrailed argent.

2. FELMS—FELTUN. Gules, two lyons passant in pale ermine.

3.* ARGENTYNE (CANTABR., added). Gules, three covered cups 2 and 1 argent.

4. ALYN CHEYNY. Gules, fretty or, a label (3) ermine.

5. BRYAN STAPELTUN (EBOR., added). Argent, a lyon rampant sable.

6. ROCHYS. Azure, three roch naiant in pale argent, finned gules.

7. M. MAYS GORNAY (MAY CORNAY in MS.). Paly (6) or and azure an annulet of the first.

8. WYLLIEM BECHAM. Gules, on a fess between six crosses crosslet or, a crescent sable.

9. JOHN BERELEY. Or, three bars and in chief two pallets all sable; an escocheon of pretence—gules, three barrulets ermine.

Folio 68b.

1. CLANBOWE (Clanvoue). Paly (6) or and azure, on a fess gules three mullets argent.

2. LANSE CLEFFERD. Chequy or and azure, a fess gules a bordure argent.

3. Azure, on a cross formée throughout per bend ermine and or, a nullet of four points counter-coloured embelif of the second and third.

4. KEDRIC SEYS (WALES, added). Azure, six plates 3. 2. 1, on a chief or, a demy lyon rampant issuant gules.

5. HOW SEGRAVE. Sable, a lyon rampant argent crowned or, over all a baston gules.

6. THOMAS LATHEM (LANC., added). Or, on a chief indented azure three plates.

7. HOW WROTTESLEY (Staff., added). Or, three piles meeting in base sable, a quarter ermine.

8. ROWS. Ermine, on a chief indeuted gules, two escallops argent.

9. MONS. (AD)DERBY. Or, a fess crenellée sable. ADDERBURY.

Folio 69.

1. SARNFIELD (written CARNYSFELD). Azure, an eagle displayed crowned or, membered gules.

2. ELMAM. Argent, a fess gules between three eagles displayed sable.

3. MORRIS (MORIEUX of THORP MORIEUX, added). Gules, a bend argent billettée sable.

2 K

4.* BANASTER (of LANCASHIER, added). Argent, a cross patonce sable. See No. 9, f.67.

5. URSWYKE (written HURSWYKE). Argent, on a bend sable three lozenges of the first each charged with a saltire gules, a crescent of the second.

6. BERNARD BROCAS (written BROKYS). Sable, a lyon rampant gardant or.

7. MARKAUNTE. Argent, fretty sable, a quarter gules.

8. BRYTAYNE (DUKEDOM, added). Ermine.

9. ROKELE. Argent, on a chevron gules, a chess rook or, in chief two lyons heads erased of the second.

Folio 69b.

1. S. HEW LEWTERELL. Argent, a bend between six martlets sable.

2.* ST. HALBOROW (? S. EADBURGA). Azure, three columbines pendant argent, slipped vert, crowned or, in base as many roses 2 and 1 gules (sic) seeded of the third, a bordure of the fifth platey.

3. COLVYLE (of BITHAM, LINC., added). Or, a fess gules.

4. S. JOHN HERON. Gules, a chevron engrailed argent, between three heron of the second.

5. WYLLM. BYCHERY. Azure, an eagle displayed or.

6. S. (ROBT.) WELYBY (LORD) BROKE. Quarterly I. quarterly 1 and 4; sable, a cross engrailed or. 2 and 3; gules, a cross moline argent; over all a crescent or. II.; gules, a cross flory or. III.; gules, four fusils conjoined in fess argent, each charged with an escallop sable. IV.; or, a chevron gules, a bordure engrailed sable.

7. S. JOHN GYSSE (GUISE of GLOUCESTER, added). Gules, eight lozenges 4. 4. vair, on a canton sable a mullet pierced or; *quarterly with*, gules, a fess between six billets or.

8. KNOLLES. Azure, crusily and a cross moline sarcellée or; *quarterly with*, per fess sable and argent, a bulls head cabossed of the second (sic), horned or; on an escocheon of pretence—gules, a chevron charged with three torteaux.

9. Argent, a chevron between three human legs couped below the knee, toes of the first to the dexter, of the others to the sinister, all gules.

Folio 70.

1. HUNTYNGFELD. Or, on a fess gules three plates.

2. BROUNE. Lozengy gules, and ermine on a quarter azure a cross moline or. (? Brune.)

3. ASCHELLYS (ATHOLL). Or, three pallets azure.

4. S. SYMOND GRENDEHAM (? MENDHAM). Argent, a chevron sable, a label (3) gules; *impaling*, or, a chevron argent (sic).

Kene

ffayreford

Lexame

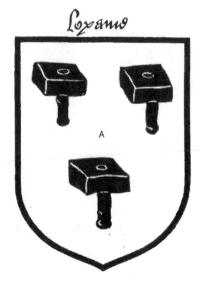

5. IPPULPEN (written PUPELPEN). Azure, on a fess between two chevronels or, three eagles displayed gules.

6.* KENE. Ermine, a cross fleurtée ermines.

7.* FAYREFORD. Argent, guttée de sang, three lyons couchant tails cowed sable, crowned gules, charged with six plates 3, 2, 1.

8. HAYDOKKE (LANC., added). As No. 6, f.66b.

9. STAVERTON. Argent, a chevron between three maunches vert.

Folio 70b.

1.* LEXAME. Argent, three mallets 2 and 1 sable.

2. HOLDE HAL (qre. OLD HALL, NORFF., added). Gules, a lyon rampant argent. See also No. 1, f.88b.

3. LADE MARE ; VERE *impaling* HOWARD. Per cross gules and or, a mullet argent ; *impaling*, gules a bend between six crosses crosslet fitchée argent.

4. MASTER HOLTUN. Argent, on a bend engrailed gules, three leopards faces of the first ; *impaled with*, argent, three false escocheons 2 and 1 sable.

John mannyngham

Gaynefford

5. JOHN WROTHE. Paly of 4 coats, (1); argent on a bend sable, three leopards faces of the field. WROTHE. (2); argent on a bend sable three vases of the field, out of each three flowers gules leaved vert. (3); argent, three chevrons azure. (4); gules, a greyhound passant argent, collared azure, studded and ringed or.

6. Gules, a fess or, over all a boar passant in fess argent, a label of three of the second.

7.* Le S. DE MANNYNGHAM (JOHN, added); Argent, a chevron sable between three peacocks azure, plumed or.

8.* GAYNESFORD (SURREY, added). Argent, a chevron gules between three greyhounds passant sable.

9. (? HURLESTON). Argent, four ermine spots per cross sable ; *quarterly with*, gules, two swords saltireways, points to the base or.

Folio 71.

1. Argent, ten escallops 3. 3. 3. 1 gules.

2. An eagle displayed———membered or.

3. Or, three cartwheels 2 and 1 argent (*sic*).

4. Or, a boars head fessways couped gules.

5. Gules, on a chevron sable (*sic*) three boars heads couped argent, a rose or, for difference.

6. Gules, a fess or, on a quarter of the second a lyon passant gardant argent (*sic*).

7. Or, a chevron wavy per pale argent and gules, between three crosses pattée fitchée at the foot of the second, a silver crescent for difference (*sic*).

8. Or, on a chevron engrailed gules, between three birds of the second, a crescent sable ; *impaled with*, gules, three (bears ?) heads ceased sable (*sic*) imperfect.

9. Grand quarterly. I. and IV. ; argent a fret gules ; *quarterly with*, gules, a saltire or. II. and III. ; or, three escallops 2 and 1 gules ; *quarterly with*, gules, a cross patonce argent.

Folio 71b.

1. SYMON MUMFORDE. Blanc. See No. 9, f.72b.

2.* CHEVERELL. Argent, on a saltire (azure) five water bougets (of the field) a chief gules.

3. SIR HUMFREY LORD DACRE OF YE NORTH. Gules, three escallops argent.

4. THOMAS LYSTAR. Blanc.

5. JOHN CANE (possibly Cave). Blanc.

Folio 72.

1. MY LORD BARYNGTON, and two other imperfect paintings.

4. WILLIAM ALYNGTON, CAMBR. Sable, billettée and a bend engrailed argent ; *quarterly with*, gules, three covered cups 2 and 1 argent ; *impaling*, quarterly. I. and IV. *in chief* ; per

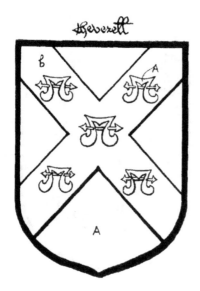

Heverett

chyche

cross argent and gules, the 2nd and 3rd fretty or, over all a bend sable charged with an annulet and a mullet of the first; *in base*; argent, a saltire gules. II. and III. gules, crusily fitchée and a bend argent, charged with an ermine spot.

5. RYCHARD NORTON. Argent, a chevron between three crescents azure.

6. *CHYCHE. Azure, three lyoncelles rampant 2 and 1 queue fourchée argent.

7. ELLYS (EBOR., added). Gules, on a cross sable five crescents argent.

BANNERS.—See also pages 127-142.

Folio 72b.

1. JESP. (Jasper) DUKE OF BEDFORDE. FRANCE and ENGLAND quarterly, a bordure azure, entoyre of martlets or.

2. THOMAS MARCS. DORSETT. Gules, seven mascles conjoined 3, 3, 1 or; *quarterly with*, (1 and 4); paly of three, Grey, Hastings and Valence as No. 1, f.73, over all a label (3) ermine. (2); ASTLEY; azure, a cinquefoyle pierced ermine. (3) WIDVILLE; argent, a fess and a quarter gules.

3. ERLE OF OXINFORD. VERE quarterly with HOWARD.

4. SYR THOMAS LOVELL (NORFF., added). Argent, a chevron azure between three squirrels sejant gules; *quarterly with*, vert, two chevrons argent, each charged with three cinquefoyles pierced gules.

5. SYR RYNOLD BRAYE. Vair, three bendlets gules; *quarterly with*, argent, a chevron between three eagles legs erased sable.

6. SYR NYCOLAS VAYS (VAUX). Chequy argent and gules, on a chevron azure, three roses gules (*sic*); *quarterly with*, gules, crusily and three lucies hauriant or.

7. SYR WELYE NORYS. Argent, a chevron sable between three ravens heads erased proper; *quarterly with*, azure, four bendlets gules; *per pale with*; or, two bars gules, a bendlet azure.

8. SYR SYMOND MOMFORD (WARR., added). Quarterly. (1); bendy (10) or and azure. (2); sable, three lyoncelles passant in pale argent. (3); argent, on a chief azure two fleurs de lys or. (4); gules, a fess between six crosses crosslet argent. BEAUCHAMP.

9. SYR T. HAWTON. Or, fretty gules, an annulet azure; *quarterly with*, argent, on a bend sable three eagles displayed or. A VERDON coat.

lorde herbard

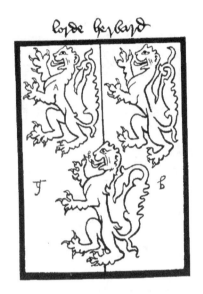

Syr Robert Grysson

Syr O Treffs

lorde ogell

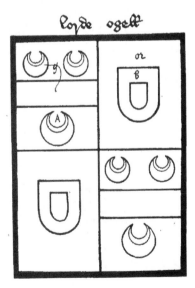

John Norys

leytelbery

Folio 73.

1. ERLE OF KENT. Barry (6) argent and azure, in chief three torteaux; *quarterly with*, HASTINGS and VALENCE, or, a maunch gules; *quartering*, burullée (12) argent and azure, eight martlets 3, 3, 2 gules. See also No. 2, f.72b.

2.* LORDE HERBARD. Per pale gules and azure, three lyoncelles rampant 2 and 1 argent.

3. LORD POWYS. Or, a lyon rampant gules; *quarterly with*, gules, a lyon rampant argent, a bordure engrailed of the last. On an escocheon of pretence; vert, a false escocheon between eight escallops bordurewise argent.

4.* SYR ROBERD CURSON. Argent, on a bend sable, between three dragons heads erased gules, as many popinjays of the first, speckled of the second, beaked or, collared of the third.

5.* SYR T. TREFFRE. Sable, a chevron between three trees eradicated argent; *quarterly with*, NORRIS, argent, a chevron sable between three ravens heads erased proper.

6. SYR THO. LEYTON. Per chevron gules and or, in chief a lyon passant gardant argent; *impaling*, per chevron or and gules. This painting may have been intended for, quarterly per fess dancettée gules and or, etc.

7. SYR ROBERD MANERS. Or, two bars azure, a chief gules; *quarterly with*, vert, three squirrels sejant argent.

8. SYR THOMAS EVERYNGGHAM. Gules, a lyon rampant vair between five fleurs de lys or; *quarterly with*, BYRKYN—argent, a fess azure, a label (3) gules.

9.* LORDE OGELL. Argent, a fess between three crescents gules; *quarterly with*, BERTRAM, or, an orle azure.

END OF BANNERS.

Folio 73b.

1. Ermine, a chief quarterly or and gules. (Fitz Nicholas or Peckham.)

2. Argent, a lyon rampant gules crowned or, over all on a bend sable three crosses crosslet fitchée of the first.

3. Gules, on a chevron argent, three talbots passant sable.

4.* JOHN NORYS. Argent, a chevron sable between three ravens heads erased proper; *quarterly with*, argent, a tower triple turretted sable; over all an escocheon of pretence; argent, three covered cups sable.

5. BOYFFELDE. Gules, a fess between three saltorelles argent; *quarterly with*, bendy (10) gules and argent.

6.* LEYTELBERY (Linc. added). Argent, two lyons passant gardant gules. See page 199.

7. SYR JOHN KYRTON, LINC. Gules, three bars ermine; painted as a banner.

8. RADMELL. Vert, on a chief indented or, two mullets pierced gules; *quarterly with*, or, on a chevron gules three plates.

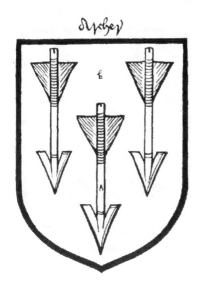

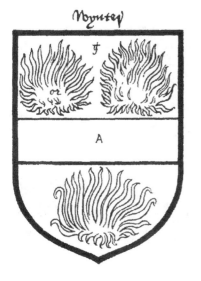

9. VARNEY (WARWICK, added). Quarterly
(1) ; gules, three crosses patée pommettée or,
a chief vaire argent and sable. (2) ; ermine on
a chevron sable three escallops argent. (3) ;
argent, three false escocheons 2 and 1 sable, a
bordure gules. (4) ; azure three stags trippant
or, a bordure argent.

Folio 74.

1. S. ROBERT PALMER. Argent, on a bend
sable four besants, and an annulet or.

2. FFELPOT (PHILPOT, HANTS., added).
Sable, a bend ermine.

3. REYNOLDE LAMOND. Argent, two bends
azure, a bordure engrailed of the last ; *quarterly
with*, gules, three garbs 2 and 1 argent.

4. *ARCHER (WARR., added). Azure, three
arrows paleways, points to the base argent.

5. CORSON. Or, on a bend argent (*sic*) three
martlets sable.

6. *THOMAS METTLEY. Argent, a chevron
between three eagles displayed sable.

7. GAYNYS (? ENGAYNE or GENNYS). Sable,
a fess dancetée between six escallops argent.

8. *WYNTER. Gules, a fess argent, between
three bushes enflamed proper. See illustration.

9. HARTWELL. Sable, a bucks head cabossed
argent, between the attires a cross pattée of the
last ; *quarterly with*, gules, eight lozenges conjoined 5. 3 argent.

Folio 74b.

1. THOMAS LEFFYN. Lozengy argent and gules ; *quarterly with*, per chevron ermine and sable, in chief two gryphons heads erased azure, in base an annulet argent.

2. COLPEPER OF KENT. Argent, a chief gules, over all a bend engrailed azure.

3. S. RICHARD NANFAN (HEREF., added). Argent, three wolves passant 2 and 1 azure ; *quarterly with*, sable, on a chevron between three wings argent, as many ermine spots.

4. OXINBYRGE. Gules, a lyon rampant argent, a bordure vert, entoyre of escallops of the second ; *quarterly with*, argent, a lyon rampant sable, a bordure entoyre of torteaux.

5. Ermine, on a chevron sable three cinquefoyles pierced or.

6. MORTON. Per cross gules and ermine, in the first and fourth a goats head erased argent, horned or. See also Nos. 1 and 2, f.107.

7. JOHN ISLEY (KENT, added). Ermine, a fess gules.

8. BELLE. Gules, three hawks bells 2 and 1 argent.

9. S. ROBERD SPENSER (DEVON, added). Sable, two bars wavy ermine ; as a banner. See also No. 7, f.73b (72b, 73), &c.

Folio 75.

1. SIR JOHN BOUTHE ; of Shrubland Hall in Suff. quartering Oke and Cogshall. 1 and 4 ; argent, three boars heads erased and erect 2 and 1 sable. (2) ; sable, on a fess argent between six acorns or, slipped vert, three escallops of the last. (3) ; argent, on a cross gules five escallops or.

2. LOWE. Argent, on a bend azure three wolves heads erased of the first, a bordure engrailed of the second.

3. SIR RAFFE LONGFORDE. Paly (6) or and gules, a bend azure ; *quarterly with*, per cross argent and gules.

4.* SMETHELEY. Gules, two bars between nine martlets 4. 2. 3 argent. See No. 3, f.83b.

5. CORSON. Argent, on a bend sable three martlets or, a mullet of the second for difference.

6. S. THOMAS BUTLER. Azure, a bend between six covered cups 3 and 3 or ; *quarterly with*, or, a lyon rampant gules.

7.* RYCHARD LEDES. Argent, a fess gules between three eagles displayed sable, a crescent of the first for difference.

8. SYMOND MANFELDE. Sable, two bars argent, on the sovereign bar a wyvern issuant wings expanded of the field.

2 L

folio 75b no3

John Lovoll

Grandyson

9. JOHN MORLEY. Sable, a leopards face or, jessant de lys argent.

Folio 75b.

1. ASHETON. Argent, a mullet sable, pierced ermine.

2. HENGLYS (HEGLISE). Ermine, on a chief or, a demy lyon rampant issuant vert.

3.* Gules, a chevron argent between three greaves embowed or.

4. POKESWELL. Sable, a chevron argent between three estoyles or.

5. RAFE RAME. Gules, three ram's heads cabossed 2 and 1 argent; *quarterly with*, sable, two bars or.

6.* JOHN LOVELL. Or, a wolf saliant azure, a bordure engrailed sable.

7. SYMOND MAWRE (S. MAURE, MORE, or MOWER). Argent, two chevronels gules; *quarterly with*, or, a lyon rampant sable.

8. JOHN MUNCHENESEY (of EDWARDSTON, SUFF., added). Or, three false escocheons 2 and 1, barry (6) gules and vair.

9. Argent, three cart wheels 2 and 1 gules.

Folio 76.

1. BEAUCHAMP. Gules, a fess between six martlets or.

2. Sable, a cross formée quarterly argent and gules.

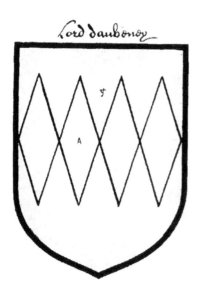

Lord daubeney

M mongomery

folio 77 no 6

3. DUFFIELD. Sable, a chevron argent, between three doves proper.

4.* GRANDISON. Argent, three palets azure, on a bend gules three eagles displayed or.

5. (? GRANDISON). Argent, three palets azure, on a bend gules three mullets or.

6. Per cross or and gules, on a bendlet sable three escallops argent.

7. JOHN PARYS. Argent, on a bend azure two bars gules.

8. Argent two flaunches sable.

9. Barry (6) or and vert.

Folio 76b.

1.* LORD DAUBENEY. Gules, four fusils conjoined in fess argent.

2. LONNAM (LOVAYN). Gules, billettée barways or, and a fess argent.

3.* S. MONGOMERY. Ermine, a bordure gules, entoyre of horse shoes or.

4. Vair, three bars gules.

5. Per cross or and sable.

6. BOWET. Argent, three reindeers heads cabossed sable.

7. Barry (6) gules and argent.

8. Gules, on a bend argent six ermine spots 1. 2. 1. 2. bendways reversed.

9. Gules, three lozenges 2 and 1 argent, each charged with a bend sable.

folio 77⁶ no1

Trafford

Bulkeley

Folio 77.

1. Sable, on a chevron argent a chevronel gules, all between three lozenges of the second, each charged with a martlet of the first.

2. Azure, a cross moline sarcelled argent.

3. Gules, a cross crosslet ermine.

4. Argent, a millrind pierced gules.

5. Argent, on a bend azure, between two lyons rampant gules, three plates.

6.* Argent, a double headed eagle per fess (enarched) gules and sable, beak and legs or. As illustration, page 243.

7. Argent, a chief per pale gules and ermine, on the dexter an owl argent, crowned and legged or.

8. Argent, three fleurs de lys bendways between two bendlets sable.

9. MELNEHOUSE. Argent, on a bend sable three fleurs de lys of the first, an annulet of the second for difference.

Folio 77b.

1.* TRAFFOW. Argent, a gryphon passant gules : A note adds "montant." TRAFFORD. See also page 313.

2. LESERTON (LESINGTON). Argent, in chief two saltorelles humettée, and in base a cross all engrailed sable; a crescent for difference of the last.

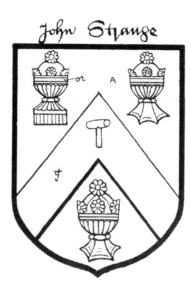

3. BOWROW (BORNE). Argent, on a bend sable three lyons passant of the first a crescent of the second for difference.

4. OLYVER. Argent, a bend gules, on a chief of the second two mullets or, a label (3) azure.

5. DENNYS. Argent, a chevron sable between three mullets gules; *quarterly with*, argent, a lyon rampant azure crowned or.

6.* BULKLEY. Sable, a chevron between three bulls heads cabossed argent.

7.* BLOSSUM. Gules, three wyverns passant in pale ermine.

8. BUTTELER. Gules, five bendlets argent.

9.* JOHN STRANGE. Argent, on a chevron gules between three covered cups or (sic). a mallet.

Folio 78.

1.* SAMON. Sable, three salmon hauriant 2 and 1 proper.

2.* Ermine, on a chief gules three dexter hands apaumée argent. See page 245.

3.* FORNEYS (SORNEYS). Argent, a talbot sejant within a bordure all sable. Md. this coat is borne, but unjustly by SIR HENRY, 1710, Furnese of Waldershare Kent kt. and baronet and by Sir Robert his son and heir baronet 1723, his father was a p . . . . at Feversham in Kent. P. Le Neve. See page 245.

folio 78 no 2

Somey

Cleyke

4. HOLKOTT. Lozengy gules and argent, a bordure azure.

5. Argent, a chief gules, three cinquefoyles 2 and 1 counter-coloured.

6. WYKE. Argent, a chevron gules, between three crosses moline sable.

7.* CLERKE. Sable, three passion nails 2 and 1 argent.

8.* OLYFE (written CLYSE). Azure, a wolf saliant argent.

9.* VAWHAN. Argent, three human heads proper, crined or, encircling each neck, a serpent azure, see illustration.

Folio 78b.

1. WELYE ROO (above it FAVOYLE, i.e., Favyle, Folville, etc.) Per fess argent and or, over all a cross moline gules.

2.* GETHYN. Argent, a chevron engrailed azure between three birds rising sable, a bordure engrailed of the second.

3. RYCHEMOND. Gules, on a mullet of nine points azure, an annulet or, pierced of the field.

4. ORSWYKE (Ursewyke). Argent, on a chevron gules five besants.

5.* SELLYNG. Vert, a chevron between three wolves heads erased or.

2Blakeborn

Hokeley

Tomas Haykoft

6. Gules, on a chevron azure (*sic*) between three cinquefoyles argent, a cross pattée of the last.

7.* BLAKEBORN. Argent, a fess undée between three mullets all sable.

8. JOHN LEYLE (LYLE, added). Or, on a chief azure three lyoncelles rampant of the field.

9. WELVE GRESLEY (DERBY, added). Vaire, gules and argent ; *quarterly with*, sable, a lyon rampant argent, collared gules.

Folio 79.

1. WELLUGOBY (WILLOUGHBY, DERB., added). Or, two bars gules each charged with as many water bougets argent.

2.* HOKELEY. Or, a lyon rampant gules.

3. Argent, two palets sable.

4. GYLYS STRANGWAYS (substituted for S. T. Strangwheygh). Sable, two lyons passant in pale argent, charged with three pallets purpure, crowned or.

5. T. OWGON. Or, on a chief sable three martlets or ; *quarterly with*, gules, on a chief or, a lyon passant sable.

6. Gules, on a chevron sable (*sic*) between three lyons heads erased argent, a mullet of the last.

7. WELVE GEYTON. Or, fretty azure ; *impaled with*, gules, two bars ermine.

8.* THOMAS HAYLTOFT (HOLTOFT of UPWELL, NORF., added). Ermine, three lozenges in triangle meeting in the fess point ermines.

9. STRECHELEY. Or, on a chevron argent (sic) three cinquefoyles sable.

Folio 79b.

1. WYLCOTYS. Azure, an eagle displayed argent, membered or : *quarterly with*, argent, a chevron engrailed between three escallops sable.

2. CORNUE. Argent, a chevron between three bugle horns stringed sable.

3.* S. THOMAS BORTUN. Sable, a chevron argent, between three owls of the second, crowned and legged or.

4. RAFE REDENEY (RODNEY, SOMERSET, added). Or, three eagles displayed 2 and 1 gules. See No. 6, f.1016.

5. RAWLYN DOTTON (DUTTON). Sable, a cross engrailed ermine.

6. TENDRING (SUFF., added). Azure, a fess between two chevronels argent.

7. BRUGFORDE. Gules, three martlets in fess between two barrulets or.

8. RAFE STROTHER. Gules, on a bend cotised argent, three eagles displayed vert, a label (3) azure.

9. RYCHARD CLETHEROW. Gules, a saltire engrailed or.

2 M

1. Argent, three crosses patonce 2 and 1 gules, an annulet of the last for difference.

2. Vert, on a bend argent, three cinquefoyles or (sic).

3.* STOKYS. Per chevron ermine and vert, a chevron engrailed counter - coloured, between three fleurs de lys 2 and 1 or. See page 249.

4.* BARTUN. Argent, three boars heads pale-ways couped 2 and 1 sable. See page 249.

5. JOHN MOORE. Azure, three leopards faces 2 and 1 or.

6. BORNAM. Or, a bend between two crosses crosslet sable.

7.* HARROW. Ermines, three harrows in triangle conjoined by a circular wreath all argent.

8.* DEYVYLL. Argent, on a bend azure, six fleurs de lys 2. 2. 2 or. "Now born by the name of Clapham of Beamsley, Ebor." P. Le Neve.

9. S. JOHN CLYFTON (of Bokenham Castell in Norf., added). Chequy or and gules, a bend ermine.

1. RAFE HONT (KENT, added). Sable, a fess between three cinquefoyles or.

2. PETER DE LEGH (CHESHIRE, added). Gules, a cross engrailed argent. See No. 7, f.91b.

3. S. JOHAN HURLESTON (HUDDLESTONE). Gules, fretty argent.

4. CROFTE. Sable, seven lozenges 3. 3. 1 argent, on the second an ermine spot.

5. JOHN WARDE. Argent, a chevron between three birds sable.

6. MORESBY. Sable, a cross argent, a cinque-foyle of the second.

7. SKELTON. Gules, two bars and in chief three mullets all argent.

8. FYLBRYG (FELBRIGG, NORF., added). Or, a lyon rampant gules.

9. Argent, two chevrons gules, on a quarter of the second, a cross patonce or.

1. Argent, on a chief sable, a crescent between two mullets or.

2. OGULL (OGLE, added). Argent, a fess be-tween three crescents gules.

3. Argent, a chevron between three mascles gules.

4. NYCOLAS HAYWODE (added above it. S. LEVIS ORELL, LANC.). Argent, three torteaux between two bendlets, a bordure all gules.

Wauton

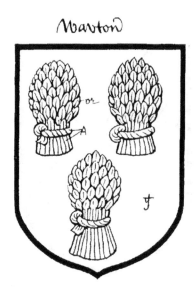

Kynvyre

5. JOHN COLSELL. Chequy or and sable, a chief argent guttée de sang; *impaled with*, gules, fretty or, a quarter argent.

6.* WAUTON. Gules, three garbs 2 and 1 argent, ears or. See also No. 7, f.193.

7. JOHN BARLEY (HERTF., added). Ermine, three bars wavy sable; *quarterly with*, or, a water bouget sable, a bordure of the second besantée.

8. PERS CABELL. Vert, fretty argent, a fess gules; *quarterly with*, gules, three cocks 2 and 1 or.

9.* KYNVYRE. Gules, a covered cup and a chief dancettée or; *quarterly with*, argent, a Sowdans head proper, a bordure azure.

Folio 81b.

1.* JOHN SYLBY. Argent, a man's head in profile gules, wreathed of the first, a chief per pale or and azure.

2. S. RYCHARD DALABERE (HEREF., added). Azure, a bend cotised argent between six martlets 3 and 3 or.

3. THOMAS HALE. Vert, a saltire engrailed argent.

4.* CORBET, SALOP. Or, a caw proper. See page 252.

5. ASTUN. (STAFF., added). Argent, a fess and in chief three lozenges all sable.

John Sylby

Corbet

Rychard Byrkehede

Zerde

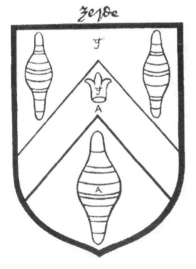

6. LORDE MORTEMER. Azure, three bars or in chief two palets between as many esquires of the second, over all a false escocheon ermine.

7.* RYCHARD BYRKEHEDE (CHESHIRE, added). Sable, three garbs 2 and 1 or, a bordure argent.

8. FELYP TONBERY (THORNBERY). Argent, a chief or, over all a lyon rampant azure.

9.* ZERDE. Gules, on a chevron between three fuseaux (spindles) argent, a cronel of the first.

Folio 82.

1. GARNYS (SUFF., added). Argent, a chevron azure, between three escallops sable.

2. BELLYNGHAM. Gules, three bendlets argent, on a quarter of the first, a lyon rampant of the second.

3. The arms cut away.

4. ARSAKE. Gules, a bend or, cotised argent.

5.* HEWE COTON (CESTR., added). Azure, a chevron between three hanks of cotton argent.

6.* COUELEY. Gules, a fess sable (*sic*) between three helmets argent.

7.* THOMAS TAPLEY. Gules, on a fess azure (*sic*) a lyon passant argent, all between three crosses botonnée fitchée of the last.

8.* JOHN ANGELL. Or, four fusils conjoined azure.

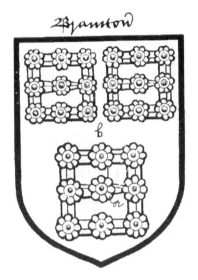

Bramton

Folio 83 no 3

9. *BRAM(P)TON. Azure, three square buckles garnished with roses, tongues to the sinister aii or. See No. 1, f.26.

Folio 82b.

1. The arms cut away.
2. PYRPOYNT. Argent, semée of mullets gules and a lyon rampant sable ; *quarterly with*, argent, six annulets 2. 2. 2 sable.
3. Gules, two bends argent.
4. Argent, two bars and in chief three mullets sable.
5. Argent, a lyon rampant gules, a bordure vair.
6. Argent, two bars sable, a baston gules.
7. Argent, on a cross azure five mullets or.
8. S. JOHN LECHE. Ermine, on a chief dancettée gules three coronets or.
9. Azure, a cross engrailed or.

Folio 83.

1. TRUSSELL (STAFF., added). Argent, fretty gules, bezanty at the joints.
2. BRUNE. Azure, a cross moline or ; *quarterly with*, ROKELE, gules, six lozenges conjoined 3 and 3 argent.
3.* Sable, billettée or, a gryphon segreant argent. [GRIFFIN.]
4. Argent, two bars gules, on a quarter of the second, a rose or, seeded gules.

5. THORPE (of ASHWELLTHORPE, NORFOLK added). Azure, three crescents argent. See page 174.
6. CHAMBERLEYN (q're. BRAY). Argent, a chevron between three eagles claws erased sable. As a banner.
7. LORD WAKE. Or, a fess gules, in chief three torteaux.
8. Gules, an eagle wings extended or, beak and legs azure, between three roses argent.
9. Vert, a lyon rampant argent.

Folio 83b.

1. Argent, a chevron sable between three greyhounds heads couped of the second, collared gules.
2.* Per fess sable and argent, a fess gules between three crosses cornished fleurtée in chief and as many plain crosses in base all counter-coloured of the first and second.
3. CHALANS. Gules, two bars between eight martlets 3. 2. 3 argent ; *quarterly with*, vair. See No. 4, f.75. (Challons of Devon.)
4. INGLOSSE, NORFOLK (substituted for Hyngylhouse). Gules, three bars gemelles or, on a quarter argent, five billets saltireways sable.
5. JERNINGHAM. Argent, three lozenge-shaped buckles, tongues to the sinister 2 and 1 gules.

folio 83ᵇ no 2

Thomas graynfelde

devenshyre

6. CRUMWELL (of TATSELE, added). Argent, a chief gules a bendlet sable; *quarterly with*, chequy or and gules, a chief ermine.

7. CORBETT. Barry (4) argent and sable, in chief and in base three crosses potent fitchée counter-coloured.

8. PYCWORRE. Gules, three picks 2 and 1 argent.

9. SIR SANCHET DABRITECOURT Kt of Garter (substituted for DABYSCORT). Ermine, three bars couped gules; sometimes blasoned, gules two bars and a bordure ermine.

Folio 84.

1.* THOMAS GRAYNFELDE. Gules, three organ rests 2 and 1 or.

2. SOWTHWELL. Argent, three cinquefoyles gules on each leaf an annulet or; *quarterly with*, ermine, two annulets interlaced sable.

3.* —— DEVENCHYRE. Gules, a fess ermine between three bundles of faggots argent, banded azure.

4. Or, three leopards faces sable, a baston azure.

5. Argent, on a fess between three crescents gules as many mullets or.

6. CONSTAINER (Constantine). Azure, six leopards faces 3. 2. 1 argent, on a canton or, a cross is indicated.

7. Or, fretty azure, on a chief gules, two annulets interlaced of the first.

folio 84 no 8

randacy

folio 84 b no 2

8.* Gules, three horses heads and necks 2 and 1 argent. ? HORSLEY.

9.* RANDACY. Sable, three fuseaux (spindles) 2 and 1 argent.

Folio 84b.

1. HARCORTH (HARCOURT, added). Gules, two bars or.

2.* Gules, a lyon passant ermine. [NERE-FORD.]

3. THI(R)KELD. Argent, a maunch gules. See No. 9, f.89b.

4. BROKESBY. Barry undée (6) sable and argent, on a quarter gules, a mullet or.

5. MESTEDE. Gules, a fess engrailed ermine between three mullets 2 and 1 or.

6. S. ———— PYLKYNGTUN. Argent, a cross patonce voided gules ; quarterly with. paly (6) argent and gules on a baston sable three mullets or.

7. THOMAS WESYNGHAM. Azure, a saltire and a chief or ; quarterly with, sable, a fess dancettée between three mullets argent.

8.* JONS. Ermine, three chess rooks 2 and 1 gules.

9. JOHN BOTTLER. Azure, a bend between six covered cups or.

Jonθ

Rynolδ Aske

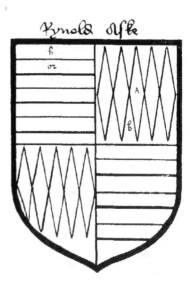

Hargrove

Folio 85.

1. RERYSBY. Gules, on a bend argent, three crosses patonce sable, a cinquefoyle or.

2. RAFFE BUTLER. Gules, two bars ermine.

3. WARTON. Argent, a chevron and in chief an annulet sable.

4. BOSSCHE. Ermine, on a chief crenellée gules three leopards faces or.

5. HARMAN (STAFORDSHERE, added). Argent, on a fess azure, three bucks heads cabossed or.

6.* RYNOLD ASKE. Azure, three bars or ; *quarterly with,* azure five fusils conjoined argent.

7.* HARGROVE. Argent, a gryphon segreant per fess engrailed gules and sable, beak and claws or.

8. BRETUN. Azure, a bend between six mullets or.

9. WALSCHE. Gules, three bars argent, on a quarter ermine five lozenges conjoined in bend or.

Folio 85b.

1. RODELL. Argent, three piles meeting in base gules, over all a bend sable.

2. HARRY NO(O)NE (of SHELFHANGER in NORFOLK, added). Or, a cross engrailed vert.

3. Sable, two bars argent, in chief three plates.

Ossebaron

Borceys

Trygonan

4. WELYE OF Ye Spycery (to HEN. 8, added).
Lozengy or and gules, a saltire counter compony
ermines and ermine. (? PEAKE.)

5. ROBERT BRENT. Gules, a wyvern statant,
tail nowed argent. See also pp. 80, 153.

6.* OSSEBARON. Argent, on a bend between
two tygers saliant sable, three fish naiant or.
See also No. 6, f.95b.

7. MERKENFELDE. Argent, on a bend sable
three bezants, a crescent for difference gules.

8. KOWLEY. Per bend crenellée sable and
argent.

9. GOLOFER. Barry undée (8) gules and
argent, on a bend sable three besauts.

Folio 86.

1.* BORCEYS. Vert, a fess gules, fretty or,
between three martlets argent.

2. WYKHAM. Ermine, a bordure gules.

3.* TRYGONAN (CORNWALL, added). Argent,
a chevron sable between three Cornish choughs
proper.

4.* THOMAS OKYN. Argent, two chevrons
vert, between three oak leaves proper.

5. LUCOMBE. Argent, a saltire sable, between four estoyles gules.

6.* DAMPORTE. Argent, a chevron between
three crosses crosslet fitchée sable.

7. T. STEVYNS. Gules, on a bend argent,
three leopards faces vert.

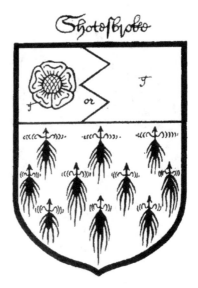

8.* AUDSELEY. Argent, a pair of lyons gambs saltireways erased gules; *quarterly with*, gules, three wallets 2 and 1 or, garnished azure. See page 259.

9. Sable, on a chief argent, three lozenges conjoined gules.

Folio 86b.

1. Gules, a bend between six escallops argent, a mullet of the first for difference.

2.* BRYGER. Argent, a chevron engrailed sable, between three crabs passant gules. See page 259.

3.* TREWART(H)E(N). Argent, a boar passant gules, tusked and unguled or.

4.* SHOTTESBROKE, BERKS. (substituted for SEUTYSBROKE). Ermine, on a chief per pale dancettée or and gules a rose of the last. See No. 3, f.16, and No. 2, f.44.

5. ROS OF KENDALL, WESTMORLAND (quartered by PARR, added). Or, three water bougets sable.

6.* WELYEM MOORE. Sable, three bears heads erased 2 and 1 argent, muzzled gules, on a quarter of the third, a crown or.

7. CHARTELEY (THONTELEY). Ermine, a maunch gules. The Coat of Calthorpe—ED.

8. JOHN MADLEY. Argent, on a chevron azure, three fleurs de lys or, a bordure engrailed sable.

Astyrfume

Bendyche

Chelden

9.* (M)ASTYRSUME. Ermine, on a chevron azure between three garbs or, a mullet for difference argent.

Folio 87.

1. S. TOMAS KERYELL. Or, two chevrons and a quarter gules.

2. CARDEMEW. Argent, on a chief sable, a lyon passant of the first.

3. CHAMPENEYS. Vert, a fess counter embattled or, between three trefoyles slipped ermine.

4. LORD FERREYS OF SHARTLEY. Vaire, or and gules. Ferrers of Chartley.

5.* BENDYCHE (ESSEX, CAMBR., added). Argent, on a chevron sable, between three rams heads erased azure, an escallop of the field. See also No. 8. f.94b.

6.* CHELDEN (SHELDON). Argent, on a bend gules, three sheldrakes of the field.

7. PORYER. Gules, three crescents argent. [Peryent.]

8. RAPE HAMMYS. Sable, on a fess or, between three cinquefoyles ermine, a crescent sable for difference.

9.* S. THOMAS FYNDERNE (DERB., added). Argent on a fess gules between three bears passant sable, muzzled of the second, as many plates. Rather Finbarne. See pages 121 and 262.

ff Thomas ffyndejrie

lovett

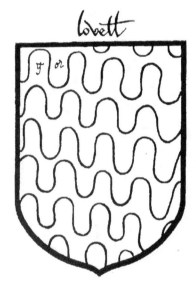

Wyclyfe

Folio 87b.

1.* LOVELL. Barry undée (8) gules and or.

2.* WYCLYFE (EBOR., added). Argent, five fusils conjoined in fess azure, between three Cornish choughs proper.

3.* KYNNYSMAN. Gules, three kine's (bulls) heads cabossed argent, horns or.

4.* WYLDSCHYRE (of HEYDON, ESSEX, added) Per chevron azure and argent, in chief five crosses pattée 3 and 2 or.

5.* THORPE (YORPE). Per pale vert and gules, three attires barways argent.

6. JOHN A. LYE (LEGH). Azure, two bars argent, on a bend gules, three crescents or.

7. JOHN ROTHYN. Paly (8) argent and gules. Also LLOYD.

8. CHEYNEY. Azure, a cross patonce or; *quarterly with*, gules, four fusils conjoined argent, each charged with an escallop sable.

9. HARPLEY. Burulee (12) or and argent, over all three chevroncls engrailed sable.

Folio 88.

1.* CLAXTON (written CALENTUN). Gules, on a fess between three hedgehogs passant argent, an ace of hearts of the first.

2. Bendy undée (8) sable and argent.

3. BEDWELL. Per saltire ermines and lozengy or and gules.

4. Ermine, a fess vaire or and gules.

5.* WELYE HORE. Argent, a stags head cabossed or, a label (3) gules.

6. BEYVYS. Chequy or and gules, a quarter ermine.

7. CAMELL. Azure, a camel passant argent : *quarterly with*, lozengy azure and argent.

8. DAN(I)ELL. Gules, a bend azure (*sic*), a bordure engrailed or, a martlet of the last for difference.

9. RYCHARD GAYNYS. Sable, a fess or between three cinquefoyles pierced argent.

Folio 88b.

1.* OLDEHALL (NORFF., added). Gules, a lyon rampant ermine. See No. 2, f.70b.

2. BYTTERLEY. Or, a fess gules and in chief three torteaux ; *quarterly with*, argent, on a bend gules three owls of the first.

3. PURSALL. Gules, two bars undée argent, over all on a bend sable three boars heads couped of the second ; *quarterly with*, bendy (8) argent and azure, on a quarter sable a lyon passant or.

4. CULPEPER (KENT, SUSSEX, added). Argent a bend engrailed gules, a label (3) azure.

5.* Sr. JOHN DE HARLYNG (of EAST HARLING IN NORFF., added). Argent, a unicorn saliant sable.

6. DAWBENEY. Gules, four fusils in fess argent.

7. T. VERNUN. Argent, fretty sable and a canton ermine.

8. S. T. RATCLAFFE. Argent, on a bend engrailed sable, a fleur de lys of the first.

9. KYRKEBY. Argent, two bars gules, on a quarter of the second, a cross moline or.

Folio 89.

1. RYTHER (EBOR., added). Azure, three crescents 2 and 1 argent ; *quarterly with*, gules, a lyon rampant argent.

2.* Argent, on a cross patonce gules, five escallops or.

3. BERKELEY. Gules, crusily pattée, a chevron and a bordure all argent.

4. ASCHELEY. Azure, on a pale engrailed argent, three crescents sable.

5. RAFFE BOSTOKE. Argent, a fess humettée sable.

Sr John de Hasþyng

folio 89 no 2

Chypman

6. S. Edmond Thorpe. Azure, three crescents 2 and 1 argent ; *quarterly with*, Baynard, sable, a fess between two chevrons or.

7. Stowell. Gules, a cross of nine lozenges argent ; *quarterly with*, bendy (6) azure and argent.

8. S. ―――― Burnell. Argent, a lyon rampant sable, crowned or, a bordure azure ; *quarterly with*, Botetourt, or, a saltire engrailed sable.

9. Thomas Blansson. Per saltire gules and azure, a chief or lozengy—imperfect.

Folio 89b.

1. Pomys. Argent, three bars azure, a bordure gules bezantée.

2.* Chypman (? Shypman, added). Sable, two lyons passant counterpassant between as many chevronels all argent.

3. Keyley. Argent, on a fess between three leopards faces sable, a mullet of the first.

4. Babthorpe. Gules, fretty argent, a quarter of Valence. See No. 1, f.73.

5. Babthorpe. Sable, seven plates between two chevronels, all enclosed by three lozenges two and one all argent.

Talbot

John Guyn

Thornham

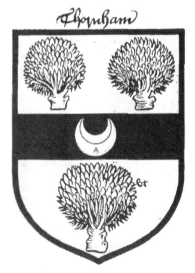

6. BLONDELL. Per pale ermine and sable, a chevron engrailed counter-coloured.

7.* TALBOT. Gules, a lyon rampant and a bordure engrailed or.

8. THORNBUR(G)H. Ermine, fretty gules, a chief of the last.

9. THYLKYLDE. Argent, a maunch gules. As on page 256.

Folio 90.

1.* JOHN GUYN. Azure, a fess gules (*sic*) between three lambs passant argent.

2. WYLLYNGHAM. Ermine, on a chevron sable an annulet argent for difference.

3.* THORNHAM. Argent, on a fess sable between three thorn bushes proper, an annulet of the first for difference.

4.* WELYE USCHER. Argent, three lyons gambs erect 2 and 1 sable.

5.* BOKELOND. Argent, a fess gules, over all two dolphins hauriant counter-hauriant or, conjoined ermine. See illustration.

6. WESYNGTUN. Gules, on a fess argent three mullets or, a label (3) of the second.

7. TRACYE. Or, two bends gules.

8.* STANDEN. Argent, an eagle close sable, beak and legs or, a bordure engrailed of the second.

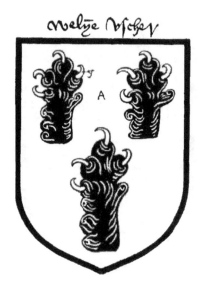

9. PYKYRKE. Sable, a cross patonce or, a bordure engrailed argent.

Folio 90b.

1. JOHN CAYLEY (NORFF., added). Per cross argent and sable, on a bend gules three mullets of the first, a label (3) silver.

2. HEWTUN (Luton). Vert, a double headed eagle displayed or, beaked and membered gules.

3. BOYS. Ermine, a cross sable.

4. GRESSELEY. Vaire, argent and gules, a label (3) sable, a bordure of the last bezantée.

5. CAUNFELDE. Argent, fretty sable. CANFIELD.

6. REDEMER. Sable, a bend argent, between six fleurs de lys or.

7. Per saltire argent and sable, in chief a cross moline of the second. See No. 7, f.35.

8. JOHN CL(I)VE. Argent, on a bend cotised sable, three mullets of the first.

9.* BELLYNGHAM. Gules, fretty argent, on a quarter of the first (*sic*) a lyon rampant of the second (*sic*), the tinctures are probably reversed in the painting. See page 268.

Folio 91.

1. MONYNTON. Argent, on a bend sable three mullets or.

Bellyngham

Stoke

Hamtun

2.* STOKE. Azure, fretty argent, on a quarter of the first (sic) a boars head barways erased of the second (sic), the tinctures are probably reversed in the painting.

3. Sable, three owls 2 and 1 argent.

4. COLLYNG. Azure, a gryphon saliant or, crowned argent, beak and claws gules.

5.* HAM(P)TUN. Gules, on a fess argent, a mullet sable ; quarterly with, argent, three bulls passant 2 and 1 sable.

6.* REDLEY. Gules, on a chevron between three kingfishers argent, speckled sable, beaks and legs or, a crescent of the last.

7. SMERES. Sable, three chevronels argent between as many mullets 2 and 1 or.

8. MYSGRAUE (MUSGRAVE of WESTMORLAND, added). Azure, six annulets 3. 2. 1 or, a martlet for difference argent.

9. CHARYLTUN. Or, a chevron engrailed sable, between three bucks heads cabossed vert, a bordure of the last.

Folio 91b.

1. RESTWODE. Per saltire ermine and gules.

2.* STONLYNG. Gules, a saltire between four lyons rampant argent, a label (3) of the last.

3. PARTRYCH. Chequy sable and argent, a bend gules.

4.* GARNYS (SUFF., added). Argent, a chevron azure, between three escallops sable.

5. HUSE (Hussey). Ermine, three bars gules.

6. CURTEYSE. Argent, a chevron sable between three bulls heads cabossed gules ; *quarterly with*, gules, a chevron vair, a chief or.

7. PET LEYTH (Cheshire, added). Gules, a cross engrailed argent. See No. 2, f.80b.

8. WALDEN. Argent, three leopards faces 2 and 1 sable.

9. ALEN LEMSTER. Argent, on a fess between three crescents gules, as many mullets or.

Folio 92.

1. HYNKPEN (INKPEN, added). Chequy argent and sable, a chief or ; *quarterly with*, gules, two bars gemelles or, a chief invected ermine.

2. GANFELDE. Or, three bars gules and a quarter ermine, over all a baston sable.

3. LECHEFORDE. Sable, a chevron between three leopards faces argent.

4. GOODBOWE. Azure, two bows crossed saltireways stringed or.

5. GOODBOWE. No. 4 within a bordure gules bezantée.

6. S. RYCHARD VARNON. Argent, fretty sable, a quarter gules ; *quarterly with*, barry (6) or and azure.

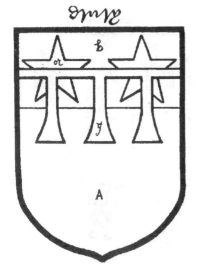

7. RYCHARD VERNON. Argent, fretty sable, bezantée at the joints, on a quarter gules a martlet or ; *quarterly with*, barry (6) argent and azure a bordure sable bezantée.

8. FOWKE VERNON. Argent, fretty sable bezantée at the joints, a quarter gules, over all a label (3) or.

9. WELYE VERNON. Argent, fretty sable, bezantée at the joints, a quarter gules, a bordure engrailed or ; *impaled with*, PYPE of DERB., azure, crusily and two pipes chevronwise or. See Brydge's Collins' peerage, vol. 7, page 400.

Folio 92b.

1. S. RYCHARD VERNON. Grand quarterly I. and IV. ; argent, fretty sable, a quarter gules ; *quarterly with*, or, a lyon rampant sable. II. and III. ; barry (6) or and azure ; *quarterly with*, azure, three lyons passant gardant argent.

2.* WARDE. Argent, a chevron between three wolves heads erased sable.

3. S. WELYE SELYNGER. Azure, fretty argent, on a chief or a mullet of the first.

4. SPEKOT (Speccot). Ermine, three lozenges conjoined in fess sable, on the second a fleur de lys argent.

5.* OSWALSTER. Argent, a lyon rampant gules, over all a bendlet sable.

Breton

Turbut

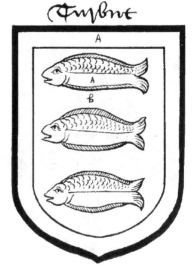

goodhande

6.* DRURY (NORFF., SUFF., added). Argent, on a chief azure, two mullets or, a label (3) gules.

7. HALSALLE. Argent, three dragons heads erased azure langued gules ; *quarterly with*, gules, three unicorns heads erased or. See next page.

8. DEN(N)Y. Gules, crusily and a saltire or.

9. CHALON. Gules, two bars or.

Folio 93.

1. Argent, two bars sable, each charged with three escallops of the field.

2.* BRETON. Argent, a lyon rampant sable ; *quarterly with*, sable, a mullet argent.

3.* TURBUT. Azure, three turbot naiant in pale argent, a bordure of the last.

4. TYLLINGIAM. Argent, on a bend gules three owls of the first. TILLINGTON.

5. SKVPTUN. Azure, on a chief of two indents argent, a lyon rampant of the first.

6. SERCHEDEN. Gules, a saltire sable (*sic*, usually silver) between four escallops argent.

7. FYFHYDE. Ermine, on a bend engrailed azure three cinquefoyles or.

8.* GOODHANDE. Argent, a chevron parted countercompony between three dexter hands aversant sable. The chevron imperfect.

Stevyn Dyer

halsale

Gyfferde

9.* STEVYN DYER. Sable, three goats passant 2 and 1 argent.

Folio 93b.

1. PARKER. Gules, three chevronels argent.

2.* HALSALE. Argent, three dragons heads erased 2 and 1 azure. See preceding page.

3.* GYFFERDE. Gules, three lyons passant in pale argent.

4. DE RANSTON. Gules, two bars argent, in chief a lyon passant gardant or. DENESTON or DENARDESTON.

5. (? WATERTON, added). Barry (6) argent and gules, three crescents 2 and 1 or.

6. BABTHORPE. Sable, a chevron or between three crescents ermine.

7. VEUER (WEAVER). Sable, two bars, the upper humettée argent, in dexter chief point a garb or, a label (3) of the last. Probably quartered by Stanley of Weaver. See page 189.

8. S. HARYNGTON. Sable, fretty argent; *quarterly with*, argent a cross patonce sable.

9.* WELYE DE HYRYSTUN. Gules, three kingfishers beaked and legged or, a bordure engrailed argent.

Watt de hyryytun

Taylboys

Folio 94.

1. MEWINS (Mewys). Paly (8) or and azure, on a chief gules three crosses pattée of the first.

2. RAFFE POOLLE. Argent, a chevron between three crescents gules.

3. MELBORNE. Argent, a crescent and a bordure sable.

4.* TAYLBOYS (Linc., added). Gules, a saltire argent, on a chief of the second three escallops of the first. The tinctures are probably reversed in the painting.

5. Gules, a lyon rampant (tail inturned) within a double tressure flory all argent.

6.* Argent, three wolves heads erased sable, langued gules. [Belson.]

7.* Argent, crusily or (*sic*) a lyon rampant queue fourcheé renowée gules, crowned of the second. See page 274.

8. Or, on a fess between three fleurs de lys gules, two like fleurs de lys argent.

9. Gules, two bars vair.

Folio 94b.

1. LUTTERELL. Azure, a bend between six martlets 3 and 3 argent. See also No. 5, f.98b.

2. Argent, a lyon rampant within a bordure engrailed all gules.

folio 94 no 6

folio 94 no 7

f welye Talbot

Tomas Stone

3.* S. WELYE TALBOT. Argent, a chevron between three talbots passant sable, a label (3) gules.

4.* TOMAS STONE. Sable, a chevron engrailed or between three flint stones argent.

5.* JOHN DALALYNDE. Gules, three bucks heads couped argent.

6.* HETUN. Argent, on a saltire azure five water bougets or, a bordure gules.

7.* S. JOHN HOLLOND. Azure, a lyon rampant gardant argent.

8.* BENDYCHE (NORFOLK, added). Sable, a cross between four lyons rampant or. See also No. 5, f.87.

9. DYYF (Dyffe). Sable, a fess between three leopards faces argent.

Folio 95.

1. DENYS. Argent, a chevron sable between three mullets gules.

2. BROKE (CHESHIRE, added). Gules, a cross engrailed per pale gules and sable.

3. Argent, on a chevron sable five mullets of the field.

4. Gules, the Navarrese net (?) or ; *quarterly with*, lozengy azure and or.

5. JOHN FLORRE. Azure, three fleurs de lys or, a crescent argent.

John dalabyndo

hetmd

f John hollond

Bendyche

6.* WOLFE. Sable, a chevron gules (sic) between three wolves heads erased argent. Reversed on page 160.

7. S. (W.) CALTHORP (NORFF., added). Chequy or and azure, a fess ermine.

8. HOLCAM. Azure, two bars undée ermine.

9. S. JOHN GRENDOR. Or, a fess between six crosses crosslet gules.

Folio 95b.

1.* KEBELL. Per fess——in chief; barry undée (6) argent and sable, on a quarter gules a crescent or; dimidiated in base with, gules, a chevron ermine between three double headed eagles displayed or.

2.* LANGTON. Azure, a double headed eagle displayed or, over all a riband sable.

3. MALARY. Or, a lyon rampant queue fourchée gules.

4. NEVELL (of HOLT, LEIC., added). Gules, a saltire ermine (5 spots).

5.* PLESYNGTON (EBOR., added, rightly LANC). Azure, a cross fleurtée between four martlets argent.

6.* Argent, three rodents (?) embelif 2 and 1 sable. [Osborne.] See also No. 6, f.85b, and No. 8, f.103b.

7. FLOURE (NORTHT., added). Sable, a cinquefoyle pierced ermine.

plesyngton

folio 95[b] no6

8. PERCY. Argent, a cross patonce gules ; *quarterly with*, argent, a lyon rampant azure.

9. BROWNE (JOHN, of Essex, late of Wiroll) ? WYRRALL in Cheshire. Azure, a chevron between three escallops or.

Folio 96.

1. CHEVELEY. Gules, a chevron argent, between in chief two boars heads erased barwise sable (*sic*), tusked argent, an apple (? acorn) in mouth or, and in base a trefoyle slipped azure (*sic*).

2. CLOWNELLE. Argent, two chevrons sable, each charged with five nails erect or ; *quarterly with*, ermine, on a chief azure three lyons rampant or. CLOVELLY and CLONVYLE.

3. CRYSTOFER SELYYOKE. Or, three oak leaves erect 2 and 1 azure ; *quarterly with*, azure, three besants 2 and 1 ; all within a bordure sable.

4.* LANGRYCHE. Gules, a lyon rampant or, in chief a fantastic gryllus, viz. :—two dragons' heads and necks issuant from a shell all or ; *quarterly with*, argent, six billets 3. 2. 1 sable. See illustration.

5. AYLMER. Argent, on a fess gules between six annulets sable, three mullets or ; *impaling*, argent, on a cross engrailed sable between four sea-aylets proper, beaks and legs gules, five besants.

langryche

Jhon Bounteyn

Piers Griffith

Edward à pris

6.* JHON BOUNTEYN. Per cross argent and sable, in the first the dexter half and in the fourth the sinister half of a double headed eagle per pale displayed of the second, in the second and third, a goat saliant of the first horned or; over all a label (3) of the last.

7. COLFOX. Argent, a chevron between three fox heads erased sable, a crescent for difference of the first.

8. BRYMYNGHAM. Per pale dancettée or and gules, a bordure azure, entoyre of mullets of the first, over all a baston sinister sable.

9. Imperfect.

Folio 96b.

1. PYERS GRIFFITH. Argent, a gryphon segreant sable.

2.* PIERS GRIFFITH. Gules, three horses heads and necks erect and couped argent.

3.* EDWARD À PRIS. Azure, three owls 2 and 1 argent.

4. JOHAN DULLON, of Devonshiere (DILLON). Argent, semée of estoyles and a lyon rampant between in chief two crescents all gules, a fess azure.

5.* Or, on a chevron sable two headless serpents of the first.

folio 96b no 5

folio 96b no 7

6. Argent, on a bend sable three gryphons heads erased in bend or.

7.* Argent, a lyon rampant queue fourchée gules. [Mallory.]

8. Quarterly per pale and per chevron reversed argent and azure, a bend sable.

9. Argent, a chevron quarterly purpure and azure, between three talbots heads erased sable.

Folio 97.

1. MAYST. LATHELL. Quarterly. (1); sable, a fess between in chief three staves erect, on the point of each, a man's head in profile proper, and in base a tun barways all argent. (2 and 3); gules, on a chevron or between three crescents argent, as many roses of the first. (4); paly (6) argent and azure, on a bend sable three pheons of the first.

2. JOHN HAYS OF DEVONSHYRE. Azure, on a pale or three bulls heads couped of the first.

3. ASHBY (ASSABY). Azure, a chevron or, between three double headed eagles displayed argent; impaling PEYTON, sable, a cross engrailed or; quarterly with, sable, a bear saliant argent, muzzled gules.

4. S. JAMES TERELL. Argent, two chevronels azure, a bordure engrailed gules, a martlet of the first for difference.

5. RYCHARD HYLL, BYSSCHYP LONDON (consecrated 1489, added). Azure, a chevron argent between three goats heads of the second, erased or, horns and beard of the last.

6. GRENEFELD. Sable, on a bend argent three (shovellers ?) of the first, beak and feet or; quarterly with, argent, a chevron between three leopards faces sable.

7. (SHERLEY, 2d coat, i.e. of augmentation). Azure, a lyon rampant or crowned gules; quarterly with, SHIRLEY, paly (6) or and azure, a quarter ermine.

8. BELLYNGHAM. Quarterly. (1); or, a bugle horn vert, stringed gules. (2); argent, on a cross engrailed gules, an annulet or. (3); argent, three bendlets gules, on a quarter vert, a lyon passant argent. (4); gules, a fess engrailed ermine between three mullets pierced or.

9. Gules, an eagle displayed argent, membered or; quarterly with, gules, a fess or between three saltorelles argent; on an escocheon of pretence, gules three bendlets argent.

Folio 97b.

1. S. EDWARD RAWLE. Argent, crusily sable and a cross moline gules; impaling GRENE, azure, three bucks trippant or.

my lord dalaweye

hary Spenser

S. dany Jnew

2. S. RAFE VERNEY, lord maior of Lond. Azure, on a cross argent five mullets or (sic); *impaling* argent, a chevron between three tails fourchée sable.

3. BROWNING OF DORSETERSHERE. Argent, three bars wavy azure; *quarterly with*, sable fretty or.

4. S. GYLBERD TALBOTE. Quarterly of six. (1); azure, a lyon rampant and a bordure or. (2); gules, a lyon rampant and a bordure engrailed or. (3); gules, on a saltire argent a martlet for difference of the first. (4); argent, a bend between six martlets gules. (5); or, fretty gules. (6); argent, two lyons passant in pale gules. *Impaled with*, sable, a chevron between three gryphons heads erased argent.

5.* MY LORD DALAWERE. Gules, crusily fitchée and a lyon rampant argent; *quarterly with*, azure, three leopards faces reversed jessant de lys or.

6.* HARRY SPENSER. Azure, three wyverns heads erased ermine.

7. S. JOHN HALWYN (ALWYN *alias* HALYWELL). Or, on a bend sable three goats passant argent, horned and unguled of the first; *quarterly with*, argent, on a chevron sable three besants. ▶

8.* S. DAVY OWEN. Gules, a chevron sable (*sic*) between three closed helmets argent, garnished or, a baston sinister of the last. See also No. 7, f.104*b*.

9. S. WELYE BRANDON. Barry (10) argent and gules, over all a lyon rampant or, crowned of the second.

Folio 98.

1. S. THOMAS MYLBURN. Gules, a chevron between three escallops argent.

2. S. JOHN TROBELFELDE (TURBERVILE, added). Argent, a lyon rampant gules crowned or.

3. S. RYS AP THOMAS (Kt. of the Garter, added). Argent, a chevron sable between three Cornish choughs proper.

4. S. ROGER TOUNSEND, Justic at Weset (Westm). Azure, a chevron ermine between three escallops argent; *quarterly with*, HAVILE, gules, a chevron between three fleurs de lys or.

5. S. JOHN BROWNE. Azure, a chevron between three escallops or, a bordure engrailed gules.

6. S. JOHN FYNKELL. Sable, a fess indented between three mullets argent.

7. S. WELYE HODY, Baron of ye cheker. Gules, a fess between six crosses crosslet argent.

8. S. JOHN SYLYARD, Justis. Argent, a chevron gules between three pheons reversed sable; *quarterly with*, gules, a chevron or, between three lyons rampant argent.

9. S. WELYE STONER (OXON., added). Quarterly. 1 and 4; azure, two bars dancettée or and a chief argent. (2); azure, six lyoncelles rampant 3 and 3, argent, on a quarter or, a mullet gules. (3); or, three torteaux 2.1.

Folio 98b.

1. S. JOHN MOUSGRAVE (WESTMORLAND, added). Azure, six annulets 3.2.1 or.

2.* S. RYCHARD FYCHLEWYS (FITZ LEWIS) of HORNDON in ESSEX, added. Sable, a chevron between three trefoyles slipped argent.

3. S. THOMAS HANSERD (LINC., added). Gules three mullets argent.

4. S. WELYE LEWCY. Imperfect.

5. S. HEW LUTTERELL (DEVONSH. NORFF., added). Azure, a bend between six martlets argent. As No. 1, f.94*b*.

6.* S. WELYE BROWNE. Argent, a chevron between three cranes passant gules.

7. S. GYLBERD DEBNAM (Suff., added). Sable, a bend between three crescents or; *quarterly with*, or, crusily and a chevron gules. See also page 220.

2 Q

Meyners

moyle

Yelnerton

8. S. NYCOLAS BYLSDON. Azure, two gemelles in bend or, in chief a gryphons head erased of the second.

9. S. THOMAS STAFFORD. Or, a chevron gules, a quarter ermine, a crescent of the first for difference.

Folio 99.

1. APPULBY. Argent, a fess between six crosses pattée fitchée sable, a crescent or, for difference.

2. S. JORGE NEVELL. Gules, a saltire argent, a baston sinister sable.

3. S. RAFFE SHYRLE(Y) (DERB., added). Paly (6) or and azure, a quarter ermine.

4. S. JOHN HODYLSTON (qy. Cambridgeshire, added). Gules, fretty argent.

5. S. SAMSON NORTON. Azure, three swords in triangle handles meeting in the fess point proper grip gules.

6.* MEYNERS (DERB., added). Sable, an eagle displayed or ; *quarterly with,* ermine a bend fusily gules.

7. WESTE. Argent, a chevron between three crescents ermines ; *quarterly with,* per cross ermine and or.

8. PAYNELL. Argent, two chevrons gules.

9.* MOYLE, Cornwall (added). Sable, a moyle passant proper, a mullet pierced or.

Folio 99b.

1.* Yelverton (Norf., added). Argent, three lyons rampant 2 and 1 and a chief gules, a mullet for difference of the first.

2. S. Amys Poulet, Knyght. Quarterly. (1); sable, three swords pileways points to the base argent. (2); azure on a chief argent, a demy lyon rampant issuant gules. (3); Azure, six mascles, three and three argent, Credy. (4); Argent, a chevron gules between three trees proper. An escocheon of pretence — argent, a fess between three cinquefoyles pierced gules.

3. Thomas Bourton (Leic., added). Argent, a chevron sable between three owls of the second, crowned and membered or.

4. S. Thomas Bryan (added). Argent, three piles meeting in base vert, a bordure azure bezantée.

5.* Master Wyseman (Essex, added). Sable a chevron ermine, between three cronels argent.

6.* Master Overey. Azure, a chevron ermine between three gauntlets aversant or.

7. Sir T. Leyton. Quarterly. (1); azure, a lyon rampant or. (2); or, a lyon rampant gules, a bordure engrailed azure. (3); quarterly per fess of two indents gules and or, a lyon passant gardant argent. (4); gules, six pears 3. 2. 1 pendant slipped or. (5); as 3. (6); argent, three boars heads couped 2 and 1 barways sable.

8. T. Burneby. Barry (4) argent and gules, in chief a lyon passant gardant of the second; quarterly with, ermine, on a chief azure two mullets or, pierced gules.

9. Pympe. Barry (6) argent and gules, a chief vair; impaling Whetley, per fess azure and argent, a pale counter-coloured; three lyons rampant gardant 2 and 1 of the second.

Folio 100.

1. Brygis (Bruges, added). Quarterly. (1 and 4); argent, on a cross sable, a leopards face or. (2); gules, on a chevron argent three bars sable, Throgmorton. (3); sable, a chevron argent between three pine cones, slipped vert (sic).

2. S. Rychard Fitz Lewis. Sable, a chevron between three trefoyles slipped argent (as No. 2, f.98b; quarterly with, azure, crusily or, a cross argent.

3. S. Robert of Browhtton. Argent, a chevron gules between three mullets of the second, pierced sable.

4. Alesaundyr Cresner (of Norff., added). Argent, on a bend engrailed sable, three crosses crosslet fitchée or; quarterly with, azure, florettée argent — an escocheon of pretence, vaire gules and or, a bordure azure, entoyre of horse shoes argent.

Roggey Button

S Rychard Ludlow

leoyd Scotey

5. WOTTON. Gules, a chevron argent between in chief two crosses crosslet and in base an annulet or.

6. WYNTER (BECKHAM, NORFF., added). Chequy or and sable, a fess argent.

7. BRAMPTON (of Brampton and Blow Norton in Norff., added). Gules, a saltire between four crosses crosslet fitchée argent.

8. ROSSELL. Azure, two chevrons or, between three roses 2 and 1 argent.

9.* ROGGER BUTTON. Per bend or and gules, a lyon rampant sable.

Folio 100b.

1.* S. RYCHARD LUDLOWE (SALOP, added). Or, a lyon rampant queue fourchée renowée sable, vulned gules.

2. MAST. LEE OF STOCKWELL (SURREY, added). Gules, a cross and a bordure both engrailed argent;— *impaling*; azure, three lozenges 2 and 1 or; *quarterly with*, argent, on a chief gules a crescent of the first.

3. S. JOHN BOWSER. Argent, a cross engrailed gules, between four water bougets sable ; *quarterly with* CHICHELE, gules, billettée or and a fess argent. *Impaled with* ; or, a chevron between three cinquefoyles gules, *quarterly with*, gules, on a chief dancettée argent three escallops sable.

folio 101 no 3

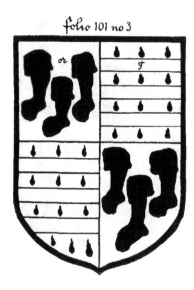

Poffce

4. S. Roger Wentworth (Ebor., added).
Per fess, in chief (1) sable a chevron between
three leopards faces or ; and in base (2). per
cross argent and gules, in the second and third
a fret or, over all on a bend sable three mullets
of the first. *Impaled with*, Howard, gules, on
a bend between six crosses crosslet fitchée
argent, an ermine spot.

5. Le(ve)nthorp (Hertf., added). Argent,
on a bend cotised gules two bars sable, a crescent
of the last for difference.

6. Hogyngton. Argent, a chevron azure,
on a chief or, three crosses formée of the second.

7. Symkyn Hoogan. Argent, on a fess
azure, between three crosses formée sable, as
many escallops or.

8. Davers of Bedfordshyre. Quarterly.
(1) ; gules, a lyon rampant or. (2) ; argent, on
a cross fleurté azure five fleurs de lys or. (3) ;
gules, a chevron between three mullets or. (4) ;
sable, a fess undée argent between six martlets
gules (*sic*).

9. Welye Haryett. Per pale ermines and
ermine, three crescents counter-coloured.

Folio 101.

1. Seynt Chadde (now the arms of the see
of Lichfield and Coventry, added by Le Neve).

Per pale gules and argent, a cross potent and
quadrate in the centre, per pale of the second
and or, between four crosses formée of the second
and third.

2.* Lloyd. Gules, on a fess or between
three eagles displayed sable (*sic*) a crescent for
difference of the last ; *impaling* Sooter, as the
illustration. The supposition that the impalement may be a dimidiation may lead to its solution.

3.* Or, three hose 2 and 1 sable ; *quarterly
with*, argent, guttée de poix, three bars gules.

4. Maystr. Fysse of Devenchyr. Sable,
three battle-axes 2 and 1 argent ; *quarterly with*,
argent, guttée de sang, a cross engrailed gules,
over all an annulet for difference or. See Denys,
page 293.

5. S. Robert Senkleer. Argent, crusily
and three fleurs de lys 2 and 1 sable.

6.* Rosshe. Purpure, on a fess or, between
three rushing horses argent, as many hurts.

7. Wotton of Boughton, Kent. Argent, a
saltire engrailed sable ; *quarterly with*, argent,
on a chief sable a lyon passant to the sinister
argent.

8. Belknap. Azure, between two bendlets
argent, three eaglets displayed the second,
membered gules.

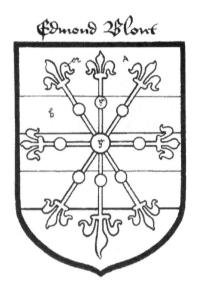

Edmond Blont

welye stede

John Reed

9.* EDMOND BLONT.   Argent, two bars azure, an escarboucle or, garnished gules.

Folio 101b.

1.* WELYE STEDE.   Sable, two lyons passant in pale argent, between as many flaunches of the second, each charged with a fess azure.

2. Azure, on a chevron gules (*sic*), between three lucies hauriant argent crowned or, as many roses of the third, seeded of the fourth.,

3. S. JOHN LAKYN (LACON, SALOP, added). Quarterly. (1) ; per cross and per fess indented argent and azure. (2) ; argent, a bend cotised azure, on a canton sable a lyon passant or. (3) ; or, a bend cotised sable. (4) ; gules, a fess undée of three sable (*sic*) issuant therefrom two conies heads and necks or.

4.* JOHN REED (Proctor, *added*).   Azure, a gryphon passant or ; *quarterly with*, or, three arquebus gules, cross-bows vert—sable.

5. WELYE LAKYN (LACON, SALOP, added). per cross and per fess indented argent and azure, in chief a falcon or ; *quarterly with*, argent, a bend cotised azure, on a canton sable a lyon passant or.

6.* RODNEY (SOMERSET, added).   Or, three eagles displayed purpure. See No. 4, f.79b.

7.* S. JOHN SEYMORE.   Gules, a pair of wings erect or.

Rodney

S John Seymore

8. SEWARD. Argent, a chevron ermine between three escallops sable.

9. VOWELL (DEVON, added). Gules, three
false escocheons argent, each charged with a
cinquefoyle pierced azure. See FOWELL.

Folio 102.

1.* FANLEROY (FAUNTLEROY, added). Azure,
three womens busts argent, crined or.

2. WALSH. Argent, three bars gules.

3.* DRYLAND. Vert, a chevron purpure (sic)
between three mushrooms slipped argent. See
page 288.

4. DENYS (DENES). Argent, on a chevron
sable between three mullets gules, a rose or.

5. THOMAS HYLLYSLAY. Argent, on a bend
cotised sable three eagles displayed argent, a
mullet pierced of the last.

6. THOMAS DYNGGELEY. Argent, a fess
sable, in chief a mullet pierced of the second,
between two pellets ; *quarterly with*, gules, three
lyons rampant or.

7.* WELYE BRYTHE. Argent, a saltire engrailed sable between four brit naiant of the
last. See page 288.

8. S. THOMAS DANVERS. Argent, on a bend
gules three martlets vert (sic), usually or.

9. RYCHARD FOWLER. *Per fess—in chief;*
ermine, on a quarter gules, a martlet with an
owls face argent ; *dimidiated in base with*,
argent, two bars gules, on a chief or, a lyon passant gardant azure.

ffanleroy

Folio 102*b.*

1. S. WAT MAYFELDE. Argent, a cross engrailed sable between four martlets of the
second ; *quarterly with*, argent, on a bend gules
four lozenges or.

2. CATERMAYN (QUARTERMAIN). Gules, a
fess azure between " quatre mains " sinister
aversant or.

3. Ermine, on a bend or three chevrons gules.

4.* FYLLYFE BYFLYTE OF BEKELS OF SOMER-
SETSHYRE. Quarterly. I. paly of threecoats ;
(1) ; azure, two swords saltireways points to the
base proper, between four fleurs de lys or. (2) ;
gules, a chevron between three hawks lures or.
(3) ; possibly an impalement, argent, a chevron
azure, on a chief of the second, two mullets
pierced of the first. II. ; sable, a lyon rampant
argent within two equilateral triangles interlaced
or, in each angle a torteau, all between three
spear heads 2 and 1 gules (*sic*). III. ; argent,
on waves azure and of the first, a bird silver
beaked gules, resting his sinister claw on a fish
naiant and holding in his dexter claw a bird(?)
all proper, a chief per fess sable and argent, the
upper charged with three hives (?) the lower
with as many trefoyles truncked, all or. IV. ;
gules, a chevron ermine between three combs
or ; the whole within a bordure also ermine.
See No. 2, f.24, and No. 1, f.49*b*.

5.* THE ABBOT OF HABYNGTON (ABYNGDON ABBOT, added). Lozengy azure and argent, on a chief or three lilies proper slipped vert.

6. S. HOLYUER (OLIVER) BORDET (BURDET, added). Azure, two bars or, each charged with three martlets of the first. See No. 2, f.36.

7. THOMAS PLYYTE OF SHROPSHYRE. Argent a chevron gules between three bugle horns of the second, garnished or, stringed sable.

8. JOHN TOMSON. Gules, a cross engrailed or, a mullet of the last.

9. JOHN TOMSON OF ETAVIL. Sable, on a chevron between three (lucies?) heads barwise erased argent, as many mullets of 12 points or (sic).

Fotio 103.

1. S. JOORG SUTTON. Argent, a chevron between three crosses flory sable ; *quarterly with*, argent, a chevron between three bugle horns stringed sable.

2* RYCHARD SUTTON. Argent, a chevron between three crosses flory sable ; *impaled with*, argent, on a chief gules a mullet of the first.

3.* Quarterly. (1) ; ermine fretty gules, on a chief of the second a crescent argent. (2) ; argent, a fess between six crosses crosslet fitchée sable. (3) ; sable, a chevron between three bulls heads erased argent, an annulet sable for difference. (4) ; ermine, on a fess gules a fleurs de lys or.

John Sibell of Kent

John Covert

Welye Huntley

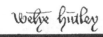

' 4. JOHN STOKWOOD, salter. Argent, on a cross sable five besants.

5.* JOHN SIBELL OF KENT. Argent, a tyger gules and mirror or.

6.* JOHN COVERT OF SOWSEX. Gules, on a fess ermine between three martlets or, an annulet sable.

7. COMENES (COMYNS, added). Azure, three garbs argent, eared or ; *quarterly with*, DYNGGE-LEY, argent, a fess sable and in chief a mullet pierced of the second, between two pellets. As No. 6, f.192.

8. FOXCOTTES. Argent, on a bend engrailed azure three plain crosses argent ; *quarterly with*, BRYTONS, gules, five escallops 2. 2. 1 or.

9. STOKES. Quarterly. (1) ; gules, a lyon rampant regardant argent, queue fourchée ermine. (2 and 3) ; sable, two lyons passant gardant in pale argent [BROCAS]. (4) ; gules, a lyon rampant queue fourchée or.

Folio 103b.

1.* WELYE HUNTLEY. Argent, on a chevron between three bucks heads erased sable, as many bugle horns gules (*sic*) stringed argent.

t. 2.* S. GYLLAM DE LA REVERS. Gules, three swords erect points to the base, 2 and 1 argent, in chief as many annulets 2 and 1 or ; *impaling*, gules, four fusils conjoined argent, each charged with an escallop sable.

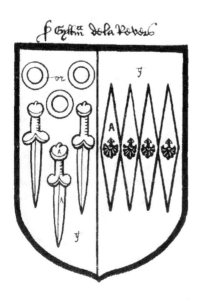

3. S. RYCHARD PODSAY (PUDSAY, added). Vert, on a chevron between three mullets pierced or, a crescent gules.

4. JOHN BUTLER ye elder. Gules, a fess counter compony or and sable, between six lozenges of the third, each charged with a cross crosslet argent; *quarterly with* KILPEC, argent, a sword in bend, point in the dexter chief sable.

5. ROGER WENTWORTH. Sable, a chevron between three leopards faces or, an annulet for difference; impaling three coats, viz., (1); HOWARD. Gules, on a bend between six crosses crosslet fitchée argent, an ermine spot as No. 4, f.100b. (2); argent, two chevrons azure, an annulet or, for difference. (3); gules, fretty argent, a fess or.

6.* THE ARMYS OF WAKEHERST (SUSSEX, added). Gules, a chevron engrailed argent between three hawks of the second, beak legs and bells or.

7. MAST. STYKKE (? if not STYLE of KENT, after of LONDON, marchant, added). Sable, a fess engrailed gules (*sic*) between three fleurs de lys or.

8.* JOHN ISLYPPE, ABBOTT of WESTMINSTER (tempe H.7 dyed 2 H.8 added). Argent, a fess gules between three weasels passant proper. See also No. 6, f.95b.

9. A quarterly coat imperfect. See No. 4, f.105.

Folio 104.

1. FYZE WATTER (FITZ WALTER). Gules, on a bend azure (*sic*) three fleurs de lys argent.

2.* LAURENCE. Argent, a chevron between three gridirons sable.

3. CRUCHEFELD. Argent, a fess between three crescents gules.

4.* SCOTT. Sable, a false escocheon between six owls 3. 2. 1 bordurewise all argent.

5.* WHYTYNGTON. Vert, three whiting hauriant 2 and 1 argent.

6. BRUARNE OF LY'CONNESCHER (LINCOLNSHIRE). Per cross ermines, and azure, in the first and second, a mullet of 10 points or. *Impaling, per fess—in chief*, (1) argent, two bars azure ; *quarterly with*, argent, three chaplets 2 and 1 gules ; *and in base* (2) azure, a bend between six martlets argent. See also No. 3, f.134.

7. THE LORD FYTHWATYR. Quarterly. (1) ; argent, a bend engrailed sable, RATCLIFFE. (2) ; or, a fess between two chevronels gules, FITZ WALTER. (3) ; gules, a lyon rampant sable (*sic*), crowned or, BURNELL. (4) ; argent, three bars gules.

8. MASTER WALDEN. Or, on a bend gules cotised azure, between six martlets of the second, three wings of the first.

9. MASTER MORE. Argent, a fess dancettée paly (6) gules and sable, between three mullets of the last ; *quarterly with*, argent, a fess between three annulets gules.

Folio 104b.

1. S. THOMAS DENYS (DEVON, added). Ermine three battle-axes paleways 2 and 1 and a bordure engrailed gules ; *impaled with*, argent, a chevron between three bulls heads cabossed sable. See MASTER FYSSE. page 285.

2. DENNY. Gules, crusily and a saltire or. See No. 2, page 231.

3. Argent a fess dancettée gules, *quarterly with*, gules, three plates 2. 1.

4. Argent, a chevron between three lambs passant sable.

5. Gules, on a chevron sable (*sic*), between three annulets, as many crescents all or.

6. Argent, on a bend sable three mullets of the field.

7. SYR DAVE OWYN. Gules, a chevron ermine between three mens heads in profile, their helmets argent ; *quarterly with*, gules, a chevron between three lyons passant or, over all a baston sinister argent. See also No. 8, t.97b.

8. MASTER ASTLEY. Azure, a cinquefoyle pierced ermine ; *quarterly with*, gules, two bars or.

9. MASTER UMFREY RUDDYNG. Argent. on a bend between two lyons rampant sable, a wyvern extended, tail nowed of the first.

Folio 105.

1. BOYS. Argent, two bars and a quarter gules.

2.* HAR[E]WELL. Sable, two lyons passant argent, crowned or.

3. S. JHON KUTTE (CUTTS, added). Argent, on a bend sable three plates ; *quarterly with*, argent, a chevron between three bugle horns, stringed sable.

4. RYCHARD WODWARD. Quarterly. (1 and 4) ; argent, a chevron sable between three grasshoppers vert. (2) ; gules, a fess between six billets or, a crescent of the first, for difference. (3) ; gules, three horses heads couped 2 and 1 or, a crescent of the first for difference. Arma JOHIS MORY qy. de Kenyngton in Com. Kanc.

5. Argent, a chevron sable, on a chief gules, three mullets argent, a bordure engrailed of the second, a crescent or, for difference.

6.* REYNILL, DEVON. Argent, masoned sable, a chief indented of the second.

7. S. JHON GRENE. Gules, a lyon rampant per fess argent and sable, crowned or ; *impaled with*, quarterly. (1) ; argent, on a chevron sable three escallops of the first. (2) ; argent, a cross between four escallops sable. (3) ; sable, six lyoncelles couchant and cowed 3. 2. 1. argent. (4) ; argent, a chevron between three Cornish choughs sable.

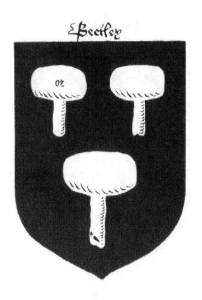

8. S. THOMAS MORE, CHANCELLOR of ENG-
LAND. Argent, a chevron engrailed sable
between three moorcocks proper; *quarterly
with*, argent, on a chevron between three unicorns heads erased sable, as many besants.

9. Gules, two chevrons argent, a mullet of the
last; *impaled with*, (1); argent, a chevron
between three falcons heads erased sable. (2);
VERE, per cross gules and or, a mullet argent.

Folio 105b.

1. (? NEVILL, EARL OF SALISBURY) imperfect;
quarterly of 8. (1); FRANCE and ENGLAND
quarterly. (2); NEVILL with a label of three.
(3); BEAUCHAMP. (4); WARWICK. (5);
MONTACUTE. (6); MONTHERMER. (7); CLARE
quarterly with DESPENSER.

2. SKEVINGTON (STAFF., added). Quarterly.
(1); argent, three bulls heads erased sable,
horned or. (2); azure, a bend between six
mullets or. (3); azure, three escallops or.
(4); argent, three martlets sable.

3. DIGBY, wife to SKEVINGTON. Azure, a
fleur de lys argent.

4. JOHN ASSHFELD. Argent, a trefoyle
slipped between three mullets all gules.

5. BATTERSBEY (EBOR., added). Vert, a
chevron between three mullets pierced or.

6. EVERARD. Gules, a fess between three
mullets argent, a crescent sable for difference.

7.* BEETLEY (BECTLEY, added). Sable, three
beetles 2 and 1 or.

8. Argent, a lyon rampant sable.

9. TYRYNGHAM (BUCKS., added). Azure, a
saltire engrailed or.

Folio 106.

1.* PRYSE. Gules, three unicorns heads
erased 2 and 1 or, a bordure engrailed
sable.

2. SOUNTYNGTON (? FUNTINGTON). Parted
sable and argent, a fess gules, the base fretty of
the first, in chief three martlets of the second.
Alternate blason, gules, on a chief sable (*sic*)
three martlets argent *dimidiated in base with*
argent, lozengy—perhaps fretty is intended.

3. WYETT. Gules, on a fess or, between three
boars heads barways couped argent, as many
lyoncelles rampant sable.

4. PIERPOUNT. Quarterly. (1 and 4); argent, a lyon rampant sable, a semée of cinquefoyles pierced gules. (2); argent, six annulets
palewise 2. 2. 2. sable, MANOURS. (3); azure,
three boars passant 2 and 1 or. HERYZE.

5. BRANDON. Sable, a chevron between
three martlets argent.

6.* REYNES. Chequy or and gules, a canton
ermine.

7. CHAMBERLEYN (of TANKARVILE, added).
Gules, a chevron between three escallops or.

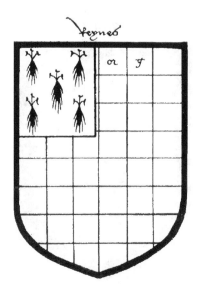

8. Ermine, two bars gules.

9. Gules, a bend argent between six martlets 3. 3 or.

Folio 106b.

1. Ermine, a chief engrailed gules.

2. Argent, two bars gules each charged with three besants, a label (3) or.

3. DOMINUS DE ZOUCHE. Gules, bezantée and a quarter ermine.

4. HADDON. Or, a human leg erect couped at the middle of the thigh azure.

5.* NORLAND. Argent, on a chevron between three lyons rampant sable those in chief combatant, as many bezants.

6. BYFELD. Sable, five bezants saltireways, a chief or.

7. THOMAS FYGE. Argent, on a bend or (*sic*) three mullets pierced sable ; and his wyffe ;——

8. Sable, a fess between three fleurs de lys argent.

9. JOHN MORETON of Mylborn Seynt Andrew, Dorset. Per cross gules and argent, in the first and fourth a goat's head erased of the second, a bordure quarterly or and azure ; *impaled with,* barry (6) argent and gules ; for Luce ux. filia T. SIDFEE.

Folio 107.

1. MORTON. Per cross, gules and ermine, in the first and fourth a goats head crased argent. See also No. 6, f.74b.

2. JOHN MORTON OF MYLBORN ST. ANDREW, DORSET. Same as preceding with the bordure, quarterly or and azure.

3. BARTYLMEW WYNDOWTT. Gules, a fess dancettée argent and six imperfectly drawn quarterings.

4.* PYGOT. Sable, three picks 2 and 1 argent. See page 295.

5.* GYFFORD. Argent, three bugle horns 2 and 1 sable, stringed and garnished or.

6. EWERSDE. Argent, a saltire engrailed sable, on a chief of the second, two mullets pierced of the first.

7. FOSTER. Quarterly per fess indented argent and sable, in the first and fourth, a bugle horn sable stringed and garnished or.

8.* HALYS. Azure, a fess indented between three garbs slipped or.

9. *Per fess—in chief;* ermine, three arbalastes gules, — *dimidiated in base with;* azure, a fess between two chevronels argent.

Folio 107b.

1. FITZ EDMUND. Sable, on a cross engrailed or, five cinquefoyles pierced of the field, a label (3) argent.

2.* BLEDLOWE. Per chevron sable and ermine, in chief two greyhounds rampant combatant argent, collared gules, a bordure azure florettée.

3.* STARKEY. Argent, a stork sable legged gules.

4. BOSTON. Argent, a fess between in chief two leopards faces and in base a trefoyle slipped, all sable.

5.* JHON HORSSEY. Azure, three horses heads couped or, bridled sable, collared platey.

6. Azure, a chevron between three crosses botonnée fitchée or.

7. W. MERBURY. Sable, a cross engrailed argent, between four nails of the second ; *quarterly with,* or, on a fess between two gemelles azure three garbs of the first ; over all a mullet gules.

8. THOMAS BLOWNT. Quarterly I. and IV. (1) ; argent, two wolves passant in pale sable, a bordure or, entoyre of saltorelles gules. (2) ; or, a tower triple turretted azure. (3) ; sable, two bars undée or. (4) ; vair ; over all a crescent gules. II. and III. ; vert, a saltire engrailed argent. HAWLEY.

9. BRYAN TUKE (KENT, added). Quarterly 1 and 4 ; gules, a chief indented azure over all three lyons passant or. (2) ; gules, a fess crenellée argent, between three leopards faces or. (3) ; gules, on a saltire argent, an annulet of the first.

Folio 108.

1. FROWYKE. Azure, a chevron between three leopards faces or ; *quarterly with,* vert, three sturgeon naiant or, over all a net gules.

2. Quarterly 1 and 4 ; azure, five fusils conjoined in fess or. (2) ; argent, three bars gules. (3) ; argent, two bars gules, on a canton of the second a cinquefoyle pierced of the first.

3. ST. JOHN, over it S. Wellyam Pollett, added. Quarterly of eight. (1) ; argent, on a chief gules, three mullets or. (2) ; gules, three lyons rampant or. (3) ; gules, two lyons passant in pale argent. DALAMARE. (4) ; gules, three water bougets argent. ROOS. (5) ; barry (6) argent, guttée de sang and gules. (6) ; argent, six martlets 3. 2. 1 sable. (7) ; azure, a fess between three fleurs de lys or. DELAMERE. (8) ; argent, lozengy. PAULET, on an escocheon of pretence ; sable, three swords pileways points meeting in base proper.

2 S

Folio 108b.

1. MASTER GOLDYNG. Azure, a chief or, over all a lyon rampant argent billettée sable.

2.* MASTER COLTE. Argent, a fess azure between three colts in full course sable.

3. MASTER ELRYNGTON. Argent, a fess dancettée sable, platey, between five Cornish choughs 3 and 2 proper; *quarterly with*, argent, on a bend gules, three fleurs de lys or. See also No. 7, f.116.

4.* MASTER STEWARDE. Argent, a lyon rampant gules over all a bend (? embatled) vert.

5. M. BYNGHAM. Azure, a bend gules (*sic*), cotised or, between six crosses pattée of the last; *impaling* COKER, argent, on a bend gules three escallops or.

6.* MASTER HALYS. Argent, on a chevron sable between three fleurs de lys gules each enclosed by a chaplet of the same flowered or, three estoyles of the first, on a chief azure as many pypes erect or.

7. CONEWEY. Azure, a lyon passant gardant paly (6) or and argent, between three dexter gauntlets aversant of the third, a bordure engrailed of the second.

8. SAVELL. Argent, on a bend sable three owls of the first, a mullet or.

9. BLABY. Paly (6) ermine and azure, on the first a billet gules.

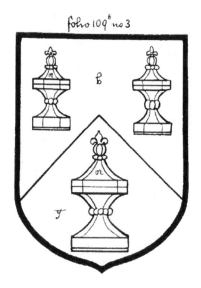

folio 109ᵇ no 3

(a) ayefter poyen)

Folio 109.

1. KING OF SPAIN. Quarterly of eight. (1) ;
gules, a tower triple turretted or. (2) ; argent,
a lyon rampant purpure. (3) ; or, four pallets
gules. (4) ; per saltire or and argent, in the
chief and base four pallets gules, in the fess two
eagles displayed sable. (5) ; gules, a fess argent.
(6) ; as No. 2. (7) ; or, five bendlets sable.
(8) ; or, a lyon rampant sable. Nos. 3. 4. 7. 8.
may be intended for an impalement.

2. KING OF SPAIN. I. and IV. quarterly of
1 and 2 as in preceding. II. and III., 3 and 4,
impaled, as in the preceding.

3. MASTER FRAUNCYS. Argent, a chevron
between three mullets pierced gules ; *quarterly
with,* barry (6) or and sable, a bend ermine.

4. STOKEWODE. "See before."

5. Imperfectly pencilled.

6. MY LADY MORE. Ermine, a fess counter
compony or and azure.

7. TWYFORD. Barry (4) argent and sable,
on a canton gules a mullet or ; *quarterly with,*
or, a fess sable between six ravens proper.

8. S. JHON DAWTRY. Azure, five fusils conjoined argent, with some quarterings imperfect.

Folio 109ᵇ.

1. S. JHON FOWELLER. Quarterly. (1) ; argent, three wolves heads erased gules, within a
bordure azure, entoyre of castles or. (2) ; ermine, on a canton gules, a martlet argent. (3) ;
argent, two bars gules, on a chief or, a lyon passant gardant azure. (4) ; vaire argent and
gules ; an escocheon of pretence for QUARTER-
MAIN (No. 2, f.102ᵇ). An impalement ; or, a
chevron between three lozenges pean ; *quarterly with,* or, a fess engrailed between six cinquefoyles 3. 2. 1 azure. See also No. 2, f.115ᵇ.

2. THE CHANDLERS ARMS, Company of
London. Per fess azure and argent, a pale
counter-coloured, three doves volant 2 and 1 of
the second.

3.* Per chevron azure and gules, three
covered cups or.

4. MASTER ERLAND. Sable, three castles 2
and 1 argent. HAVELAND bears the reverse.

5.* MAYESTER PEYEN (Pine). Sable, a chevron ermine between three pine cones or, slipped
vert.

6. Argent, five fusils conjoined in pale gules.

7. MASTER OF THE HOSPITALERS (St. JOHN of
Jerusalem). ? argent, three (billets ?) gules, on
a chief of the second a cross of the first. See
page 301.

8. WELLYM WILBRAHAM (VELBROUNN). Azure, two bars argent, on a quarter sable a wolf's head erased of the second.

Folio 110.

1. MY LORD HARY (FITZROY, DUKE OF RICHMOND AND SOMERSET). FRANCE and ENGLAND quarterly; a border also quarterly, (1); ermine. (2 and 3); counter compony or and azure. (4); gobony azure and argent. Over all an escocheon of pretence, per cross gules and vaire argent and of the first, over all a lyon embelif of the second; on a chief azure [for THE EARLDOM OF NOTTINGHAM], a castle between two bucks heads cabossed all silver.

2. Argent, a chevron sable between three ravens proper; *quarterly with*, argent, on a cross sable five besants, in the cantel a spear head gules.

3. NEVILL. Quarterly. (1 and 4); gules, a saltire argent. (2); gules, three lyons passant or, a bordure argent. (3); or, fretty gules a canton argent.

4. WALTER SCOTTE, squire. Per pale indented argent and sable, a saltire counter-coloured; *impaling*, gules, a fess cotised or, between two frets argent; *quarterly with*, gules, crusily pattée 1.3.3. between three boars heads barways couped 2 and 1, all argent.

5. M. WARING (WEIRYN). Quarterly. (1); gules, on a fess or between three bucks heads cabossed argent, as many unstrung bugle horns sable. (2); argent, two palets sable each charged with three crosses crosslet fitchée at the foot or. (3); or, a lyon passant gules, a mullet for difference argent. (4); sable, three bars argent, in fess three popinjays vert, beaked and legged gules, on a canton gules a saltorelle of the second.

6. Argent, on a bend between two lyons heads erased gules, a dolphin embowed or enclosed by two birds of the same, collared azure; *impaling*, sable, on a cross quarter pierced argent four eagles displayed of the first; *quarterly with* vair; old form.

Folio 110b.

1. Or, three pallets azure, on a chief gules three crosses patée convexed of the first.

2. Barry nebulée (12) azure and argent, on a saltire sable five martlets or; *impaled with*, argent, a chevron between three crescents ermines; *quarterly with*, per cross ermine and or.

3. Argent, on a fess between three annulets sable, as many mullets pierced of the first.

Folio 111.

1. THE GOLLSSMETTS (company) HAREMES. gules, a leopards face or, *quarterly with*, azure, a covered cup and in chief two chaplets or.

2. THE FESSMOUNGER (company) HAREMES. Azure, three dolphins naiant embowed 2 and 1 argent, on a chief gules three pairs of crossed keys saltireways, handles downwards or. See pages 4 and 286.

3. HABERDASHERS COMPANY. Barry nebulée (6) azure and argent; a chief quarterly 1 and 4 gules a lyon passant gardant or; 2 and 3 or two roses gules.

4. SKYNNERS COMPANY. Ermine, on a chief gules, three princes crowns, imperfectly represented.

5. Azure, on a fess gules (*sic*) between three fleurs de lys or, a martlet argent.

Folio 115b.

1. S. HARRY WENSSOWER (LORD WYNDSOR, added). Quarterly of five. (1); gules, crusily or, a saltire argent. (2); argent on a bend cotised sable, three mullets of the first. ANDREWS. (3); azure, a cross moline quarter pierced argent. MOLINEUX. (4); argent, on a cross sable five bezants. STRETTON. (5); gules, five lyons rampant per cross or. BENTWORTH.

2. S. RCHARD FOWLER. As No. 1, f. 109b. *impaling* WINDSOR, quarterly of five as last.

3. Azure, on a fess cotised or, three roses gules, *impaling*, chequy or and azure, a fess gules fretty argent.

4. *Per fess ── in chief*, gules, two lyons passant gardant or, sans forelegs; and ──*in base*, sable three boars heads couped 2 and 1 or; *impaling*, sable, a fess gules (*sic*) between three shovellers argent beaked and membered of the second.

5. Or, a cross voided gules.

6. Or, on a cross engrailed gules five cinquefoyles pierced argent.

7. Azure, a bend gules (*sic*) cotised or, between six crosses pattée of the last; *impaled with*, argent, on a bend gules three roses or.

8. MASTER WAYISCOTT. Argent, on a bend sable an annulet or, a bordure engrailed gules bezantée.

9.* (IRONMONGERS COMPANY). Argent, on a chevron gules between (three billets ?) sable, as many links *vel* handcuffs or. As illustration.

Folio 116.

1. S. WELLYM FITZ WILLIAMS. Lozengy gules and argent, with 15 quarterings.

2. (? GARDNER of Co. Linc.) Quarterly. (1 and 4); or, on a chevron gules between three gryphons heads erased azure two lyons rampant respecting each other argent. (2); ermine, on a fess gules, three fleurs de lys or. (3); argent, a cross moline gules; *impaling* Fitz William, Clarell and 3 other quarterings.

3. Argent, a bend between two cinquefoyles pierced sable; *impaling*, argent, a fess azure.

4. MASTER ELLMARE (Aylmer), Master of St.
John of Jerusalem. Argent, on a cross engrailed
sable between four sea-aylets of the second,
five besants ; *quarterly with*, argent, on a fess
gules between six annulets 3. 2. 1 sable, three
mullets or ; *impaled with*, LANGRYCHE, *quarterly* as No. 4, f.96 ; over all, on a chief gules, a
cross argent, for St. John of Jerusalem.

5. GERRARD. *Per fess* (1) *in chief*, vert, a lyon
rampant argent crowned or ; and (2) *in base*,
argent, on a cross sable five besants, *impaling*,
YENXLLEY, argent, a chevron sable between
three mullets of 12 points gules.

6. S. THOMAS SEYMOUR. Sable, on a fess
counter embattled argent, between three wings
or, as many pellets ; *impaling* BOURCHIER,
argent, a cross engrailed gules between four
water bougets sable.

7. ELRINGTON. Argent, a fess dancettée
sable, platey, between five Cornish choughs 3
and 2 proper ; *impaling* SEYMOUR, as last coat.
See also No. 3, f.108b.

Folios 116b and 117b.

1. [POLE BARON MONTAGUE 1529-39]. An
atchievment of 12 coats. (1) ; per cross azure
and gules, a label (3) argent, on each file a
(canton ?) gules ; intended for GEORGE DUKE
OF CLARENCE. (2) ; per pale or and argent, a
saltire engrailed counter-coloured [POLE]. (3) ;
NEVILL. (4) ; BEAUCHAMP. (5) ; WARWICK.
(6) ; MONTAGU. (7) ; gules, three lyons passant
gardant in pale or, a bordure argent, KENT ;
quarterly with WAKE. (8) ; MONTHERMER. (9) ;
CLARE, *quarterly with*, per cross argent and gules,
a baston sable, probably intended for DES-
PENCER. CREST incomplete, a golden eagle
preying. SUPPORTERS, incomplete : a black bull
and a golden gryphon.

Folio 118b.

1. LORD MARQ. DORSET. Quarterly I. and
IV. (1 and 4) ; party per tierce, (i) barry (6)
argent and azure, in chief three torteaux, GREY
(ii) HASTINGS and (iii) VALENCE. (2) ; ASTLEY,
azure, a cinquefoyle pierced ermine. (3) ;
WIDVILE, argent, a fess and a quarter gules.
II. and III. QUINCEY, gules, seven mascles conjoined 3. 3. 1 or. CREST. A unicorn ermine,
horned and crined or.

2. LORD OF OXYNFORD. Per cross gules and
or, a mullet argent ; *quarterly with*, HOWARD,
gules, a bend between six crosses crosslet
fitchée argent. CREST. on a chapeau gules
turned up ermine, a boar azure, crined and
tusked or.

3. LORD OF ARONDELL. Gules, a lyon rampant or ; *quarterly with*, sable, fretty or. CREST.
Out of a ducal coronet gules, a gryphon's head
argent, beak or.

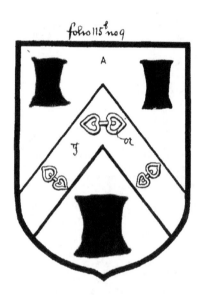

folio 115b no 9

4. LORD OF SCHREWSBERY. Quarterly. (1) ;
azure, a lyon rampant and a bordure or. BEL-
LESME. (2) ; gules, a lyon rampant and a
bordure engrailed or. TALBOT. (3) ; NEVILLE
with a martlet gules for difference. (4) ; argent,
a bend between six martlets 3 and 3 gules.
FURNIVALL. (5) ; or, fretty gules. VERDON.
(6) ; argent, two lyons passant gules. STRANGE.
CREST. On a chapeau gules turned up ermine,
a lyon passant or.

Folio 119.

1. LORD OF SUFFOLKE, Great Chamberlain
(1447). Azure, a fess between three leopards
faces or, POLE ; *quarterly with*, CHAUCER, argent,
a chief gules, over all a lyon rampant queue
fourchée or. CREST. A man's head in profile
gules, collared azure, bordured gold, and wreathed
about the temples or.

2. LORD OF DERBY. Quarterly I. and IV.
(1 and 4) : argent, on a bend azure three bucks
heads cabossed or. (2) ; or, on a chief dancettée
azure three plates. LATHOM. (3) ; chequy or
and azure. WARREN. II. and III. gules, three
armed legs conjoined in triangle argent, for
MAN. On an escocheon of pretence ; azure, a
lyon rampant queue fourchée argent. CREST.
An eagle, wings endorsed or, preying on an infant
swaddled gules, face proper, banded gold.

3. LORD OF SORREY (SURREY). Quarterly.
(1) ; gules, three lyons passant gardant in pale
or. ENGLAND. (2) ; gules, a lyon rampant
argent, FITZALAN ; the Lyon should be, or. (3) ;
chequy or and azure. WARREN. (4) ; gules, a
bend between six crosses crosslet fitchée argent.
HOWARD. CREST. On a chapeau gules turned
up ermine, a lyon purpure crowned or. Created
DUKE OF NORFOLK.

4. LORD DENAM (Dynham). Gules, four
lozenges conjoined in fess ermine. CREST. On
a chapeau gules turned up ermine, a hound
argent between two spears or.

Folio 119b.

1. LORD WELLYS. Or, a lyon rampant
queue fourchée sable ; *quarterly with*, ENGAINE ;
gules, a fess dancettée between six crosses
crosslet or. CREST. A demi gryphon wings
elevated argent, ducally gorged, chain and ring
or, in his beak a horse shoe gold.

2. LORD BROKE. Quarterly I. and IV. ;
sable, a cross engrailed or ; *quarterly with*, gules,
a cross moline argent, over all a crescent gold
for difference. BEKE. II. ; gules, a cross
flory or. LATIMER. III. ; gules, four fusils
conjoined in fess argent, each charged with an
escallop sable. CHEYNEY. IV. ; or, a chevron
gules, a bordure engrailed sable. CREST. A
Saracen's head in profile sable, ducally crowned
or.

• 3. LORD DAWBENEY. Gules, four fusils conjoined in fess argent. *CREST, see illustration.
A holly bush proper.

4. S. EDWARD PONYNGS. Barry (6) or and
vert, a bendlet gules ; *quarterly with* [? FITZ-
PAYNE], gules three lyons passant in pale argent;
on an escocheon of pretence ; or, three piles
meeting in base azure. CREST. A demy dragon
wings endorsed sable, langued gules.

Folio 120.

1. LORD SCROPP OF BOLTON. Azure, a bend
or ; *quarterly with*, TIBETOT, argent, a saltire
engrailed gules. CREST. Out of a ducal coronet or, a plume of feathers azure.

2. LORD OF DEVENSCHYRE. Quarterly. (1) ;
or, three torteaux 2. 1. (2) ; gules, a lyon rampant azure. REVERS. (3) ; gules, a cross
patonce vair. DE FORS. (4) ; per pale,
chequy or and azure ; and vert ; over all two
barrulets argent. OKEHAMPTON. CREST. Out
of a ducal coronet or, a plume of feathers argent.

3. S. GYLBERT TALBOTT. Same atchieve-
ment and Crest as No. 4, f.118b, with a crescent
azure for difference.

4. S. JOHN CHEYNY. Azure, six lyoncelles
rampant 3. 3. argent, a canton ermine ; *quarterly with*, SHOTESBROOK, ermine, on a chief per
pale indented or and gules, a rose of the last.
CREST. A bulls horns and scalp or.

my lorde ffrater

f harry folett

Folio 120b.

1. S. RYCHARD GYLFORD. Or, a saltire between four martlets sable; *quarterly with*, argent, a chief sable over all a bend engrailed gules. CREST. On a chapeau sable turned up ermine, an ostrich feather argent, pen or, issuing out of an escallop gold.

2. S. JOHN FORTESCUE. Azure, on a bend engrailed argent, plain cotised or, a mullet pierced sable. CREST. A wolf statant argent, langued gules.

3. S. JOHN MORTYMER. Azure, three bars or, a false escocheon argent, in chief two palets between as many esquires of the second. CREST. Out of a ducal coronet or, a garb azure.

4. S. ROBERD POYNYS. Quarterly per fess indented argent and azure; *quarterly with*, per cross gules and or, a bend argent. *CREST, see illustration. Out of a mound (?) azure, four branches proper, fructed with five pine cones or, fretted gules.

Folio 121.

1. S. JHAMYS BLONTE. Quarterly. (1); argent, two wolves courant in pale sable, a bordure or, entoyre of saltorelles gules. AYALA. (2); or, a tower triple turretted azure. SANCHEZ. (3); barry undée sable and or. (4); vair. [BEAUCHAMP.] CREST. Out of a ducal coronet, a pair of bulls horns all or.

2. S. JOHN REYSELEY. Barry (10) argent and azure, over all a gryphon segreant or, beak and members gules. CREST. A man's head affrontée sable, from each ear two annulets interlaced or.

3. MY LORDE FL'ATER (FITZ WALTER.) Or, a fess between two chevrons gules. *CREST. The Fitz Walter fetterlock supporting an estoyle slipped or, between a pair of wings gules. See RATCLIFFE; BANNERS and STANDARDS VOLUME, page 211.

4. S. THOMAS COKESAY. Quarterly of six. (1); sable, a cross and a bordure both engrailed or. (2); azure, crusily and a lyon rampant or. (3); argent, on a bend azure, three cinquefoyles pierced or. COKESAY. (4); argent, a bend sable, a label (3) gules. (5); argent, a bend gules, a bordure counter compony or and azure. (6); argent, on a bend gules, three annulets or. CREST. A garb or, banded gules.

Folio 121b.

1. S. ROGER LEWKENORE. Azure, three chevronels argent. CREST. A unicorns head couped azure.

2. S. HARRY HAYDON (NORFF., added). Quarterly argent and gules, a cross engrailed counter-coloured. CREST. A talbot statant ermine.

3.* S. HARRY COLETT (MAIOR OF LONDON, added). Sable, on a chevron between three colts trippant argent, as many annulets of the first. CREST. A colt as in the arms.

4.* S. Welyem Capell (Maior of London, added). Sable, crusily fitchée and a lyon rampant or. Crest. A demy lyon rampant or.

Folio 122.

1. S. John Byron. Argent, three bendlets enhanced gules; *quarterly with*, argent, on a bend azure three annulets or, in sinister chief a cross crosslet fitchée of the second. Crest. A mermaid, comb and mirror all proper.

2.* S. JOHN VERNEY. Azure, on a cross argent five mullets or, (rightly, gules). CREST. A phœnix argent—incomplete.

3. S. EDMONDE BE(D)YNGFELDE (NORFF., added). Ermine an eagle displayed gules, membered or. CREST. An eagle displayed or.

4. S. RYCHARD DELABERE. Azure, a bend argent cotised or, between six martlets of the last. CREST. Out of a ducal coronet or, a double plume of feathers argent.

Folio 122b.

Folio 123b.

1. S. JHAMYS BASKERVYLL. Argent, a chevron gules between three hurts. CREST. Four branches of rosemary vert.

2. S. JAMYS AUDELEY. Gules, fretty or; *quarterly with*, ermine a chevron gules. CREST. A Saracens head in profile argent, wreathed or.

3. S. ROBERDE CLYFFORD. Chequy or and azure, a fess gules. CREST. Out of a ducal coronet or, a wyvern rising tail nowed gules.

4. S. EDWARD ABOROW (BOROUGH of GAINS-BOROUGH, LINC., added). Quarterly. 1 and 4; azure, three fleurs de lys ermine. 2 and 3; or, a lyon rampant azure; *quarterly with*, paly (6) or and azure. CREST. A falcon rising ermine, ducally gorged and beaked or.

Folio 123.

1.* S. WELYE TROUTBEKE. Azure, three trout fretted in triangle tête-a-la-guise argent; *quarterly with*, argent, three moor's heads in profile couped 2 and 1 proper, a fleur de lys of the last for difference. CREST. A moor's head proper as in the arms.

2. S. GEORGE HOPTON (NORFF., added). Argent, a chevron azure, a label (3) ermine. (SWILLINGTON's coat). CREST. A monk's head proper, hood.

3.* S. THOMAS GREEN. Azure, three bucks trippant 2 and 1 or; *quarterly with*, gules, a chevron between three crosses crosslet or, in chief a lyon passant argent. CREST. A buck's head in profile, couped or.

1. S. EDWARD NORYS. Argent, a chevron between three ravens heads, erased sable; *quarterly with*, or, three bends azure, within a bordure gules. CREST. A martlet sable.

2. S. WELYEM SANDYS (DE LE VINE, HANTS., added). Argent, a cross ragulée sable, a label (3) gules. CREST. A goat's head in profile argent, horns or, between a pair of wings gold.

3. S. MORYS BERKELEY (SOMERSET, added). Gules, a chevron between nine cinquefoyles pierced argent. CREST. A bear's head argent muzzled gules.

Folio 124.

1.* S. WELYEM TYRWYTT (LINC., added). Gules, three tyrwhits passant or. CREST. A tyrwhits head and neck, in profile or. See page 308.

2. S. EDWARD PYKERYNGE. Ermine, a lyon rampant azure, crowned or. CREST. A lyons gamb erect azure, armed or.

3. S. WELYE CAROW. Or, three lyons passant in pale sable. CREST. A round top or, thereout a demy lyon rampant issuant sable.

4. S. ANTONYE BROWNE. Sable, three lyons passant between two bendlets engrailed argent; *quarterly with*, per cross gules and sable, in the first and fourth a lyon rampant and in the second and third a fret, all or. CREST. ? Three vine branches proper, fructed gules.

Folio 124b.

1. S. JOHN PASTON (NORFF., added). Or, six fleurs de lys 3. 2. 1 azure, a chief indented argent. CREST. A gryphon sejant wings endorsed, tail cowed or, holding in the beak a chain gold.

2. S. RYCHARD POOLL. Per pale or and sable, a saltire counter-coloured. CREST. An eagle wings elevated or, preying on a fish argent.

3.* S. WELYEM VAMPAGE. Azure, an eagle displayed argent, beak and legs gules, within a double tressure flory of the second. CREST. A demy lyon rampant or, langued and armed gules.

4. S. HOMFRY SAVAGE (CHESHIRE, added). Quarterly. 1 and 4; argent a pale lozengy sable. (2); or, on a fess azure, three garbs of the first. (3); gules, a chevron between three martlets argent. CREST. A unicorns head erased argent, horned and tufted or, on the neck a crescent azure for difference.

, *Folio* 125.

1. S. WATER HARBERD. Per pale azure and gules, three lyons rampant 2 and 1 argent. *CREST, see illustration. A woman's bust three quarter face sable, crined wreathed and tassled or.

2. S. THOMAS ASHETON (LANC., added). Argent, a mullet pierced sable. CREST. A mower habited per pale sable and argent, scythe proper.

3. S. WELYE GASGON (GASCOIGNE, EBOR., added). Quarterly. (1); argent on a pale sable a lucies head couped erect or. (2); gules, a saltire argent. [TIBETOT.] (3); gules, a lyon rampant argent, a bordure engrailed gobonated or and of the first. (4); vaire, or and gules. CREST. A lucies head erect as in the arms.

4. S. THOMAS BUTLER (LANC., added). Azure, a bend between six covered cups 3 and 3 or. *CREST, see illustration. A covered cup or.

Folio 125b.

1. S. WATER HONGERFORD. Sable, two bars argent, in chief three plates; *quarterly with*, argent, a lyon rampant sable, langued and armed gules, a bordure azure. CREST. Out of a ducal coronet or, a golden pepper garb, enclosed by two sickles erect proper.

2. S. EDWARD BERKELEY. Gules, crusily and a chevron argent, within a bordure of the second ; *quarterly with*, argent, on a saltire gules, five estoyles or. *CREST, see illustration. A mitre lined argent.

3. S. THOMAS POLTENEY. Argent, a fess indented gules, in chief three leopards faces sable. CREST. A lyons head sable.

4. S. HEW CONWEY. Sable, on a bend cotised argent, a rose gules enclosed by two annulets or (*sic*) ; *quarterly with*, azure, a cross double voided or. CREST. A moor's head in profile proper wreathed, etc., argent.

Folio 126.

1. S. THOMAS POMEREY. Or, a lyon rampant gules crowned (————) a bordure engrailed sable. CREST. A lyon sejant tail cowed gules, holding in the dexter paw a bezant.

2. S. RAFE SHELTON (NORFF., added). Azure, a cross or. *CREST, see illustration. A Saracens head argent, habited or.

3. S. NYCOLAS LYSLE. Or, on a chief azure three lyoncelles rampant argent. CREST. A stag argent, attires or, ducally gorged, chain and ring gold.

4.* S. RYCHARD NANFAN (see next page).

Folio 126*b*.

1. THERLE OF NORTHEHUMBERLAND. Quarterly I., quarterly, 1 and 4 ; or, a lyon rampant azure. [LORAINE.] 2 and 3 ; gules, three lucies hauriant argent. [LUCY.] II.; barry (6) or and vert, a baston gules. [POYNINGS.] III. ; azure, five fusils conjoined in fess or. [PERCY, ancient.] IV. ; gules, three lyons passant in pale argent. [FITZ PAYNE.] On an escocheon of pretence—or, three piles meeting in base azure. [BRYAN.] CREST. On a chapeau gules turned up argent, a lyon azure.

2. MY LORDE LATYMER. Quarterly of six. (1) ; gules, on a saltire argent, an annulet or. [NEVILL.] (2) ; BEAUCHAMP. (3) ; WARWICK. (4) ; gules, crusily and a chevron argent. (5) ; gules, a lyon passant gardant argent, crowned or. (6) ; gules, a chevron argent. STAFFORD CREST. A gryphon passant or.

3. S. WELYE GRYFFYTH. Quarterly. (1) ; gules, a chevron between three mens heads couped in profile argent ; *quarterly with*, azure, crusily and a lyon rampant argent. (2) ; argent, on a bend azure three stags heads cabossed or. (3) ; argent, on a bend azure three mullets or. (4) ; gules, a chevron sable (*sic*) between three bucks heads cabossed argent. CREST. A bucks head cabossed per pale or and argent.

Folio 126.

4.* S. RYCHARD NANFAN. Sable, a chevron ermine, between three wings argent; *quarterly with*, argent, three wolves passant 2 and 1 azure. CREST. A talbot statant argent.

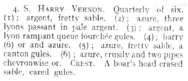

2. S. JOHN HASTYNGS. Or, a maunch gules ; *quarterly with,* FOLIOTT, gules, a bend argent. *CREST, see illustration. A mermaid proper crined gold, comb and mirror or. See also page 137.

3. S. WELYE TYNDALL (NORF., added). Quarterly. (1 and 4) ; argent, a fess dancettée on each point a crescent all gules. (2) ; or, a lyon rampant gules, langued and membered azure. (3) ; gules, six escallops 3. 2. 1 argent. *CREST. Out of ducal coronet or, a garb ermine. See illustration, next page.

4. S. EDMOND GORGE. Quarterly. (1) ; lozengy or and azure, a chevron gules. (2) ; argent, on a chief gules three bezants. (3) ; gules, a lyon rampant argent. (4) ; argent, a chevron sable between three billets of the second each charged with four guttée d'eau. *CREST, see illustration, next page. A greyhound's head proper, collared gules, studded bordered and ringed or.

Folio 127b.

1. THE LORDE DACRE OF YE SOWTHE. Azure, three lyons rampant 2 and 1 or ; *quarterly with,* gules, three escallops 2 and 1 argent. CREST. An eagle's head, in the mouth a gemmed ring all or.

4. S. HARRY VERNON. Quarterly of six. (1) ; argent, fretty sable. (2) ; azure, three lyons passant in pale argent. (3) ; argent, a lyon rampant queue fourchée gules. (4) ; barry (6) or and azure. (5) ; azure, fretty sable, a canton gules. (6) ; azure, crusily and two pipes chevronwise or. CREST. A boar's head erased sable, eared gules.

Folio 127.

1. *MY LORD STOURTON. Sable, a bend or between six fountains. CREST. A demy friar habited sable, holding in the dexter hand a scourge of three lashes with knots proper, staff or. See also No. 2, f.10.

2. THE LORD FYTHWAREN. Quarterly. 1
and 4; BOURCHIER, *quarterly with*, LOUVAINE.
2 and 3; FITZWAREN and HANKFORD (impaled)
argent, two bendlets undée sable. CREST. A
wyvern sans feet wings endorsed and tail
nowed or.

3. S. GERVYS OF CLYFFTON (NOTTS., added).
Quarterly. 1 and 4; sable, a lyon rampant,
semée of cinquefoyles pierced all argent. 2 and
3; argent, a lyon rampant queue fourchée sable.
CREST. Out of a ducal coronet or, a peacock's
head and neck sable beaked and crested gold.

4. S. ROBERT HARRECOURT. Gules, two bars
or. CREST. Out of a ducal coronet or, a peacock close proper.

Folio 128.

1. S. JOHEN ARUNDELL. Sable, six hirondelles 3. 2. 1 argent; *quarterly with*, azure, a
bend or; over all on an escocheon of pretence
——gules, a false escocheon between 11 martlets
bordurewise all argent.

2. S. WATER GRYFFYTH. Gules, a fess
dancettée argent between six lyoncelles rampant 3 and 3 or; *quarterly with*, azure, crusily
and three eagles displayed or; over all on an
escocheon of pretence——azure, a false escocheon
barry (6) argent and gules, between ten martlets
bordurewise or. CREST. A woman's head
couped at the shoulder proper, crined or,
habited gules.

3. S. ROGER NEWBORGH. Quarterly. 1 and
4; or, three bendlets azure. (2); argent, three
lyons heads erased or, collared ——. (3); argent,
two bars gules. CREST. A more's head in
profile proper.

4. S. RAUFFE RYDER (EBOR., added). Gules,
a lyon rampant argent; *quarterly with*, azure,
three crescents 2 and 1 or. *CREST, see illustration. A man's leg embowed sable, spurred or.

Folio 128b.

1. S. HERRY MARNEY. Gules, a lyon rampant gardant argent, crowned or; *quarterly with*, azure, two bars argent. CREST. Out of a chapeau sable, turned up argent, a pair of wings silver.

2. S. THOMAS BAWDE OF ESSEX. Gules, three chevronels argent; *quarterly with*, gules, three wings bendways 2 and 1 or. *CREST, see illustration. A satyr's head in profile sable.

3. S. EDMOND TRAYFORD, LANC. Quarterly. 1 and 4; argent, a gryphon segreant gules. (2); argent, on a bend azure three garbs or. (3); argent, on a bend gules, three cinquefoyles pierced or. CREST. A husbandman per pale gules and argent, holding a thresher or. See also TRAFFORD, page 244.

4. S. ROBERD LYTTON OF KNEBWORTH, HERTS. Ermine, on a chief dancettée azure three crowns or. *CREST, see illustration. A bittern holding a branch of lillies all proper.

Folio 129.

1.* S. JOHN SPEKE (see next page).

2. S. HUMFREY FULFORD (qr. wrong). Sable, a chevron between three bears heads erased of the second, muzzled of the first (FITZ URSE); *quarterly with* BOZOM; azure, three bird bolts erect argent. CREST. A bears head erect and erased argent and muzzled.

3. S. THOMAS FAYRFAX, EBOR. Argent, three bars gules, over all a lyon rampant sable; *quarterly with* [BECKWITH], argent, a chevron between three hinds' heads erased sable. CREST. A hind's head erased sable.

Folio 129.

1.* S. JOHN SPEKE (SOMERSET, added). Argent, two bars azure ; over all a double headed eagle displayed gules (*sic*), beaked and legged or (*sic*). CREST. A porcupine sable. See also page 219.

4. S. RYCHARD KNYGHTLEY, NORTHTS. Per cross or and ermine, on the first and fourth three palets gules, all within a bordure azure. CREST. A stags head in profile argent, attires or.

Folio 129b.

1. S. PERE EGECOMBE (DEVON, added). Gules, on a bend sable (*sic*) cotised or, three boar heads couped argent ; *quarterly with*, azure, florettée and a lyon rampant argent. CREST. A boar's head couped in profile argent, tusked and eared or.

2. S. ROBERD CLERE (NORFF., added). Argent, on a fess azure three eagles displayed or ; *quarterly with*, argent, on a cross moline gules, an annulet or. CREST. Out of a ducal coronet or, a plume of feathers argent.

3. S. EDWARD DARELL. Azure, a lyon rampant or, crowned argent. *CREST, see illustration, page 313. Out of a ducal coronet or, a Saracen's head argent, wreathed argent and azure, in his ear a golden ring, on the head a fretted chapeau or.

4.* S. THOMAS OF WOLTON. Argent, three hawks' heads erased sable, beaks gules. CREST. A salvage man with club over sinister shoulder all argent.

Folio 130.

1.* S. RYCHARD CROFTE (HEREF., added). Quarterly per fess indented argent and azure, in the first a lyon passant gardant gules. CREST. A wyvern extended sable, vulned in the side gules.

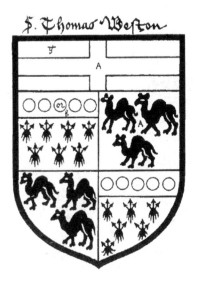

S. Thomas Weston

1. MASTER PARR. Or, three water bougets 2 and 1 sable; *quarterly with*, barry (8) argent and azure, a bordure engrailed sable. CREST. A pear tree in blossom, etc., as drawn.

2. S. GORGE MANNERS. Quarterly——imperfect.

3. S. JHON DRATORY (DAWTREY), imperfect.

1. Argent, on a fess between six cinquefoyles sable, three crosses crosslet of the first; *quarterly with*, gules on a chevron vert (*sic*), three eagles heads erased argent. CREST. An eagle's head between two wings gules.

2. TRENCHARD. Imperfect.

3. MASTER REDE OF KYNTE. Azure, a gryphon segreant or; *quarterly with*, argent, an arquebus, staff or, bow vert, stringed gules. CRESTS. (1); an eagle displayed sable, beaked and legged or. (2); A garb or, banded gules.

1. MASTER RAYMOND. Sable, a bend vair between two shovellers or, on a chief of the third three cinquefoyles gules; *quarterly with*, 1 and 4; gules, a chevron argent between three (gryphons) heads erased or. 2 and 3; argent, a fess between two chevronels gules, over all ? an annulet for difference. CREST. A leopard sejant gardant per pale or and sable, spotted counter-coloured.

2. S. WELYE MERYNG. Argent, on a chevron sable three escallops or. CREST. A boars head and neck couped ermines. SUPPORTERS. Two females proper habited gules, their heads encircled by a —— or. "posted to paper of supporters," in P. Le Neve's handwriting.

3. S. —— SEYMEUR. Argent, crusily and a lyon rampant azure; *quarterly with*, argent, two chevronels gules. CREST. A wolf proper ——.

4. S. THROGMORTON. Quarterly. (1); gules, on a chevron argent three bars gemelles sable. (2); argent, on a fess crenellée between six crosses crosslet fitchée gules, three crescents of the first. (3); sable, a chevron between three crescents argent. (4); gules, three bird bolts 2 and 1 erect argent. CREST. An elephant's head proper.

2.* MY LORDE OF SAYNTE YON (SR. THOMAS WESTON, Lord of St. John of Jerusalem, temp. H. 8). Ermine, on a chief azure five bezants; *quarterly with*, argent, three camels 2 and 1 passant sable; on a chief gules a cross argent, for the hospital of ST. JOHN. CREST. A Saracen's head wreathed—imperfect.

1. ROBERT ROYDON (RYDOON). Per pale argent and gules a gryphon segreant counter-coloured. CREST. Out of a ducal coronet or, a demy gryphon segreant, as in the arms.

2. RYCHARD DOLAND OF CO. LANC. Gules, two lyons rampant counter-combatant argent, within a double tressure flory counterflory or, CREST. A demy lyon rampant gules, holding in his dexter paw a battle-axe proper.

John Bruarne

3.* JOHN BRUARNE OF LYNCOLNESCHER. Quarterly ermines and azure, in the first and second a star radiated or. CREST. A hand argent cuffed azure, holding a fan-brush argent, handle gules. See also page 292.

Folio 336.

Master Dalbe

56° MASTER DALLBE, *Gules*, a chevron argent between three buckles or *(argent) on the chapter, sable*, a griffon [...] A cap of degrees sable. CREST. A bird's head and neck erased or, between two oak leaves vert, in its mouth a book gold.

Robert Dalby, a Roman Catholic priest, was executed [...] on the "Dice Nes Base"

INDEX

For names of Saints, Kings, Strangers, Prelates, Abbots, the Nine Worthies, Knights of the Round Table (and other fabulous coats), Lord Mayors of London, Companies, Cities, and Towns (see pages vii and viii).

* An asterisk denotes an illustration.

UNNAMED ILLUSTRATIONS—Pages 39, 49, 53, 54, 65, 69, 71 bis, 72, 73, 74, 75, 79, 88, 90, 91, 96, 97 bis, 98 (3), 99 (3), 100 bis, 101 (3), 102 bis, 103 bis, 104, 105, 106, 119, 120 bis, 121, 168, 169, 171 (3), 181, 186, 188, 207, 225, 231 bis, 232, 242, 243, 244, 246, 254, 255 bis, 256 bis, 265, 273, 274, 277, 279 bis, 285, 299, 301.

PRINTED BY THE LONDON COLOUR PRINTING COMPANY, EXMOOR STREET, NORTH KENSINGTON.

CPSIA information can be obtained
at www.ICGtesting.com
Printed in the USA
LVHW031556140223
739490LV00004B/131